Reconciling People

RECONCILING PEOPLE

COVENTRY CATHEDRAL'S STORY

Edited by

Christopher A. Lamb

CANTERBURY PRESS

Norwich

© The Contributors 2011
© Illustrations Martin R. Williams except where indicated otherwise.

First published in 2011 by the Canterbury Press Norwich
Editorial office
13–17 Long Lane,
London, EC1A 9PN, UK

Canterbury Press is an imprint of Hymns Ancient & Modern Ltd
(a registered charity)
13A Hellesdon Park Road, Norwich,
Norfolk, NR6 5DR, UK

www.canterburypress.co.uk

British Library Cataloguing in Publication data

A catalogue record for this book is available
from the British Library

978 1 84825 093 2

Typeset by Regent Typesetting
Printed and bound in Great Britain by
CPI Antony Rowe, Chippenham, Wiltshire

CONTENTS

* *Asterisks in the text denote an entry in the Glossary*

ABOUT THE CONTRIBUTORS

Colin Bennetts was Bishop of Coventry during 1998–2008. Previously he held three parochial posts, as a college chaplain, a director of ordinands, and Area Bishop of Buckingham. In retirement he serves as Honorary Assistant Bishop in the Guildford Diocese and travels on behalf of the Archbishop of Canterbury as a Pastoral Visitor to the Anglican Communion.

Louise Campbell is Reader in the History of Art at the University of Warwick and a member of Coventry Cathedral's Fabric Advisory Committee. She devised the exhibition 'To Build a Cathedral' (Mead Gallery, 1987), and is author of *Coventry Cathedral: Art and Architecture in Post-war Britain* (Oxford University Press, 1996), and co-author of *Sir Basil Spence: Buildings and Projects* (Royal Institute of British Architects, 2011).

Richard Farnell is Emeritus Professor of Neighbourhood Regeneration, Coventry University, and a lay Canon Theologian of Coventry Cathedral. His research interests focus on the engagement of churches and other faith groups with public policy in local neighbourhoods. He served as Chair of Midland Heart Housing Association, the Extra Care Charitable Trust and as a Church Urban Fund Trustee.

Christopher A. Lamb is a retired parish priest and Canon Theologian Emeritus of Coventry Cathedral. During 1987–1992 he was Community Relations Adviser to the diocese of Coventry, based at the Cathedral, before becoming Secretary for Interfaith Relations in the Board of Mission (now part of the Archbishops' Council) of the Church of England.

Paul Oestreicher was born in Germany in 1931, grew up in New Zealand and graduated in political science. After ordination he worked first at the BBC, then in the International Department of the British Council of Churches, specializing on relations with Eastern Europe and Southern Africa. He has been Chair of Amnesty International UK. From 1986 to 1997 he was Canon and Director of International Ministry at Coventry Cathedral.

Michael Sadgrove has been Dean of Durham since 2003. Having been a theological educator and parish priest, he became Precentor and Vice-Provost at Coventry in 1987 where he had the oversight of the Cathedral's liturgy and music. In 1995 he was appointed Provost of Sheffield. He is married with four adult children.

Margaret Sedgwick is a lay Canon of Coventry Cathedral, a Reader and member of the cathedral community since 1974, a member of the Cathedral Council from 2006 and Chapter Clerk (2000–06). She was Deputy Head of Coventry Blue Coat Church of England School, 1977–92.

Martin R. Williams ('Adam') has lived in Coventry since childhood. He attended Bablake School, Coventry, read law at the University College of Wales, Aberystwyth, and today practises locally as a family solicitor. He is a lay Canon of Coventry Cathedral.

ACKNOWLEDGEMENTS

The story of Coventry Cathedral over the last 50 years, since the new building was consecrated, is remarkable by any standards. Perhaps even more extraordinary is that we have been able to contact and listen to so many of those who for some, or even for all, of their lives have been a part of the cathedral community.

A precursor to this book was an oral history project known as the People's Story (a working name we also adopted for the wider undertaking, including the book itself). We are most grateful to the interviewing team, and in particular Jane Corrigan, who between them recorded some 20 interviews with members of the community with 'stories to tell'. To enable the interviews and the book to be produced everyone has given willingly and freely of their time and memory, and for that we are indeed most grateful.

To make a full list of all who have made some contribution to this book would be an almost impossible task; however, apart from the chapter and insert authors whose names appear alongside their text, special mention should be made of: John Irvine and St Michael's Committee who in 2006 had the foresight to give the enterprise their blessing and encouragement; the Friends of Coventry Cathedral who have provided financial backing along with the Hymns Ancient and Modern Trust and a number of private individuals; the cathedral archivists – John Rathbone, Shirley Willis and Heather Wallace; Christine Smith and her staff at Canterbury Press; John Brassington and Heather Wallace who proofread the manuscript meticulously; Martin Williams who assembled all the illustrations and took the photographs not otherwise credited; and Christopher Lamb who as one of the authors as well as editor has ensured that everyone has brought their contributions in on time, and then welded them successfully together. Finally, special thanks are due to the People's Story/Editorial Committee of Richard Chamberlaine-Brothers, John Rathbone, Martin Williams and John Willis, whose commitment and enthusiasm over the past five years in guiding the whole project has been exemplary.

Ted Hiscocks
Chairman, Editorial Committee

PREFACE

by the Dean of Coventry Cathedral
The Very Revd John Irvine

It is an enormous privilege to be Dean of Coventry and to contribute to its story.

Arriving in Coventry for the first time, I was immediately struck by how the buildings shouted the gospel of Jesus Christ from the ruins of destruction, through the cross to resurrection and the hope of glory. In my mind's eye, I had almost immediately the picture of a new cathedral on fire with the love of God in the centre of the country – a model to the rest of the Church of how to worship God in a variety of ways while reaching out to a generation that had become disaffected with Church.

It was this idea that prompted me to accept the call to Coventry. I took up post in 2001 and was immediately struck by both the wonder of the past and its millstone weight. Almost everyone I met was constantly looking backwards to the destruction of 1940, or to the glory days of the new Cathedral, or to some particular leader or other. It seemed clear to me that there needed to be encouragement to look forward. With the help of facilitators and committed members of the existing cathedral community, Jane and Peter Woodward, a process was crafted whereby we sought God's leading through groups and consultation with many people. Some of these were not directly connected with the Cathedral but all had a concern for it. The Cathedral's fiftieth anniversary in 2012 was already on the horizon and gradually it became clear that we should think towards that date. An eight-year vision plan seemed the right sort of period to aim at.

The end result, summed up in the vision statement brochure *The task is great . . . but God is greater*, took many months to formulate but has proved a helpful filter ever since. We are still aiming to be 'a place of spiritual renewal, a world centre of reconciliation, a resource for City, Diocese and Nation and the home of a vibrant community'.

I am very happy to see this book appearing with its many contributions from such a distinguished collection of individuals. I would not necessarily agree with all that is written but that is the delight of the Christian community in general and Coventry Cathedral in particular. We are a group of ordinary people with very different experiences and ideas, but we have been reconciled through Jesus Christ and that means we can work together for his glory. Long may this story continue.

John Irvine
March 2011

Coventry Cathedral at the heart of its city in the 1960s. © Richard Sadler FRPS.

INTRODUCTION

How Did We Come to Have Cathedrals and What Are They For?

CHRISTOPHER LAMB

Houses or temples?

In Europe our rural and urban landscapes are dotted with churches, and we expect great cities to have landmark Christian buildings, of appropriate size and splendour. We travel on holiday to see and admire comparable mosques, temples and places of worship in other parts of the world. Yet in the earliest days it was not obvious that Christians would build such places. The first Christians worshipped in one another's homes. Paul sends greetings to those who meet in the house of Aquila and Prisca – or Priscilla – (Romans 16.5 and 1 Corinthians 16.19), and to Nympha (Colossians 4.15). His reference to 'Chloe's people' also seems to indicate that a congregation met in her home (1 Corinthians 1.11), probably under her leadership. At times they may have moved around to different homes in order to avoid the attention of the Roman authorities. In the same way Christians worshipping today in some parts of the Muslim world never meet in the same house twice running.

Today, too, some Christian groups in the West prefer to meet in hired places and so remain unburdened by the cost and responsibilities of maintaining a building of their own. Such provisional arrangements, they feel, also give a certain authenticity to their communal lifestyle. There is the upper room of the Last Supper and the first Jerusalem church (Acts 1.13) to serve as their prototype, and the early house churches mentioned above. A permanent building used exclusively for worship and the meetings of a religious community inevitably acquires a distinctive character of its own. Continuous association with the business of holiness makes the building itself a special place, even if some users would hesitate to call it a 'house of God', insisting that the whole world is God's habitation. Most Christians and other believers, of course, have no such qualms, and state emphatically that their place of worship is a space where they can be confident of meeting God, and they adorn it accordingly. Yet the Old Testament records what is expressed as God's rejection of any attempt to locate him, much less confine him in a permanent structure:

> I have not lived in a house since the day I brought up the people of Israel from Egypt to this day, but I have been moving about in a tent and a tabernacle . . . Did I ever speak a word . . . saying 'Why have you not built me a house of cedar?'
>
> *2 Samuel* 7.6, 7

Perhaps we should assess whether a community is still a movement or has fossilized into an institution by the place where it chooses to meet.

Nevertheless, the Bible records the apparently unstoppable development in Israel of both kingship, also seriously questioned in 1 Samuel 8, and a permanent house of God. Although David was refused God's permission to build it, the Temple was built by his son Solomon, and soon became regarded as the only place where authentic worship, in the form of sacrifice, should be offered to Israel's God. 1 Kings 5–8 records the enormously detailed arrangements and lavish expense which went into its construction. Even so, Solomon was well aware of the paradox involved in building a house for God. 'But will God indeed dwell on the earth? Even heaven and the highest heaven cannot contain you, much less this house that I have built!' (1 Kings 8.27). The prophets warned that the Temple, as God's house in their midst, would be no protection against the consequences of deserting God's way. God would not guarantee his house permanence irrespective of the moral state of the nation. There followed the trauma of the Temple's destruction by the Babylonians, and its first slow rebuilding under Haggai and Zechariah. By this stage the earlier prophetic misgivings about the Temple had given way to a sense of its focal importance.

> Thus says the Lord of hosts: these people say the time has not yet come to rebuild the Lord's house. Then the word of the Lord came by the prophet Haggai, saying: Is it a time for you yourselves to live in your panelled houses, while this house lies in ruins? . . . Go up to the hills and bring wood and build the house, so that I may take pleasure in it and be honoured, says the Lord. *Haggai* 1.2–3, 8

Later there was massive expansion and adornment to the Temple under Herod the Great. One of his disciples said to Jesus, marvelling at Herod's work, 'Look, Teacher, what large stones, and what large buildings!' But Jesus was not impressed: 'Do you see these great buildings? Not one stone will be left here upon another; all will be thrown down' (Mark 13.1–2). And so it happened, at the hands of the

Romans in AD 70. The Gospel of John, in particular, notes Jesus' conviction that he himself, rather than the Temple, was the place where God would be encountered. The Church, his Body, was to take the place of the Temple at Jerusalem. The Letter of Peter urges its readers to become 'living stones . . . built into a spiritual house . . . to offer spiritual sacrifices', not animal ones (1 Peter 2.5). The Letter to the Hebrews spells out all the ways in which the sacrificial system of the Temple had been fulfilled and made redundant by the death of Jesus on the cross. The loss of the Temple, it implies, need not concern his followers.

A mixed message about buildings

The Christian tradition, then, in both Old and New Testaments, conveys a mixed message about great and impressive buildings dedicated to the worship of God. They cannot guarantee authentic worship, or the presence of God. The true residence of God is to be found in the hearts and minds of the believers. They constitute the spiritual temple, the living stones of God's house. Yet the Church has great and impressive buildings in abundance. It seems to be a deep human instinct to want to create a solid, enduring structure in honour of God and as a mark of faith, and also as a way of expressing in stone and human ingenuity the articles of that faith. This longing for a permanent and appropriate place on earth for God sits uneasily with the earliest Jewish conviction that Israel's God was for ever mobile. Surrounding nations, addicted to idolatry, might have their temples and their images of the divine, but the innermost sanctuary of the Temple at Jerusalem had no representation of God at all, and the prophets of Israel ridiculed idols made of wood and precious stones. Isaiah declares that the idol-maker 'feeds on ashes; a deluded mind has led him astray, and he cannot save himself or say, "Is not this thing in my right hand a fraud?"' (Isaiah 44.20). The name of God given to Moses was 'I am who I am' or 'I will be what I will be' (Exodus 3.14), a vivid warning against any attempt to tie him down, in words or in stone.

So how did church buildings come about? Archaeological remains have revealed no purpose-built churches before Constantine's Edict of Milan in AD 313. Some domestic buildings used as house churches appear to have been altered internally for church use, but without any external changes, no doubt for security reasons. The old idea that Christians worshipped secretly in the catacombs is now rejected, although Christians, like others, made use of the opportunity to bury their dead there privately rather than in the mass graves.[1] Once the Emperor Constantine had begun to favour Christianity and build churches, the remains of the martyrs and those of other Christian leaders were brought to the surface and the buildings named in their honour. Many of these were modelled on the Roman basilica, the seat of the magistrate or imperial officer, which were used for tribunals. They were generally long rectangular buildings with a rounded end or apse* where the magistrate sat with his assistants. This form lent itself easily for use by the Church, where the altar was the focal point in the apse and the magistrate's seat became the bishop's throne behind it, facing the congregation. The association with secular power and authority would not be lost on people long familiar with the state controlling religious activity. Not only did Constantine privilege Christianity as the dominant faith of the Roman Empire, but in the fifth- and sixth-century decline of the Empire in Western Europe, the Church found itself taking over government functions such as building roads and walls, operating public baths and administering cities.[2]

Large buildings not only make an impression on the public mind, they invariably have the effect of thrusting their owners and trustees into public debate and decision-making, if it is only to determine their effect on public order. For centuries buildings like churches have been subject to gradually increasing regulations over things like water, power, public safety and parking. Members of the first-century house churches would be astonished at the civic responsibilities undertaken by their religious descendants, and the way in which property law and planning decisions affect church communities. Today the process of church engagement with the state continues in such details as national regulations framed to safeguard children and vulnerable adults, and the requirement for those catering in a church to hold a food hygiene certificate. The effect of possessing and managing a large building which is accessible to all comers is to develop and shape a partnership with the public authorities, both local and national. Richard Farnell describes such a relationship between Cathedral and City in Chapter 5 of this book.

A serious house

So turning to the subject of this book, what sort of building is in focus here? In his rather acerbic poem 'Church Going', the Coventry-born poet Philip Larkin seems irritated by his own attraction to church buildings, wondering why he stops to look inside them. Like many of our generation he doesn't want to be caught up in any actual worship:

Once I am sure there is nothing going on
I step inside

Yet by the end of his musings he reflects that

It pleases me to stand in silence here;
A serious house on serious earth it is . . .
. . . someone will forever be surprising
A hunger in himself to be more serious,
And gravitating with it to this ground,
Which, he once heard, was proper to grow wise in,
If only that so many dead lie round.[3]

To stand at Hill Top in the centre of Coventry is to be at the site of three cathedral buildings with a long complex history, and a revolving-door relationship with Lichfield. The story begins with Leofric, Earl of Mercia, and his wife Godiva founding a Benedictine monastery at Coventry in 1043. The Diocese of Mercia had been founded as early as 669 with its seat at Lichfield, but Lichfield itself was badly damaged in tenth-century Viking raids, so in 1102 the diocese was renamed the 'Diocese of Coventry', with the Coventry monastery as its cathedral. This was enormously enlarged during the twelfth century, and completed in 1220, but in 1228 the diocese was renamed again as the Diocese of 'Coventry and Lichfield'. Later still, after the monastery had been dissolved in 1538 with so many others by Henry VIII, and fell into ruins, the Dean and Chapter of Lichfield were given the title of the Chapter of the diocese, which was again renamed with its title reversed as 'Lichfield and Coventry'. In 1836 Coventry itself was absorbed into the Diocese of Worcester, and Lichfield was on its own. With the huge growth in population throughout the Midlands, the Diocese of Coventry was revived in 1918, and the parish church of St Michael, adjacent to the ruined monastery, became the second cathedral. The third is of course the subject of this book. Appropriately, it bridges the ruins of the first and the second of its predecessors. Louise Campbell describes the process of settling on its design in Chapter 1.

The Benedictine tradition that Coventry Cathedral is heir to magnificently fulfils Larkin's criterion of 'a serious house on serious earth, which it is proper to grow wise in'. The *Rule of St Benedict* was written in southern Italy in about 540, but still inspires monastic life nearly fifteen hundred years later. It begins 'Listen, child of God, to the guidance of your teacher', and goes on to provide guidance for a way of life devoted to daily worship, strenuous manual work, the study of the Bible and other sacred literature, and the care of guests. There is a practical realism which is evident on every page:

The greatest care should be taken to give a warm reception to the poor and to pilgrims, because it is in them above all others that Christ is welcomed. As for the rich, they have a way of exacting respect through the very fear inspired by the power they wield.[4]

Margaret Sedgwick, in Chapter 4, describes how the Benedictine tradition of concern for the whole of life has inspired the outreach of the contemporary Coventry Cathedral.

As is well known, in time the monasteries of medieval England themselves became rich and powerful, not only through the donations of devout lay people but through the careful husbandry of land and property, and through the preservation of classical learning. The medieval monastery had enormous influence on its own locality, being at once hostel, hospital and school. The development of the wool trade owed much to the Cistercians, and the Coventry monks, with those at Coombe and Stoneleigh, specialized in the breeding of sheep and the marketing of wool, the foundation of Coventry's weaving industry. In the cathedral destroyed in 1940 were guild chapels for the Cappers, the Dyers, the Weavers, the Mercers and the Smiths. These guilds, and others like the Shearmen and Taylors, performed the annual Mystery Plays*, for which Coventry was famous, and which are still enacted in the Ruins of the old Cathedral. Although abuses had crept into monastic life by the sixteenth century, and had never been entirely absent from it, Henry VIII's dissolution of the monasteries now appears as a cynical asset-stripping exercise which destroyed a great contribution to English society and handed the proceeds to men on the make.

The Church of England in the twentieth century

By 1940, the year of the destruction of the old Coventry Cathedral, the Church in the West had passed through centuries of accumulating power and wealth, through the struggle for autonomy from jealous monarchs, through division and fratricidal conflict, and slowly growing intellectual opposition. The German theologian Friedrich Schleiermacher found it necessary in 1799 to write a book entitled *On Religion: Speeches to its Cultured Despisers*, while in 1867 Matthew Arnold wrote the much-quoted lines:

> The Sea of Faith
> Was once, too, at the full, and round earth's shore
> Lay like the folds of a bright girdle furled.
> But now I only hear
> Its melancholy, long, withdrawing roar.[5]

He mourned a world 'where ignorant armies clash by night'. 'An army of illiterates' was one of the jibes used about the successful movement against Anglican liturgical revision in 1928. The House of Commons, whose agreement was needed, twice defeated proposals that were passed overwhelmingly in the Church Assembly (the precursor of the General Synod) but were popularly presented as a sell-out to Rome. Nevertheless, *The Prayer Book as Proposed in 1928* was widely used until revision was finally authorized in *The Alternative Service Book 1980*. Michael Sadgrove describes in Chapter 2 how Coventry Cathedral developed the Anglican liturgical tradition. Despite the parliamentary snub of 1928, the Church of England in 1940 remained an immensely powerful force, and was about to have in William Temple (1881–1944) its most distinguished Archbishop of Canterbury for generations. True, the historian Adrian Hastings' judgement on the scholarly Dean Inge of St Paul's Cathedral (1860–1954) could stand for a number of Anglican clergy of the time: 'The gap between the demanding nature of the gospel and the comfortable state of its proclaimer is made a lot worse by the tendency of the upper-class cleric to pontificate about matters on which he is a complete amateur.'[6] In retrospect, a greater surprise is the acquiescence by Archbishop Lang, William Temple and other Anglican bishops, including George Bell, in the relief and gratitude expressed to Chamberlain on his return from Munich with the ignominious agreement he had concluded with Hitler in September 1938.[7] The fact that they were thus in tune with the feelings of almost the whole nation only highlights the cultural captivity of the Church, and its failure to think and speak prophetically. 'A word of critical warning', wrote Hastings, 'might have been most unpopular, yet most opportune.' The Church could not carry the nation with it on the matter of its own form of prayer, but sided with it when it proved to be quite mistaken about how to deal with tyranny.

One who had seemed to be a prophet in those years was Dick Sheppard, Vicar of St Martin-in-the-Fields, pioneer broadcaster and ardent pacifist, the moving spirit behind the Peace Pledge Union. From 1934 his personal charisma swept many prominent clerics and lay people from different churches into the PPU. On most, perhaps, the memories of the First World War lay heavy, and there was a widespread longing for an end to all armed conflict. For a while those who searched for peace through appeasement and those who were absolute pacifists joined together to decry rearmament. Then in 1937 Sheppard died, and the movement fell apart. But something of its spirit must have persisted, no longer starry-eyed about Hitler or blind to the real evils of Fascism, but no less determined to make space for peace wherever possible. Jock Forbes was a stonemason and caretaker of the grounds of Coventry Cathedral. On the morning after 14 November 1940 he walked into the ruined Cathedral with Provost Dick Howard, and finding two fallen charred beams fashioned them together into the form of a cross. That response, together with the three nails fastened into a cross by the Revd A. P. Wales, and Howard's contribution of the words 'Father Forgive', began in Coventry Cathedral a unique Ministry of Reconciliation which has defined its work ever since, most prominently in the international sphere, as detailed in Chapter 6 by Paul Oestreicher. In 1940 there began to be a Reconciling People.

The Church of England in the 1950s

The 1950s, when the new Coventry Cathedral was being built and its ministry planned, was a confident period for the British churches as a whole, with steady recovery from the War bringing growing prosperity and a sense of things returning to normal. In 1956 the number of infant baptisms in the Church of England was 602 per 1,000 live births – the same level as 1900. (By 1997 it was down to 228.) It was at this time that Billy Graham brought his evangelistic crusades to the UK, and in the Harringay Arena and elsewhere many young people found a new experience of faith. The late 1950s and early years of the 1960s were peak years for ordinations in the Church of England, before the rapid decline in church attendance through the later 1960s, a decline which has continued ever more steeply since.

> All of the indicators show that the period between 1956 and 1973 witnessed unprecedented rapidity in the fall of Christian religiosity amongst the British people . . . Across the board, the British people started to reject the role of religion in their lives.[8]

Coventry Cathedral in the 1960s and early 1970s was an exception to this general picture, something that encouraged most Anglicans while irritating a few. The very controversy surrounding the building ensured that visitors would come, while the undoubted energy, talent and creativity of its clergy and congregation drew committed worshippers, as 'Adam' describes in Chapter 8 on the story of the Cathedral's congregation. In Chapter 3, cathedral members chronicle the equal energy and creativity of the musicians and artists drawn to the new Cathedral.

But what is a cathedral really for, and can a spiritual renewal like that of Coventry Cathedral in the early 1960s be sustained for fifty years or so without drawing talent and energy away from neighbouring churches? Without pursuing the maintenance of its image at the expense of developing real substance? Without becoming in its turn a monument to past glories? These are the questions this book tries to answer, particularly by Bishop Colin Bennetts in Chapter 7. The first question of the purpose of a cathedral is something that every cathedral has to ask itself, so it is not difficult to find attempts at answers.

What are cathedrals for?

Feeding such a question into a search engine like Google brings a shoal of answers. The first received was from the website of Norwich Cathedral in its Mission Statement, part of the section called 'About Us'. [9] After noting that cathedral congregations generally have increased while parish congregations have declined in recent years, it continues:

NORWICH CATHEDRAL IN THE NEW MILLENNIUM

Here in Norwich we try very hard to make good use of our resources (the building, its contents and its people) and our freedom to be a laboratory of the Church of England. We seek to be creative about how we carry out our core role in ways that serve the needs of this new millennium.

- We devise services combining the best of new music and new liturgy with old traditions, and always strive for the highest musical standards.
- We lead interfaith initiatives.
- In our learning initiatives we seek to let the Cathedral speak to children and adults on many levels and not let them concentrate just on facts about the building's history and architecture.
- With both the Refectory and Hostry we have created new buildings to enhance our role as a place of welcome and mission.
- We raise issues of importance to today, and are not dismayed that this can sometimes cause controversy; this is because the Cathedral is here to help us think as well as to pray.
- We commission new works of art – such as statues, windows, misericords – combining the great tradition of religious art with encouraging the culture of today.
- We go out into the community to enable the Cathedral to engage with those who have never set foot here, for example with our music outreach programme and the Mile Cross Intergenerational Project.

Other cathedral websites may be less specific but have many of the same aims. They often recognize explicitly that the visitor may be more interested in art and architecture than in religion. They are proud of their attractions and their antiquity.

> Welcome to Hereford Cathedral. This beautiful building is the home of a community which has worshipped and worked together here continuously for well over 1200 years.
>
> It is a place where the mission of the church to proclaim Christ's love is central, and therefore the community has always warmly welcomed visitors. We all hope that you enjoy your visit.[10]

Worship is invariably central, as at Exeter:

> The Cathedral understands its essential mission to be an open house of God, proclaiming, living and singing of His love for all creation which was shown in Jesus Christ, and to be a place where bishop, diocese, county, city, tourist, worshipper and pilgrim can, in different ways, be supported and nurtured.[11]

There is pride in the building and the community:

> Welcome to Liverpool Cathedral website. This Cathedral is an awesome, spectacular, beautiful building and yet also a vibrant living church attempting to live the Christian Gospel; a community of daily prayer and worship; a home to great art and music with our 60 boy and girl choristers, a full events programme and exciting, new visitor facilities. On behalf of our staff, volunteers and congregation we hope that this website will give you enough information to make the decision to come and enjoy this place whether as a worshipper, an enquirer into our Christian faith, a client or visitor. This is your Cathedral – and now awarded Liverpool City Region's Best Large Visitor Attraction![12]

Some are admirably succinct, as at Sheffield:

> If you want a place to think, to pray, to learn about God or just to marvel at the architecture, we welcome you.[13]

In this company, which rings the changes on a number of important themes, Coventry Cathedral manages to offer something different. John Irvine, the Dean, puts reconciliation at the heart of the Cathedral's life and welcomes the visitor with the hope that through it he or she will encounter God.

Coventry Cathedral has been a place of worship for over 900 years. Today, it is our vision to be a place of spiritual renewal, where people can be reconciled to God through faith in Jesus Christ, and to be a world centre for reconciliation where creative, often challenging, work goes on to bring people together to find ways to live and work without conflict and hatred. It is our prayer that our story will affect and inspire every visitor, whether you visit us in person or through this website. The Cathedral is home to a vibrant Community, where visitors are always welcome. We hope that you will enjoy Coventry Cathedral, and that here you will encounter God.[14]

In the pages that follow the reader can judge for him- or herself how that vision has been seized and made part of the life of this unique cathedral, and how those drawn to work and worship in it have been a Reconciling People. As the authors each tell their own version of the last fifty years and more, there are quite properly overlaps and repetitions, particularly of some choice quotations – David Eccles' decisive letter of 1954 enabling work to proceed on building the Cathedral, and Joseph Poole's description of the place of music in worship, among others. No attempt has been made to harmonize the contributions, so the question is whether what emerges is a coherent vision of Reconciliation successfully sustained over half a century. The reader must judge.

* Denotes an entry in the Glossary

Notes

1 The chapter by Bradley Blue, 'Acts and the House Church', is a useful overview of the whole topic. See D. W. J. Gill and C. Gempf (eds), *The Book of Acts in its Graeco-Roman Setting*, Eerdmans, 1994, ch. 6.

2 A. Casiday and F. W. Norris (eds), *The Cambridge History of Christianity: Volume 2 Constantine to c. 600*, Cambridge University Press, 2007, p. 723.

3 Philip Larkin, 'Church Going', *Collected Poems*, Faber & Faber, 1988, pp. 97–8.

4 *St Benedict's Rule*, chapter 53, York: Ampleforth Abbey Press, 1997, pp. 63f.

5 Matthew Arnold, 'Dover Beach', from *New Poems*, published in 1867, though the poem may have been written as early as 1851.

6 Adrian Hastings, *A History of English Christianity 1920–2000*, SCM Press, 2001, p. 177. W. R. Inge was Dean of St Paul's Cathedral, 1911–34.

7 Hastings, *A History of English Christianity 1920–2000*, p. 348.

8 Callum G. Brown, *The Death of Christian Britain: Understanding Secularisation 1800–2000*, Routledge, 2001, p. 188.

9 www.cathedral.org.uk (accessed 10 March 2010).

10 www.herefordcathedral.org (accessed 9 March 2010).

11 www.exeter-cathedral.org.uk (accessed 9 March 2010).

12 www.liverpoolcathedral.org.uk (accessed 9 March 2010).

13 www.sheffield-cathedral.org.uk (accessed 9 March 2010).

14 www.coventrycathedral.org.uk (accessed 9 March 2010).

1 ARCHITECTURE, WAR AND PEACE

Coventry Cathedral and the Arts of Reconstruction

LOUISE CAMPBELL

I have not tried to create an exciting building, such as can be done so readily with modern materials of construction. A cathedral should not arouse excitement but a deep emotion, and it must express the canons of the Christian faith.

Basil Spence, 1955[1]

At the time of the competition for Coventry Cathedral, Basil Spence (1907–76) was working on the Sea and Ships Pavilion for the Festival of Britain. Despite his success as exhibition designer, Spence admitted to a growing impatience with lightweight materials and modern technology, which he judged to be inappropriate to the new Cathedral.[2] Looking back, Spence related his approach to the privations and uncertainties of the post-war period, and an emotional response to the site.[3] An end to austerity and Spence's own growing confidence as a designer helped to confer a sense of drama and triumphalism on the developing Cathedral, befitting its status as the premier building of Britain's post-war reconstruction. Despite the innovative features which Spence incorporated in his design during the late 1950s, Coventry Cathedral continued to represent – as had originally been intended – a token of continuity at a time of rapid change. This, the defining characteristic of Spence's cathedral, was to be the key to its success.

Coventry Cathedral is inextricably linked to the sufferings of Coventry and its citizens during the Second World War. But for Spence and his generation, the previous war also cast a long shadow. The roots of Coventry Cathedral's design lie in churches and chapels built after World War One, which as well as functioning as places of worship also served to commemorate the dead. Two were of particular importance:

Sir Basil Spence before the entrance porch of Coventry Cathedral.
© Richard Sadler FRPS.

the church of Notre Dame du Raincy outside Paris, and the Scottish National War Memorial in Spence's native Edinburgh. The church at Le Raincy was built in 1922–23 by Auguste Perret as a memorial to the victims of the Battle of Ourcq, its beautifully proportioned concrete framework containing magnificent stained glass by the artists Maurice Denis and Marguerite Huré. The Scottish National War Memorial, designed by Robert Lorimer in 1923–28, was a showcase of craft techniques – stained glass, sculpture, metalwork – and an amalgam of old and new buildings. It created a hall of remembrance and chapel by grafting a new apse* and entrance onto a pre-existing barracks at Edinburgh Castle, thus transforming the skyline of the city. Perret and Lorimer represented two very different approaches, the former combining modernist materials with modern art, and the latter deploying artists, craftsmen and craftswomen to create a shrine within an historic framework. Spence was to draw on both approaches to create a building which would serve as an enduring monument to the losses of the war.

In 1937, the architectural writer John Gloag published a novel called *Sacred Edifice*. It concerns an English cathedral partly destroyed by a zeppelin raid during the First World War, whose ruins were being incorporated by an inspired architect into a daring glass and concrete structure. Standing in a tranquil close in a city nestled into the South Downs, the new cathedral – a structure of concrete and glass – combines a vision of the future with a dean straight out of Trollope. As in Victor Hugo's novel *Notre Dame de Paris* of 1831, the image of the cathedral served to structure and dominate the narrative. However, Gloag's novel showed the modernist edifice – alarmingly vulnerable to air attack – reduced to ruins in a subsequent war. His book vividly evokes the anxieties of the generation growing up between the wars. Basil Spence – part of that generation, who participated in the Allied landings in Normandy in 1944 – wrote the Foreword to the second edition in 1954, calling it 'a most interesting prophecy'.[4]

Although modern-day cathedrals serve different purposes and represent different things from medieval ones, becoming civic and national signifiers rather than demonstrations of the absolute authority of the Church, a residue of nineteenth-century romanticism encouraged expectations of height and of a dominating position. What Paul Winninger termed 'the monumental complex' seems to have exerted an insidious influence on concepts of the twentieth-century cathedral.[5] Although suggesting that architecture was no longer 'the social, the collective, the dominant art' which it had been before the fifteenth century, Hugo felt that it acquired a new significance in the aftermath of France's 1830 revolution, with Notre Dame providing evidence of the creativity of the medieval mind. This suggestion that architecture represented 'the most majestic and permanent repository of the national memory' – a book of stone revealing the mentality of a period – was further developed in the writings of A. N. W. Pugin (1812–52), eloquent exponent of the Gothic revival in Britain, and the critic John Ruskin (1819–1900).

During the Second World War, the survival of Britain's historic buildings became the focus of considerable anxiety. Just as in novels, where cathedrals functioned as fixed points around which swirl the forces of change, so in wartime publications the fate of Britain's monuments, cathedrals and churches was often identified with that of the embattled nation. Such sentiments helped to shape attitudes to the Cathedral when in 1940 Coventry became the first city outside London to suffer a sustained air attack.[6]

Giles Gilbert Scott and Coventry

On 14 November 1940, in the course of a prolonged air raid which devastated the city, Coventry's Cathedral was gutted by incendiary bombs and left a smoking ruin. Visiting the site on the morning after the raid, Provost Howard vowed that the Cathedral would be rebuilt. His words ensured that Coventry Cathedral became associated with the city's fate and the country's battle against Fascism. Via some adroit propaganda, the cathedral scheme became part of the discourse of British reconstruction. But while the City and its architect linked a new approach to planning and architecture with a dynamic and prosperous future Coventry, the promoters of the new Cathedral embraced a more traditional vision. Howard's choice of architect was Sir Giles Gilbert Scott, with whom he had worked at Liverpool on the long building campaign for the Anglican cathedral.[7] Not until Neville Gorton arrived in Coventry as Bishop in early 1943 were relations between City and Cathedral scrutinized, and thought given as to the ways in which a new generation might be attracted to worship there.

As architect, Scott represented a safe pair of hands. Asked to redesign the House of Commons after its destruction at the height of the London Blitz in 1941, he did so to a design that echoed the old layout, but with improved sight lines, ventilation and acoustics. At Coventry, Scott proposed to set the new Cathedral north–south, across the Ruins, and to adapt the ruined apse* as a lady chapel and the nave walls as a cloister walk. However, Bishop Gorton was concerned with what he called a co-operative 'Christian social attack' on contemporary problems.[8] He also had a lively interest in ecumenism. He asked Scott to incorporate novel features like a Christian Service Centre and a Chapel of Christian Unity. Although Scott proposed to differentiate the new buildings from the old fabric by using a paler stone and a more sparing ornament, he used a similar streamlined gothic style to that he used at the new Commons Chamber. Gorton – convinced that the style of the new Cathedral was a crucial factor in attracting a younger congregation – was unenthusiastic, and pressed Scott to modernize his design. Scott then produced an extraordinary interior with concrete arches and dramatic shadows. At the Bishop's request, he also placed the altar in the centre of the new nave, an arrangement which Gorton had used in 1938 when reordering the chapel at Blundell's School around an altarpiece by Eric Gill. However, Scott balked at modifying the exterior, and Gorton made his position increasingly difficult. 'Only one thing in life I really have done – on my own . . . to have got rid of Scott for Coventry', Gorton later confessed.[9] In 1947, after the Royal Fine Art Commission strongly criticized the contrast between the design of the interior and the exterior of the new cathedral, Scott resigned his post as architect.[10]

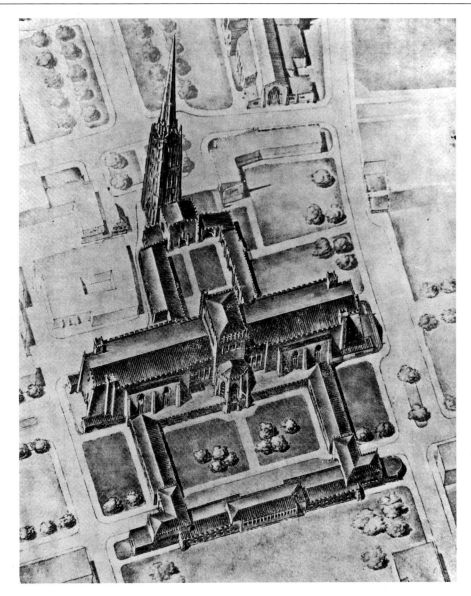

*Birds-eye view of the proposed cathedral based on Sir Giles Gilbert Scott's
plan in 1944.*

The aftermath of the resignation was tactfully managed, and an advisory com-
mission chaired by Lord Harlech attempted to retrieve the situation. The Harlech
Commission, reporting in July 1947, stressed the potential significance of the new
Cathedral in the reconstructed city, but gave a more traditional steer to the scheme.
Gorton had described the beauty of the interior spaces of the shadow factories which

5

filled the city in order to encourage Scott to take a more imaginative approach.[11] However the Harlech Commission – which took extensive soundings in the City – recommended building a new cathedral that combined a traditional layout, a finely crafted roof and a 'wealth of stained glass'.[12] The Ruins were deteriorating fast, and the city architect Donald Gibson advised that they were too weak to build on. Harlech for his part felt that they did not merit extensive rebuilding because they had been extensively restored during the 1880s.[13] A groundswell of local opinion, which wished to see the Cathedral restored or rebuilt as it was, seems never to have been seriously considered. The report recommended demolishing the Ruins, except for the majestic tower and spire, and building a new cathedral on or near the site 'in the English Gothic tradition', using red sandstone, its architect selected by competition. After protests from the architectural profession, the Gothic proviso was dropped, and no stylistic restrictions were included in the conditions of the competition announced in 1950. Nonetheless, the cathedral project was haunted by a residual conservatism which restricted Gorton's ideas about architecture and internal layout and shaped the approach of competitors. Although a Christian Service Centre and Chapel of Unity were to be included, the Cathedral was to be the dominant element. Significantly for the future, Harlech recommended appointing a strong building committee of lay men (as at Liverpool) to draw up the competition brief and oversee the building campaign, with few clergy representatives.

The architectural competition

During the 1940s, the Ruins of the Cathedral had acquired an enormous significance. It was there that a ceremony was held each November to commemorate the dead of the 1940 Blitz. On Christmas Day 1940, the Empire broadcast ended with the Coventry carol, sung by the cathedral choir under the tower of the ruined Cathedral. Open-air services were regularly held in the Ruins by Bishop Gorton. On VE day 1945, Provost Howard recalled that 'the people of Coventry completely took possession of the Ruins, by day and by night', placing the names of the fallen in a bowl on the altar, 'a spontaneous tribute of thanksgiving and commemoration'.[14] The rubble was cleared from the Ruins, and grass was laid inside the nave in 1948 to create a garden of remembrance. In 1941 Howard had asked the cathedral stonemason to erect a rubble altar, a cross of charred timbers in the Ruins. In 1948 a silvered cross of nails was placed there on a pedestal, and the words 'Father Forgive' carved on the sanctuary wall. Eight 'hallowing places' were created in the ruined nave, enclosures planted with flowers and marked by wooden boards inscribed with prayers; each represented an aspect of daily life which was sacred to God.

*In the months following the bombing, the Cathedral Ruins
became a place of pilgrimage and remembrance for the people of
Coventry. © Associated Press.*

In 1941 the government's War Damage Commission had promised funds to build
'a plain replacement'. The proposal to sweep the remains of the old Cathedral away
and construct a new cathedral building seemed to Gorton and Gibson a token of
faith in the future. However, it ignored the strong affection for the Ruins in Coventry. Their preservation, wholly or in part, was a topic of intense debate, encouraged by proposals to preserve as 'a potent source of emotional experience' the Ruins
of the most badly bombed of London's city churches as gardens of remembrance.
'Could there be a more appropriate memorial of the nation's crisis than the preservation of fragments of its battleground?' asked a letter to *The Times* in 1944.[15]

The competition brief attempted to bridge significant differences of opinion, both as regards the treatment of the Ruins and the character of the new Cathedral. The Bishop and Provost stated their priorities in a foreword: the Cathedral should be centred on the Eucharist and the preaching of the Gospel, and should contain an inviting and accessible altar.[16] Gorton's desire for a Chapel of Unity and a Christian Service Centre were merged with the more conventional priorities of the building committee (renamed the Reconstruction Committee) under its chairman Ernest Ford, which stipulated features like a chapter house, Lady chapel, guild chapel, children's chapel, and a chapel of the resurrection for private prayer. Significantly, too, it specified that the altar should be 'placed toward the east'.[17]

The architects who assessed the competition – the president-elect of the Royal Institute of British Architects Howard Robertson and experienced church designers Edward Maufe and Percy Thomas – and the city architect had their own views. They advocated preserving the Georgian houses of Priory Row and photographs of these were included in the competition conditions. Gibson for his part supplied drawings of the proposed new city centre for inclusion. So many requests for clarification were received that supplementary guidelines for competitors were issued in January 1951. When the 219 entries were scrutinized in July, there was a palpable feeling of anti-climax. Restricting entry to architects who had already qualified meant that no one born after about 1925 could compete; it was limited to British and Commonwealth citizens. This meant that the competitors had vivid memories of the war, and understood the symbolic significance of Coventry for Britain's reconstruction. Although the competition specified that only the tower and crypt chapels of the bombed cathedral should be retained, many competitors chose to retain more rather than less of the Ruins, but experienced difficulty squeezing this and a new cathedral building onto the site, even with some extra land to the north purchased in 1948. The assessors were confronted with a number of neo-Gothic designs and ones whose scale and design showed little sensitivity to the Ruins and the buildings of the cathedral close. Although none struck them as outstanding, they agreed that number 91 (by Spence) demonstrated 'qualities of spirit and imagination', was beautifully detailed and capable of development.[18]

Spence had responded astutely to the conditions of the competition, both written and unwritten, and his design revealed a strategic blend of tradition and modernity. Although he had no previous experience of church design, Spence's work as an exhibition designer had taught him how to convey ideas with space, light and materials. He had also become a knowledgeable connoisseur of contemporary art.[19] The statement accompanying Spence's drawings explained that he had made the basis of his design the integral relationship between old and new. He wished, he said, to preserve the Ruins almost intact 'as an eloquent memorial to the people of

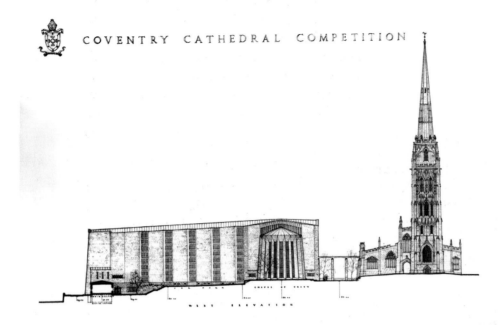

COVENTRY CATHEDRAL COMPETITION

Sir Basil Spence's 1951 competition design for Coventry Cathedral – west elevation.
© Phoenix At Coventry, Basil Spence.

Coventry' and to make the altar visible from the nave of the old cathedral.[20] Spence proposed to use sandstone for a robust, low-slung cathedral, its nave set at right angles to the Ruins, to which it was linked by a columned porch. The elongated plan was conventionally divided into nave, choir and sanctuary. Angled side walls, lit by narrow windows, created recesses for the Hallowing Places. A cylindrical Chapel of Unity was attached, the counterpart to a smaller Guild Chapel at the north end. A Christian Service Centre was housed in a substantial annexe to the west. Spence suggested moving the rubble altar and cross of timbers from the Ruins and placing it in the new Cathedral. His delicate drawings show them backed by a tapestry of the crucified Christ. Yet modern materials were also present: a glass screen at the entrance designed to retract into the ground, a sheet steel font cover, spun copper light-fittings, and slim concrete columns in the nave. Thus Spence (who while making his competition drawings was busy detailing the Sea and Ships Pavilion) simultaneously evoked a technological future and the Gothic past, the co-existence of modern and traditional forms and materials creating a richly allusive whole.

Developing the design

Winning the cathedral competition transformed Spence's career as architect. He moved from Edinburgh to London in 1953, where he built up the office he needed to detail and supervise the cathedral project to completion. Crucially, too, he got to know Provost Howard and Bishop Gorton and working together with them developed the key concepts of the cathedral design.

The theme of sacrifice and resurrection (which was not explicit in Spence's competition report) emerged with Howard's encouragement. Howard and Gorton had asked competitors to offer clear and forceful messages:

> It is a Cathedral of the Church of England. In terms of function, what should such a Cathedral express? It stands as a witness to the central dogmatic truths of the Christian Faith. Architecturally it should seize on these truths and thrust them upon the man who comes in from the street.[21]

Spence's design allowed a clear vista of the altar through the glass of the entrance screen, and the passage from old to new was encouraged by the accelerated perspective of the nave columns and the light directed towards the altar from the nave windows in a carefully orchestrated spectrum. However, the iconography and meaning were not as yet fully developed. Following Howard's suggestion that the subject of the tapestry should be Christ in Majesty rather than the crucifixion, Spence suggested making a new altar and hanging the tapestry above it, leaving the rubble altar and charred cross in their original position in the Ruins. They provided a powerful image of the resurrection as counterpart to past suffering, represented by the journey through Ruins. Caroline van Eck suggests that the Church of England has a tradition of architectural rhetoric, with its emphasis on the church as auditorium, its use of elements like font, pulpit and altar to convey key aspects of doctrine, and its stratagem of persuading by establishing a common ground of shared experience.[22] Coventry Cathedral's interior is an excellent example of this rhetoric in practice, with architecture providing a reminder of the past (the Gothic tradition of church and cathedral building and the shared experience of war) and a token of the emergence from suffering and death to afterlife. The symbolism of the windows and the Tablets of the Word lining the walls of the new cathedral emphasize this progression.

Bishop Gorton – who had bowed to the Reconstruction Committee's preferences at the time of the competition – soon resumed his campaign for a centrally positioned altar, and asked Spence to revise his design accordingly. Drawings of late 1951 show the altar brought forward, raised only three steps above the nave floor, with the choir placed behind and clergy stalls arranged around it in a U shape. The clergy

Sir Basil Spence's perspective of the chancel with the altar in a forward position,
November 1951. © Phoenix At Coventry, Basil Spence.

seated below the tapestry would echo the figures of the apostles being planned for
the base of the tapestry above, with the bishop's throne directly below the figure
of Christ. However, the Reconstruction Committee and Cathedral Council refused
to tolerate the change and insisted that Spence revert to the layout in his competition design.[23] Although the altar could not be moved from the east end of the nave,

Spence attempted to telescope the space of the nave visually, by establishing links between the imagery of the tapestry and that of the glass screen at the other end of the nave. Early sketches for the tapestry produced by Sutherland showed 'the worshipping multitude of the saints triumphant' behind the figure of the risen Christ.[24] Spence and Howard then asked the glass engraver John Hutton to cover the west screen with the figures of saints in their life on earth. In place of a layout that brought the altar physically closer to the congregation, Spence planned to echo figures in the tapestry with figures engraved on the screen. Although later revisions to the design of the tapestry and the position of the clergy seats were to blur that linkage, Spence's desire to orchestrate art with architecture remained strong.

Other features of the competition design were altered in the light of criticism in the architectural press. The silhouette of the Cathedral was strengthened by raising the 'east' end, increasing the height of the glass screen at the 'west' end (now made fixed and not movable), and redesigning the porch as a grand, triple-bayed structure. This helped reinforce the north–south axis linking the old and new cathedrals and the east–west axis between new shopping precinct and the cultural zone, and provided a monumental canopy for the approach stair. The internal vaulting was also changed, with the solid concrete vault supported by two rows of columns replaced by a delicate ribbed structure carried on a single row of tapered columns. The nave recesses were reshaped, their walls projecting at sharper angles, and a group of designers from the Royal College of Art was asked to produce stained glass for the nave windows, following the colour sequence which Spence proposed. His original idea was to have pairs of windows arranged in a graduated colour scale as Perret had at his church at Le Raincy. Mindful of Howard's concern with the theme of sacrifice and resurrection, Spence asked that the windows symbolize the passage from birth to death and modified the sequence of colours, which were to range from green to silvery white. In 1953 the three designers – Keith New and Geoffrey Clarke and their tutor Lawrence Lee – began work on the ten windows. Spence had to commission these windows, the tapestry, and the engraved panels of the great glass screen early enough to give the artists time to complete this enormous job. They suggest the integral role of artists in Coventry Cathedral, the first British cathedral to deploy modern art. Although a token of the architect's confidence in the power of art to raise the emotional temperature of the Cathedral and reinforce its meaning, they also had the unfortunate effect of fixing prematurely some key aspects of the architectural design.

Cathedral versus City

When the result of the competition was announced in August 1951, there was no prospect of an immediate start on building. Shortages of material and labour meant that major building projects required a licence, with priority given to schools and housing. However, in 1953, following the passage through Parliament of an Act authorizing the construction of the new Cathedral, it seemed possible that the Cathedral might receive preferential treatment. Gibson was an admirer of Spence's design, but his employers in Coventry's City Council, disappointed in their bid for government help in building the new commercial centre, felt otherwise. The Council resolved in February 1954 that 'the present time is not opportune for the rebuilding of the new Cathedral to be commenced'.[25] A deputation from the Council visited the Minister of Works to ask that the licence for the Cathedral should be postponed for ten years while the City moved ahead with its own building programme. They told him that Coventry needed housing, schools and health clinics rather than another place of worship, and that there would be serious repercussions for the labour situation in Coventry if it went ahead.

However, the Minister of Works, David Eccles, reminded the delegation of the national and international attention which was focused on the cathedral scheme. He sent a carefully worded letter to the Council, which was simultaneously released to the press. Eccles pointed out that the Cathedral would not delay other building work, having different requirements in terms of materials and skills; he emphasized the opportunities that it promised for 'fine craftsmen who have had a hard time during the years of utility'. He suggested that the Cathedral was important as a symbol for post-war Britain:

> Can we be sure that a Cathedral would be so useless? Is it always right to prefer things seen to things unseen? . . . The Cathedral is not a building which concerns Coventry and Coventry alone. The echo of the bombs which destroyed your city was heard around the world. We cannot tell how many people are waiting in this country and abroad for this church to rise again and prove that English traditions live again after the blitz. The threat of far worse destruction is with us today . . . We have never had a greater need for acts of faith.[26]

A cathedral was proposed as a reassuring bulwark to set against the anxieties and uncertainties of the decade of the test-bomb and the Cold War.

Eccles' reference to craft skills and to English traditions creates a striking polarity between the cathedral scheme and the City's own innovative building programme, which used prefabricated homes and industrial techniques to meet immediate needs. Robertson too, in his Presidential address to the RIBA in 1952, had stressed the need for constructing some buildings of fine quality, for a new tradition of monuments to replace those destroyed in the war.[27] Even Bishop Gorton now seemed to embrace a more traditional vision of a cathedral. 'Here was . . . the chance of creating nobility for its own sake, and to which could be harnessed all the skill, craft and talent of our time', he declared in a radio broadcast in February 1954. The battle to obtain a licence to build encouraged Spence to stress the use of traditional craft skills and media in the new Cathedral.

By 1954, while the battle to obtain a licence to build was raging, Spence had begun to cast around for a sculptor to produce the figure of the Cathedral's patron saint for the entrance of the new Cathedral. Spence's competition drawings showed a carved group of St Michael and the devil beside the approach stair. Provost Howard produced a vivid description of the essential qualities of the saint of the Cathedral and his adversary:

> The Devil represents all evil – in the universe and man.
> Active against man, individually and socially.
> Destructive of body, mind and soul.
> Malignant.
> Defeated.
> Michael (and all angels) is the Servant and Messenger of God.
> He is (sinless
> > (in constant vision of God
> > (adoring God
> . . .
> Qualities: Sudden breaking through.
> > Flashing brightness.
> > Strength and beauty.
> > Confidence – Freedom from malignity.[28]

In view of the changes he had made to the Cathedral's design, Spence began to feel the need for a large-scale sculpture (rather than a relief carving) beside the entrance. He took Gorton to see Jacob Epstein's sculpture of the *Madonna and Child* in Cavendish Square, London, and by late 1954 they had approached the sculptor. Epstein, asked to produce a maquette* for the Reconstruction Committee and with Spence's approval, forged ahead regardless with a full-size group, modelled in clay as preliminary to eventual casting in bronze.[29] Gorton had presented the options facing Coventry's citizens in terms of a choice between material and spiritual values. In the aftermath of the victory over the City Council, the commission acquired a special resonance.

ST MICHAEL AND THE CASKET OF JEWELS

The Cathedral would be like a plain jewel-casket with many jewels inside.

Basil Spence, Phoenix at Coventry

The jewels to emerge from Spence's vision, albeit expressions of individual creativity from some of the leading artists of the day, work together with that casket to project a coherent visual embodiment of Coventry's spiritual personality and its mission.

From the Middle Ages, St Michael was typically depicted as either a Roman or medieval warrior bedecked in shining armour, sword raised to strike at the snake, dragon or demon, writhing beneath his feet; in paintings of the Last Judgement, he might carry scales for the weighing of souls. In about 1920, Alec Millar (1879–1961) was commissioned to sculpt a figure of St Michael as a war memorial for Coventry Cathedral. The outcome was a traditional image of our universal protector against the forces of evil, standing tall and resplendent in his medieval armour, shield before him and sword raised high in a gesture of triumph.

For his bronze at the entrance to the rebuilt Cathedral, Jacob Epstein suppressed the metaphor of armed combat in favour of the spiritual, choosing the moment when St Michael proclaims the defeat of Satan. He retains the air of an archangel with a full spread of wings, but is no longer the warrior of medieval and Victorian art; he wears no armour and his only weapon, a spear, is neither poised over nor thrust into a writhing serpent or dragon, but held forth in a gesture of moral victory. His head, modelled on Epstein's own son-in-law, Wynne Godley, is at once human and celestial, noble and serene. The image of Satan, naked, wretched and in chains beneath St Michael's feet, is all the more potent for also having been cast in human form. Following Provost Howard's brief that 'The Devil represents all evil – in the universe and in man', Epstein has produced a work that no longer asks us to witness our protector St Michael vanquishing the forces of evil, but internalizes the conflict as one between opposing tendencies present in each of us. It shows the battle we have to fight within ourselves and has thus become a mirror to the human soul. Satan has not been destroyed, but cast down at St Michael's feet is a prisoner, loosely bound in chains. Prisoners can and do escape. In the same way, the malevolence personified in Satan is not extinguished, but lies in wait for new opportunities to feed on human frailty.

Carrying this image with us into the bombed ruins, it resonates with the words of the Litany of Reconciliation and we are well prepared to start a visually inspired pilgrimage through the Cathedral, allowing the architecture and art to lead us into questions as relevant today as in the 1950s, when Spence's vision of a jewel-casket was conceived.

John Willis
Editorial Committee Member

In June 1954, four weeks after the licence to build was issued, work began clearing the site in preparation for laying the foundations of the Cathedral. In the process, the enormous footings of the Benedictine priory of St Mary were discovered at the west side of the new nave. Perhaps fearing a further delay to the start of building, no great fuss was made about these, and they were incorporated into the paving of the car park beside the Chapel of Unity.

The crisis of 1956 and its aftermath

By the end of 1955, it was apparent that the cost of building the Cathedral to Spence's designs would exceed the funds available. Spence knew that vigorous fundraising was needed to pay for the elements like stained glass, tapestry, sculpture, and fine materials which he regarded as essential. However, as the foundations were being clad with stone up to the level of the nave during 1955, it emerged that – owing to increased costs of materials and labour – building the Cathedral's superstructure was likely to be far dearer than the original estimates.[30] That autumn, Spence, Gorton and the Reconstruction Committee exchanged worried letters. Gorton argued that there was no justification for commissioning expensive works of art if there were insufficient funds for essential features of the Cathedral. Howard had just asked John Piper to design the baptistry window. 'A Piper baptistry might cost another £30,000!!! And prevent us building the Chapel of Unity,' Gorton warned.[31]

In 1954 Gorton had commissioned Spence to design three small concrete churches for the new housing estates at Willenhall, Tile Hill and Bell Green (Spence described them as 'simple, direct, topical and traditional') to a tiny budget.[32] The Bishop's unexpected death in November came as a devastating blow. Charismatic, dynamic and a lover of art, Gorton had proved a stimulating patron, a modernizer and a moral support. Had he lived, it would have been characteristic of him to propose returning to the drawing-board when confronted with a financial crisis. Without him, Spence responded pragmatically. Constrained by the fact that the tapestry, nave windows and engraved west screen were being designed, and that the foundations of the Cathedral were well advanced, Spence stuck to his plan, but cut costs by drastically reducing the amount of stonework in the Cathedral.

After attending the ceremony in which the Queen laid the foundation stone of the new Cathedral in March 1956, Spence decided to simplify the porch design. The royal procession had used a temporary ramp passed through the window of the ruined Cathedral to gain access to the new. Spence decided that instead of jutting into the space of the Ruins like a triumphal arch, the porch should be retracted and the perimeter wall of the ruined nave left intact. The stonework of the new porch was pared away, leaving only the concrete porch canopy to hover over the ruined nave like a hand outstretched in blessing. The Chapel of Unity was reduced in size, and redesigned in concrete, with an external cladding of green Westmorland slate. Concrete and slate were also substituted for stone in the Chapel of Industry and link passages between the chapels and the main Cathedral were simplified. The Christian Service Centre was shelved, and the stonework planned for the interior walls of the Cathedral was eliminated, and replaced by concrete breeze blocks, roughly rendered. Helped by a resourceful new surveyor, revised estimates suggested that the cathedral budget could be brought back under control. Gorton's successor, Cuthbert Bardsley, a calmer presence than Gorton, proved equally supportive of Spence and a highly effective fundraiser.

Between 1956 and 1958, a period when Spence travelled widely, he revised the cathedral design in the light of the latest developments in church design. Internally, profiles and details were tightened and made tauter, and in late 1957 the side walls were redesigned to rise above the nave windows, creating jagged external profiles. The vaulting system was revised using a mathematical grid in which the rows of nave columns were not set out in parallel lines, but converged slightly. The effect was to enhance the link with the old Cathedral, to make the new one appear longer than it was, and focus attention on the 'east' end.

Existing commissions were reviewed and co-ordinated with one another, and with Spence's design. Six of the ten windows for the nave were completed by 1956, and exhibited at the Victoria and Albert Museum. Spence wrote in his book that the advantage of off-white internal walls over red sandstone ones was that stained glass could be viewed to advantage.[33] But because of the angle at which the windows were set, they were invisible on entering, revealing themselves only when standing with one's back to the altar. This meant that they had to compete with the glare from the west screen. More demanding still was called by one of the designers the 'black grid problem' – the dominant grid of stone necessary to stiffen the windows meant producing glass whose motifs and colours were strong enough to hold their own. Although Spence's competition report described the glass in abstract terms, Lee and his team recalled that 'we decided that some Christian symbolism would give a recognizable content for the spectator – each designer being free to construct his own interpretation'.[34] New worked hard to give his windows movement and to act as an extension of the architecture: his pair of green windows beside the entrance contained emblems of fertility, regeneration, baptism and the family group. Lee's two red windows combined symbols of 'Passion. Marriage. Mature conceptions. Flowering' with emblems of the Old and New Testament contained in tight, jewel-like compositions. In Lee's golden window, the Heavenly Jerusalem is represented as a skeletal structure, its main shafts echoing the framework of the window. In New and Clarke's multi-coloured windows half-way up the nave, larger-scale motifs represented man's triumph over evil. Clarke's two purple windows and the gold window near the altar (a joint venture) were more abstract and bolder in conception. Spence wrote that the six windows he saw in 1956 'were much better than I ever hoped'. The sequence of ten completed windows are among the outstanding achievements in post-war stained glass.[35]

John Hutton worked out with the Provost the imagery of the west window in 1953. Howard suggested that the saints represented there would be a counterpart to images of the heavenly host being planned for the tapestry.[36] Bishop Gorton encouraged him to intersperse these with rows of angels.[37] Old Testament saints and prophets were to be at the top, followed by New Testament saints, saints connected with the British Isles, and local saints like Chad and Osburga in the lowest row. St Michael was placed in the top row of angels, and the Madonna and Child directly below him. After finalizing with Howard the choice of saints and their attributes, Hutton devised an arrangement which created lively rhythms across the whole window. The angels were designed in vigorous action, flying, playing trumpets and dancing, in contrast with the static poses of the saints. At the same time the framework of the window was simplified and refined in order not to interrupt the delicate lines of the figures. Engraved onto the glass by Hutton, they were intended to form a pale web of figures through which visitors could see the interior of the Cathedral from the porch. Spence wrote of his original concept, 'I could not see the altar clearly but through the bodies of the Saints.'[38] The style of the figures and their draperies – reminiscent of Henry Moore's wartime sketchbooks with figures of Tube shelterers cocooned in a nest of lines – evoked the ghosts of those who had died in the war. Another possible source is the Hiroshima Panels, representing the victims of the atom bomb. These panels, depicting the naked figures of the dead, the scorched, and the survivors of the atomic bomb, drawn in brush and ink upon rice-paper by Iri Maruki and Toshiko Akamatsu, toured Britain in 1955 and were shown in St Mary's Hall in Coventry, drawing large crowds.

The tapestry was revised in 1956 to take account of the changed wall colour. Spence had decided in 1953 to dispense with the wall separating nave and Lady

Chapel; the tapestry was to hang on the back wall of the Cathedral, away from the coloured light of the nave windows, lit by clear glass windows in the side walls of the Lady Chapel. Sutherland produced a first cartoon in December. The figure of Christ was surrounded by the four beasts described in the book of Revelation – the lion, the calf, the man-faced beast, the eagle – against a green ground, and with a predella* depicting the Deposition. In the light of comments from Howard and Gorton, a second version was made in 1954–55, showing Christ's upper body and drapery looking 'less sepulchral and more regal, because . . . the body is a resurrection body'.[39] The figure of Christ was shown with arms outstretched and the colour of the background was made more vibrant. The base was modified to include scenes of the annunciation and visitation. A third and final version of 1957–58 shows a more stylized and hieratic* image of Christ with arms upraised, enclosed in a yellow-rimmed mandorla* which contrasts with the vibrant green ground; the four beasts, framed by boxy compartments, are attached. The reredos* – now containing a single scene of the crucifixion – is screened from the sight of those in the nave by the high altar, but visible to those in the Lady Chapel. The cartoon was dispatched to France, where the long process of weaving by expert tapestry-makers at Felletin began in January 1959.

The hallowing places, a concept of which Gorton had been privately sceptical, were developed into highly effective elements of the cathedral interior. In place of the sculpture which Howard and Spence had originally envisaged for the recesses of the nave, Spence proposed using a young letter-carver, Ralph Beyer, who was asked to design simple emblems and inscriptions for eight stone slabs fixed to the inner walls of the Cathedral. The texts, chosen by Howard, were taken from the New Testament, and their scale very carefully considered with regard both to viewers in the cathedral nave and to the enormous image of Christ which dominated the tapestry behind the altar. Beyer produced irregular, capitalized lettering forming a unity with the images of chalices, fishes and crosses which he carved on stone panels set into the nave walls. Inspired by the inscriptions on the walls of the catacombs in Rome, the 'Tablets of the Word', as they became known, introduced a natural material to the rough-rendered concrete walls of the cathedral interior, and helped establish a human scale. Much was made of the idea of craftsmanship in the new Cathedral; but although masons and others worked on the fabric of the building for seven years, Beyer pointed out that he and his assistant were the only artists to execute their work *in situ* in the Cathedral, making small adjustments in the process where necessary to the shape and size of letters and symbols.

The baptistry window was the last major element of the Cathedral to be finalized. The commission to Piper stalled during the financial crisis of 1956. In 1957, Spence contacted Piper again to ask him to estimate the cost of stained glass to fit the huge window of the baptistry. The rigidity of the window, which helped carry the weight of the roof over this part of the Cathedral, depended on its stonework. Great louvres of stone alternated with voids, producing a chequerboard effect even more dominant than the grid of the nave windows. Piper had to work around this, and instead of Spence's earlier suggestion of very pale glass or the flying angels, he proposed a design which conveyed its message entirely by colour. A light central area would be set off by a belt of deep colour, an effect which Piper described as 'a blaze of light, framed and islanded in colour . . . symbolising the Holy Spirit' and 'a great burst of light and grace'.[40] The very simple design, involving gradations of colour from red at the upper side margins of the window to areas of deep blue at top and base, was conceived as a contrast to the detailed and figurative designs of the nave windows nearby, and paid for with funds from a private donor. Beginning in 1958, he worked with the stained-glass artist Patrick Reyntiens to make the 198 lights required for the apertures of the window. Because of the orientation of the new Cathedral, the window catches the early morning sun, as in a traditional 'east' window, its blaze of white light providing 'a dazzling, elemental trumpet call'.[41]

Epstein's work on the figure of St Michael prompted Spence to make a final revision to the porch design. After seeing his small maquette* in 1957, Spence drew a perspective which showed Epstein's group in terms of sculpture in the round. Spence incorporated his latest ideas about the entrance steps and the canopied porch, which he showed casting strong shadows, as complementary to the robustly modelled forms of Epstein's adjacent sculpture. In February 1957, Spence alluded to the sculpture as representing a moral conflict, between the forces of good and evil. The clergy shared this view, with Howard referring to the figure of the devil as 'modern man chained by his own limitations'.[42] Modelled in several sections, it was cast in bronze in 1958–59, a process which was almost complete when Epstein died in August 1959. The theme of the sculpture seems to have had a significance which went beyond the victory over the City Council in 1954. The psychological tension which he established between the two protagonists was powerful enough to sustain interpretation of many different kinds and on different levels by those involved in the cathedral scheme: the clergy, the architect, the Reconstruction Committee, the citizens of Coventry and the Ministry of Works.

Jacob Epstein died in August 1959, less than twelve months before his evocative bronze of St Michael and the Devil was mounted by the main entrance to Coventry Cathedral. It was unveiled by Lady Epstein in June 1960. © Cathedral Archives.

The Cathedral achieved, 1958–62

Spence became President of the RIBA in 1958. This position, Spence's flair for publicity and the place of the Cathedral in the public imagination ensured very wide coverage in the media. Unfortunately, it also brought Spence into conflict with the man appointed to succeed Provost Howard on his retirement in 1958. The new Provost Bill Williams was a churchman of charisma, who had steered the rebuilding of a bomb-damaged church in Southampton. Williams had firm views on the ideal plan of a church, and was appalled to find that most of the key decisions as regards the shape and organization of the new Cathedral had already been made.

Spence felt that Williams was unsympathetic to much of the art in the Cathedral; Williams for his part, trying to establish a ministry in the new Cathedral, felt that many aspects of the design were unsuited to modern habits of worship. He was not alone in criticizing the Cathedral as a place of worship. The liturgical movement which gathered pace in Britain in the 1950s brought together like-minded clergy and architects to consider the design and function of new churches such as St Paul, Bow Common. Peter Hammond, parish priest and architectural writer, denounced the Cathedral as old-fashioned in layout and conception, despite its innovative art works. The growing interest in new styles of worship coincided with a radical approach to materials and structure on the part of young architects concerned with close relationships between function and design. Coventry, with its long, narrow plan and a structure that combined load-bearing walls with a ceiling, which – although echoing Gothic vaulting – was an entity independent of both walls and roof, grated on these concerns.[43]

Williams initiated a more sophisticated and cosmopolitan phase of the Cathedral's life, developing the international ministry of the Cathedral, and refining its role as a venue for reconciliation. The final phase of the Cathedral's design echoed a growing internationalism in art as in theology. Spence's original choice of artists stemmed from his involvement in the Festival of Britain and other post-war exhibitions, and a concept of the Cathedral as a showcase of British art. But as the cathedral design matured, a much broader spectrum of artists was employed, several from overseas. This could be controversial, as Ralph Beyer, the German-born son of an émigré scholar, discovered. Beyer, whose Jewish mother had died in Auschwitz, was deeply hurt to read criticism in the local paper of the decision to employ a German artist at the Cathedral.

Spence's visits to some of the new churches of Switzerland and France in 1956, and a visit to Cologne in 1957, fostered a tougher architectural approach, especially to the chapels and chancel. This last phase of the Cathedral's design produced the distinctive silhouette and spiky glamour which became a distinctive feature of the

Cathedral. The first move of Provost Williams was to ask Spence to create a place in the undercroft of the new Cathedral as a place for the cathedral congregation to worship. The long narrow space was equipped as a temporary chapel with an altar and a cross and candlesticks designed by Geoffrey Clarke in nickel bronze and crystal; the design of the cross, incorporating an integral light-fitting, echoed the charred timber cross. The chapel was inaugurated on the last day of December 1958, a symbolic occupation of the new Cathedral by its congregation.

A temporary Chapel of Unity was established by Gorton in the west crypt of the old Cathedral in 1945. Administered by a Joint Council of Anglicans and Free Churchmen, it was an entity independent of the Cathedral, yet physically attached to it. In Spence's revised design of 1956, the new chapel was given a more compact shape, with walls which inclined inwards and ten hollow concrete buttresses radiating from a circular core. In this chapel, the altar was positioned centrally, a cross suspended above it. The artist Margaret Traherne was commissioned in 1958 to design windows of thick slab glass set into concrete blocks, to fill the narrow apertures. She produced designs based on the deployment of colour, rather than images: 'a feeling of elation was intended to be conveyed by the rising and gradually lightening of colour scale as the eye travels up the narrow columns of glass'. She added, 'I suppose a musical feeling was also at the back of my mind'.[44] The windows were paid for with a donation from the German Evangelical churches.

The Guild Chapel – envisaged as the architectural counter-balance to the Chapel of Unity – hung in the balance as a result of forced economies in the late 1950s. However, as the ministry to industry gained momentum, funds were found to build what was from now on to be known as the Chapel of Christ the Servant. Here the impact of the new churches on the Continent was registered in the centrally positioned altar, the spare, sombrely coloured surfaces, and the clear glass of the windows. The robust shapes of the altar, plinth and monumental pottery candleholders, over which hung an aluminium canopy-cum-candelabrum designed by Clarke on the theme of the cross of nails, formed a sculptural unity.

Between 1960 and 1962, Spence and his assistants embarked on the final stage of the design of the cathedral interior. There were two priorities: Provost Williams' desire for as much space as possible around the altar, and the need to prevent the sanctuary and altar from being visually overwhelmed by the tapestry nearby. Spence began by enlarging the altar, and commissioning a dramatic high-altar cross from Geoffrey Clarke. Clarke's cross was a dramatic, twisted form, reminiscent of both the charred cross and of the root-like forms in the tapestry, and was to hold a silvered cross of nails. A poignant contrast was established between the delicate little cross and the powerful form which enwraps it. The whole eloquently evokes the gesture of making the sign of the cross. By giving the cross a protective cowl or shield, it suggested its vulnerability and a sense of lurking danger. The cross was set upon a marble plinth behind the altar, and the candlesticks were cantilevered over it, leaving the altar surface uncluttered. Six huge pottery candleholders were made by Hans Coper to flank the altar. They gave scale to the chancel and helped establish the importance of the sanctuary as the place where the drama of the liturgy is staged. Its identity was reinforced by the floor colouring. Originally envisaged as richly patterned, the floor design was greatly simplified around 1960; the nave was floored in black marble, with simple inset patterns of grey and creamy marble; chancel and sanctuary were floored in black.

John Piper had been asked to design vestments in 1959; the results were a spectacular set of heavy silk robes in six liturgical colours, with appliqué motifs like crosses, flames, bird-like forms cut from fabrics of contrasting texture and colour and stitched on. Spence wrote to Williams describing the way in which he hoped they would strike a note of vitality in the redesigned chancel: 'the movement of the clergy must be imagined against a background of austere simplicity – the black floor, the white walls, the simple wood of the choir stalls, the richness of the tapestry behind'.[45] In contrast to this austere zone, the Chapel of Gethsemane, designed by Steven Sykes, with its reliefs set with mosaic, glass, mirror and gold leaf, caught the eye at the head of the south aisle, providing a vision of an angel holding a glittering chalice appearing to Christ as his disciples slept.

The canopy over the choir and clergy stalls were redesigned as thorny, three-armed structures, christened 'triads' by Spence's office. The young Elisabeth Frink produced sculptures of a mitre and a flame in beaten copper to mark the seats of the Bishop and the Provost.

Handing over the Cathedral

In April 1962, an RAF helicopter lowered in position onto the new cathedral roof a lightweight bronze flèche*; two days later Clarke's 12-foot aluminium sculpture of a winged Mercian cross was threaded onto a spindle at the tip. The sculpture, suggestive of both flame and winged creature, is dynamic and phoenix*-like, and visible from a distance. It served to signal the presence of the Cathedral in the city (which had so far failed to clear the dilapidated buildings around it) and as a token of the modernity of 'Britain's first space-age cathedral'.[46] The episode – recorded on film and in photographs – helped to heighten the excitement which surrounded the completion of the Cathedral.

On 24 May, the original cross of nails from the altar of the old Cathedral, which had been carried to every parish church in the diocese over the previous 40 days, returned to Coventry. Bishop Bardsley carried it into the Ruins of the old Cathedral, passed it to Provost Williams, who carried it down the steps into the new Cathedral and inserted it into the high-altar cross. After an overnight vigil of prayer in the Wyley crypt chapel, the new Cathedral was consecrated the following day.

The ceremony of consecration was devised by the cathedral precentor, Joseph Poole. Since few English cathedrals had been consecrated since the Middle Ages, this required composing a new liturgy. Elements of the pre-Reformation Latin rite were spliced with new translations and specially composed fanfares. It was a ceremony designed to evoke the cathedral-building campaigns of the Middle Ages, to which Spence himself explicitly alludes as the antecedent of his sparkling new building. The Bishop darted around the Cathedral, striking altar, font and lectern with his crozier, invoking the Holy Spirit's blessing: 'Be here, *be* here to bless the prayers and sacraments of thy church . . . This house is thine . . .'

Five days later, Benjamin Britten's *War Requiem* – specially written for the Cathedral – had its performance there. It used the Latin Mass for the Dead, interspersed with Wilfred Owen's First World War poems. The three leading choral parts were

The Consecration Service, 25 May 1962. Bishop Cuthbert Bardsley signing the 'Sentence of Consecration'. © Coventry Telegraph.

assigned to singers from Britain, Germany and Russia – Peter Pears, Dietrich Fischer-Dieskau and Galina Visnevskaya.[47] In Part Two, the *Dies Irae,* the chorus sings, 'the trumpet, scattering its awful sound/Across the graves of all lands/Summons all before the throne'. The score was prefaced by Owen's words, 'My subject is war and the pity of war.' The ceremony marked an extraordinary trajectory in the post-war imagination, from the nationalistic and patriotic commemorative project of the 1940s, to the renewal of national architectural and craft traditions of the 1950s, to the internationalism of the 1960s and the solemn and moving indictment of war in all lands.

The life of the new Cathedral, which began so dramatically with the Consecration, was to be enriched by musical, dramatic and artistic events. Williams ensured that drama and music played an important role in the new Cathedral. Plays were staged in the porch and on the steps of the Chapel of Unity and in the Ruins in the 1960s, and major art exhibitions were held, continuing and extending the adventurous artistic patronage of the Cathedral to the benefit of the City's cultural life.

Aftermath

As formal jurisdiction over the Cathedral passed to the Provost, tensions between architect and provost resurfaced. Williams feared that the publicity that enveloped the new Cathedral threatened to overshadow the significance of his own plans for the ministry of the new Cathedral. For his part, Spence was deeply hurt by criticisms of the Cathedral which the Provost voiced in a television programme in September. These tensions were exacerbated by events soon after the Consecration. Spence, mortified not to be consulted over arrangements for securing the porch with gates, accused Williams of indifference to aesthetics. Williams, attempting to mollify him, wrote: 'I think that your feelings must be not unlike the feelings of the father of a very beloved daughter when the time comes for the daughter to be married.'[48] Apprehensive about the Cathedral's future, Spence offered to act as advisor in return for a small annual fee. He advised on the screen for the Lady Chapel and on enlarging the bookshop, and was paid a separate fee for extending the refectory and designing the youth hostel, John F. Kennedy House in Hill Top. However, on hearing that the Bishop's study in the Cathedral with its fine oak-panelled ceiling had been altered without consultation, Spence relinquished even his watching brief.[49]

The significance of Coventry Cathedral for the general public was indicated by the crowds of visitors who flocked there. For those unable to queue for hours to get in, newspapers, magazines and television footage provided extensive and enthusiastic coverage. By contrast, architectural writers criticized the cathedral interior for its lack of structural clarity (its elegant nave columns and ribs do not support the weight of the roof but carry only the timber ceiling), for its traditional layout and for an overly rich mix of art. The writer Reyner Banham called his article on the completed Cathedral 'Strictly "Trad, Dad"', arguing that Coventry with its long nave and choir, and its fixed altar position, was liturgically inflexible and anachronistic.[50] Such criticism ignored the fact that its layout was dictated by a conservative-minded lay committee, and that over and above its function as a place of worship it served to commemorate the dead of a recent war and to meet a new appetite for spectacle and public ceremonial. However, Coventry Cathedral's role as a key monument of post-war reconstruction was recognized by the American writer Henry Russell Hitchcock. Writing in 1964, he argued that although the Cathedral was architecturally and spatially not an avant-garde building, its character was determined by its role as triumphant symbol of the end of austerity and a celebration of the fruits of peace: 'In contrast to the visual penury . . . of much English architecture, this is a twentieth-century building of assured sumptuousness, handsome in its materials, gorgeous in many of its accessories, and happily symbolic in its broader significance.'[51]

Coventry Cathedral today

The criticisms of Williams and Banham are often echoed in present-day reactions to the building, reactions that focus on the Cathedral's inflexibility as a space of worship. Yet, as was demonstrated in the 1970s, the altar can be set up in the nave with some success.[52] That the cathedral plan was long and thin rather than circular is due to the demands of the Reconstruction Committee. Spence later acquired the reputation of being stubborn in achieving his vision of an immaculately crafted, tightly integrated ensemble of art and architecture. But Spence was in the 1950s highly responsive to his clients and their wishes. As we have seen, the Cathedral was the fruit of an extraordinarily intense consultation process between Spence, Howard and Gorton, and the artists commissioned to work there.

Coventry is a city with a vibrant post-war record of architecture and design, a record that goes well beyond the Cathedral and the three little Spence-designed churches. Unfortunately, its innovative pedestrianized shopping precinct, its pioneering public art programme and its technically daring school buildings have been poorly maintained, clumsily altered and partially demolished. It is likely that they will soon vanish altogether. The Cathedral, although more careful of its twentieth-century architectural heritage than the City has been, could take a more robust and imaginative approach to it. It has had to confront several major difficulties. The first is the tension between different concepts of 'heritage'. In Coventry, the lure of

ADDENDA OR *ERRATA*?

I saw the old Cathedral as standing clearly for the Sacrifice, one side of the Christian faith, and I knew my task was to design a new one which should stand for the Triumph of the Resurrection.

Basil Spence, *Phoenix at Coventry*

The artworks commissioned by Spence cannot be separated from the Cathedral's architectural form. Together they evolved and together they lead us on that journey from sacrifice to the triumph of the resurrection. As we progress through the Ruins into the new Cathedral, however, we become aware of works that were not part of the original concept, but were added in later years. We might be prompted to ask, what are they saying to us and how do they relate to the wider concept?

Jacob Epstein's *Ecce Homo* was carved speculatively in the 1930s from a particularly hard piece of Subiaco marble. Its lines are uncompromisingly angular and brutal and it failed to find a buyer. After the sculptor's death in 1959, it stood in Battersea Park until Lady Epstein offered it to Coventry. It was installed in the cathedral Ruins in 1969. *Ecce Homo* ('Behold the man!') were the words spoken by Pilate as Christ, scourged and crowned with thorns, was presented to the crowds who were calling for his crucifixion. With a gaze described by Epstein as one of 'pity and prescience in our unhappy world', this primitively hewn image of Christ's suffering and degradation stands in a place itself dedicated to the suffering of war. From its plinth in the Ruins, it looks through the west screen, towards Graham Sutherland's tapestry of Christ in Glory, perfectly signalling Spence's journey from 'sacrifice' to the 'triumph of the resurrection'.

Less obvious as a station on that journey is the *Head of Christ Crucified*, fashioned by the American sculptor Helen Jennings out of the mangled metal of a crashed car. Provost Williams was moved by a photograph of the piece to accept the offer of its shipment to Coventry, where it now sits at the entrance to the Chapel of Unity. The artist explained that, like Coventry Cathedral, it was 'resurrected from a wreck – from tragedy to triumph'. The origins of the *Christ Crucified* sculpture proved particularly emotive following the death of Diana, Princess of Wales.

Clark Fitzgerald's sculpture, *The Plumbline and the City*, a gift in 1971 from Christ Church, Cincinnati, is a rather selective interpretation of two verses of Amos, an Old Testament book which tells of God's condemnation and punishment of the people of Israel. Its relevance to Coventry undoubtedly lies with the 1968

'People and Cities' conference and the subsequent setting up of the Centre for Urban Studies. Its significance to the wider themes of the Cathedral might prove obscure to today's visitor.

The Cathedral has a story to tell and art is a powerful storyteller. But as these examples show, we have to be clear what it is we wish it to tell.

John Willis
Editorial Committee Member

the medieval past vies with the concern for the experience of the Second World War, and both have tended to overshadow the appreciation of the legacy of the more recent past: Coventry Cathedral's heritage of mid-twentieth-century art and architecture. An example emerged during the 1990s, when the excavation of the pre-Reformation Priory Church of St Mary and the creation of a millennium garden disinterred a lost chapter in Coventry's history, a prequel to the story of St Michael's. Unfortunately, retrieving and displaying the remains of this was achieved at the expense of demolishing John F. Kennedy House, the youth hostel built by Spence and his office in 1965. Kennedy House, a building sensitive to its location among the buildings and gardens bordering Hill Top, was a stylish example of Spence's work in the 1960s, and – testament to the international dimension of the Cathedral's youth work in the 1960s – formed an integral part of the cathedral complex. Although the hostel had structural problems, its disappearance represented both an architectural and a historic loss.

The second difficulty arose from the Cathedral's own pioneering role in incorporating major works of contemporary art. The successful exhibitions organized in the Ruins during the 1960s stimulated major gifts of sculpture to the Cathedral, including Epstein's *Ecce Homo* and Frink's small bronze *Crucifix* (attached to the pulpit), but also several less distinguished pieces. These now threaten to clutter the space of the Cathedral, and to compromise the impact of the Ruins and their importance as a zone of memory, and essential prelude to the experience of the new Cathedral.

The dignified interior spaces of the new Cathedral have also proved vulnerable to other kinds of clutter, ranging from unsympathetic signage to the furniture and storage facilities required by changing styles of worship and the equipment needed for them. It is vital that a proper balance be achieved between these practical demands and the need to respect and maintain the aesthetic unity and integrity of the Cathedral.

The third problem concerns changed patterns of tourism. For visitors in 1962, Coventry Cathedral represented the recovery from a long and damaging war and a triumphant celebration of the arts of peace. They have been succeeded by a generation which has at its disposal a range of glamorous modern buildings and spaces which were inconceivable 50 years ago. Coventry Cathedral no longer draws the admiring crowds of tourists who flocked there soon after its consecration. But while its role as a place for mediation and the reconciliation of international and sectarian conflicts has grown, the Cathedral's status as a tourist venue is less certain. For the visitor today it has neither the romance of an older cathedral nor the glamour of an iconic contemporary building, but occupies an uneasy place in between. In its current presentation, the story of the Blitz and the ruined Cathedral must compete for space with the story of the project to build a new one. The consequence is that the audacity and excitement of that project and its profound artistic, social and spiritual significance for its time is understated. The Herbert Art Gallery possesses a fine collection of paintings by Sutherland related to the cathedral tapestry, as well as works by Spence, Hutton and Piper. Its extension in 2008, and the creation of a new piazza between the Herbert and the Cathedral, raises the possibility of initiating an integrated approach to the display of their collections. The Cathedral could enhance the visitor's experience and understanding of the building and draw those with a special interest in twentieth-century British art and architecture by finding space in the undercroft for a display which charts in detail the genesis of the new Cathedral and the works of art made for it. This might be complemented by a gallery designed to display works of art donated by well-wishers for which there is no suitable place in the Cathedral itself.

The Cathedral tells us much about the condition of the arts in the post-war era, and also suggests some more general lessons about the vital relationship between place, memory and making in the modern world. In its optimism and vitality, Coventry Cathedral affirms the symbolic significance of architecture around 1950, representing hope for the future and the longed-for arrival of peace, and the material, spiritual and aesthetic rewards which accompanied it. This optimism deserves to be remembered and celebrated.

* Denotes an entry in the Glossary

Notes

1 Basil Spence, 'The Cathedral Church of St Michael Coventry', *RIBA Journal* 1955, p. 151.

2 Basil Spence, *Phoenix at Coventry: The Building of a Cathedral*, Geoffrey Bles, 1962, p. 25.

3 John Donat, 'Sir Basil Spence OM. on his work', *Listener*, 18 February 1965, p. 253.

4 Basil Spence, Foreword to John Gloag, *Sacred Edifice*, 2nd edn, Cassell, 1954, p. vii.

5 Paul Winninger's phrase 'le complexe du monument' is cited by Peter Hammond, *Liturgy and Architecture*, William Clowes & Sons Ltd, 1960, p. 48.

6 See Nicola Lambourne, *War Damage in Western Europe*, Edinburgh University Press, 2000.

7 Provost Howard's approach to Scott overrode the advice of the Central Council for the Care of Churches, which in 1942 recommended building a new cathedral inside the restored walls of the old (the Esher Report).

8 Quoted Louise Campbell, *Coventry Cathedral: Art and Architecture in Post-War Britain*, Oxford University Press, 1996, p. 22.

9 Letter from Gorton to Spence, 12 May 1955, Spence Archive, RCAHMS.

10 Scott wrote to Howard on 2 January 1947: 'It is unlikely that a modernist or a transitional design will ever meet the approval of all parties . . . these differences of opinion . . . harass the unfortunate artist and hamper the production of the work.' Quoted in Louise Campbell, *To Build a Cathedral*, A. H. Jolly, 1987, p. 18.

11 Gorton to Scott, 21 December 1944, quoted Campbell, *Coventry Cathedral*, p. 29.

12 Harlech Report (1947), p. 21.

13 '. . . since they are not of sufficient architectural merit to justify the complete rebuilding which would be necessary', Harlech Report, p. 20.

14 R. T. Howard, *Ruined and Rebuilt: The Story of Coventry Cathedral 1939–1962*, Council of Coventry Cathedral, 1962, pp. 82–3.

15 Quoted Campbell, *To Build a Cathedral*, p. 38.

16 'The Cathedral should be built to enshrine the altar', quoted Spence, *Phoenix at Coventry*, p. 16.

17 Spence, *Phoenix at Coventry*, Appendix B, 'Schedule of Requirements'.

18 Spence, *Phoenix at Coventry*, Appendix D, 'Report by Assessors'.

19 See P. Long and J. Thomas (eds), *Basil Spence Architect*, National Galleries of Scotland, 2007.

20 Spence, *Phoenix at Coventry*, Appendix C, 'Architect's Report'.

21 Spence, *Phoenix at Coventry*, Appendix B.

22 Caroline Van Eck, *Classical Rhetoric and the Visual Arts*, Cambridge University Press, 2007, ch. 4.

23 On 25 June 1952, Ford, then Chairman of the Reconstruction Committee, told the Cathedral Council, 'It is wrong aesthetically, practically, psychologically and traditionally', quoted Campbell, *To Build a Cathedral*, p. 92.

24 Statement by the Provost, December 1951, quoted Campbell, *Coventry Cathedral*, p. 98.

25 Quoted Campbell, *Coventry Cathedral*, p. 137.

26 Quoted Campbell, *Coventry Cathedral*, p. 139.

27 'Inaugural Address by the President', *RIBA Journal*, November 1952, pp. 3–6.

28 Howard, October 1953, quoted Campbell, *Coventry Cathedral*, pp. 143–4.

29 Approval had to be hastily obtained from the Reconstruction Committee.

30 See Howard, *Ruined and Rebuilt*, ch. 17.

31 Gorton to Thurston, 31 October 1955, quoted Campbell, *Coventry Cathedral*, p. 145.

32 Spence to Gorton, 23 July 1955, Spence Archive.

33 Spence, *Phoenix at Coventry*, p. 105.

34 Lee in Campbell, *To Build a Cathedral*, p. 50.

35 Spence to M. Berthold, 19 November 1956, Spence Archive.

36 Howard, quoted in Andrew Revai, *Sutherland: Christ in Glory in the Tetramorph: The Genesis of the Great Tapestry in Coventry Cathedral*, Pallas Gallery, 1964, p. 92.

37 See *The West Window at Coventry Cathedral*, English Counties Periodicals, p. 6.

38 Spence, *Phoenix at Coventry*, p. 18.

39 Howard to Sutherland, quoted Campbell, *Coventry Cathedral*, p. 109.

40 Quoted in F. Spalding, 'John Piper and Coventry, in War and Peace', *Burlington Magazine*, vol. CXLV, July 2003, p. 498.

41 Spalding, 'John Piper and Coventry', p. 500.

42 Howard, *Ruined and Rebuilt*, p. 113.

43 Hammond, *Liturgy and Architecture*.

44 Quoted Campbell, *To Build a Cathedral*, p. 39.

45 Spence to Williams, 25 May 1960, quoted Campbell, *Coventry Cathedral*, p. 212.

46 *Manchester Evening News*, 25 May 1962.

47 Visnevskaya could not get a visa, and her part was taken by Heather Harper.

48 Quoted Campbell, *Coventry Cathedral*, p. 241.

49 Spence resigned in 1967.

50 Reyner Banham, *New Statesman*, 25 May 1962.

51 Henry Russell Hitchcock, 'English Architecture in the Early 1960s', *Zodiac* 12, 1964, p. 39.

52 Howard to Spence, 16 October 1972, Spence Archive, describes setting up a central altar in the nave on the tenth anniversary of the Consecration. Colin Semper also experimented with this arrangement during the 1980s.

2 THEOLOGY, WORSHIP AND SPIRITUALITY

MICHAEL SADGROVE

Introduction

In 1995 a little-noticed but thoughtful novel about Coventry was published, *The Glass Night* by John de Falbe. It is a story told by a father to his son in the aftermath of a tragedy affecting them both. Dan, the father, is a Holocaust survivor, a German Jewish émigré. He is rescued as a baby from the Nazi *Kristallnacht** of 1938 and comes to England, where he is brought up in wartime Coventry. The Blitz of November 1940 and its aftermath are therefore at the core of his personal memory. When, years later, his daughter-in-law lies in a coma, Dan becomes preoccupied with recovering and mapping his childhood memories, discerning the relationship between past and present, discovering how his personal narrative connects with, and in some ways symbolizes, that of his adopted city.

While Dan is growing up, the city's reconstruction is being fiercely debated. There is talk of building a new Cathedral, and this too is a matter of heated debate. De Falbe gives us a cameo of many a conversation that must have taken place in the drawing rooms of suburban post-war Coventry.

'And what do you think should be done with the Cathedral, Julius?'

'No question about it,' David intruded. 'It should be rebuilt.'

'As was,' opined his father . . .

'Personally' [said Julius], 'I don't think it should be rebuilt. After the war we're going to need houses in Coventry, not a huge, expensive new Cathedral.'

'But you can't just let the Cathedral be destroyed!' Mr Shearer insisted.

'It's destroyed already.'

'That's not the point. We've got to show 'em!'

'Show who? What?'

'Show that we've still got the spunk in us, boy, show that we can still *do* it! Otherwise they'll stop bringing their industry here and we won't be able to afford your precious houses!' . . .

'In any case, what's this about "our" Cathedral? I thought we were all good Methodists,' [said Julius] . . . winking cheekily at his mother.

David saw the wink but chose to ignore it. 'The point of the Cathedral is not that it's Anglican or Methodist or anything else. It's symbolic of the city.'

'And would it still be symbolic of the city if the majority of the population weren't Christians?'

'You're being deliberately difficult, Julius.'

'No, he's got a point', said Mr Phelps unexpectedly. 'It would be different in that case, I think. But the fact is that we aren't all heathen. We're Christians. I've never been much of a one for theology myself, but it's obvious to me that the Cathedral occupies an important place in the heart of an English city.'

'At most, it's symbolic of what the city was,' said Julius. 'And as far as reconstruction goes, speaking for myself, I'm interested in what the city is and will be, not in what it was.'

'It will never be anything if you ignore what it was,' said David.[1]

Important issues are raised here about the nature of the new Cathedral and what it might symbolize: confidence or defiance, hope or nostalgia, civic pride or social need. These are not all antitheses; but they do hint at different assumptions about what a cathedral is *for*, and specifically what the religious or 'spiritual' role of a new Coventry Cathedral might be. Although the language is conversational and informal, De Falbe's protagonists are debating issues about meaning and symbolism that are utterly central to the new Cathedral's purpose. To put their question in a more focused way: in post-war Coventry, a place that both we and the novelist know was destined to become one of England's ethnically diverse and secularized cities, what would it mean to build a cathedral that represented the sacred at the heart of human life and activity?

In an important recent study, John Inge explores the meanings of sacred 'space' and 'place' in Christian theology. He argues for a sacramental view of place that is constructed as a result of how a community's experience, memory and spiritual awareness coalesce around it. 'Place' is 'space' that is charged with meaning because of the associations it carries, especially encounter with fellow human beings and, above all, with God.

The encounter is built into the story of the place for the Christian community as well as the individual, and this is how places become designated as 'holy'. Holy places are thus associated with holy people, to whom and in whom something of the glory of God has been revealed. The existence of such holy places should facilitate a sacramental perception and serve as a reminder that all time and place belong to God in Christ – the part is set aside on behalf of, rather than instead of, the whole.[2]

It is the meanings that belong to Coventry Cathedral as sacred space that are my concern in this chapter. I want to consider the Cathedral as a specifically *religious* place set apart for worship, prayer and the nurture of the spiritual life. My question is, how far has the Cathedral as a religious space proved able to guard the sacred and to explore its connectedness to the whole of life? What does its architecture symbolize, consciously and unconsciously, for the citizens of Coventry, for its visitors, for those who work and pray in it? How has the building functioned as a holy or, in Inge's terms, 'sacramental' place for worshippers, pilgrims and those who, even if not conventionally religious, look to it to nurture a more aware, reflective approach to life? Fifty years on, can we identify its strengths and weaknesses when it comes to celebrating the liturgy in and around the building? I shall approach these questions by looking in turn at the building as a *theological* statement, as a space for *liturgy*, and as a place of *spirituality and prayer*.

The Cathedral as a theological statement

The brief for those submitting designs in the 1950 competition to find the architect for the new Cathedral laid out its theological agenda.

> The Cathedral is to speak to us and to generations to come of the Majesty, the Eternity and the Glory of God . . . It stands as a witness to the central dogmatic truths of the Christian Faith. Architecturally it should seize on those truths and thrust them upon the man who comes in from the street.[3]

This is to recognize that form follows function and that architecture embodies values that have a profound effect on human beings. One of the charges sometimes laid against Coventry Cathedral is that as an expression of this theological brief, its symbolism is both too 'obvious' and too self-conscious. It also seems strangely untroubled by the doubts and ambivalences that the painful history of Coventry's destruction might have evoked. But I want to argue nevertheless that the Cathedral is a rich and surprisingly complex theological symbol-system with many layers of meaning attaching to the 'sacred'. Out of many possible approaches I want to explore two dimensions of this complexity: what the Cathedral says about *the death and resurrection of Jesus,* and about *the immanence and transcendence of God.*

The theme of the Cathedral as a sequence of spaces that embody the Christian story of death and resurrection was there from the beginning. Provost Howard recalled in 1962: 'As I went . . . into the ruined Cathedral on the morning after the destruction, there flashed into my mind the deep certainty that as the Cathedral had been crucified with Christ, so it would rise again with Him.'[4] The placing of the new building outside the footprint of the bombed-out church, but in clear axial relationship with it as its narthex*, was consciously meant to signify the journey from crucifixion to resurrection. Spence writes: 'I saw the old Cathedral as standing clearly for the Sacrifice, one side of the Christian Faith, and I knew my task was to design a new one which should stand for the Triumph of the Resurrection.'[5]

But the two buildings, taken together as the architect intended as a single theological entity, read in a more complex way than this. (I need to underline here the importance of understanding 'Coventry Cathedral' as both buildings together, even though it is understandable that we easily slip into the inaccurate but convenient parlance of 'old' Cathedral and 'new'.) It is more complex because the Ruins, in so far as they represent a past and finished act of destruction, are more like an empty cross than a crucifix bearing the body of a dead man. In Christian iconography, the empty cross is not so much a symbol of the death of Jesus as of his death-and-resurrection, understood as a single redeeming event. Empty and open to the sky, the Ruins are an eloquent symbol of life-through-death, of Easter hope and ascent through sacrifice. The custom, dating back to the Second World War itself, of celebrating the Eucharist at the altar in the Ruins early in the morning on Easter Day and Whit Sunday (now Pentecost), was an expression of this.

If there is resurrection as well as passion in the Ruins, there is passion as well as resurrection in the new Cathedral. The avenue of thorns created by the canopies of the canons' stalls form a kind of via dolorosa* for communicants on the pilgrimage to the high altar. Here, so close to the tapestry as to make its huge images dissolve, the dominating feature is Geoffrey Clarke's great altar cross. Set within it is the original cross formed out of the medieval nails that littered the Ruins after their destruction. This is the most eloquent symbol of the taking into the new building the central truth about the old. But it is far from being the only one. Sutherland's tapestry contains as its lower section one of the bleakest representations of the crucifixion in contemporary art. The sequence of nave windows tells of suffering and death leading to transfiguration. This all indicates how in both old and new buildings, death and resurrection are understood as a conjoined 'paschal' or Easter reality.

PRAYER FOR THE WEEK

A witness to forgiveness after the 1940 Coventry raid inspires Steve Aisthorpe.

*All have sinned and fallen short of the
glory of God.*
The hatred which divides nation from
nation, race from race, class from class
Father forgive.
The covetous desires of people and
nations to possess what is not their own
Father forgive.
The greed which exploits the work of
human hands and lays waste the earth
Father forgive.

Our envy of the welfare and happiness of others
Father forgive.
Our indifference to the plight of the
imprisoned, the homeless, the refugee
Father forgive.
The lust which dishonours the bodies of
men, women and children
Father forgive.
The pride which leads us to trust in
ourselves and not in God
Father forgive.
Be kind to one another, tender-hearted,
forgiving one another, as God in
Christ forgave you.

The Luftwaffe's *Blitzkrieg* began on the evening of 14 November 1940. At dawn, the immensity of the destruction became clear: residential areas reduced to ruins; Coventry Cathedral just charred timbers and smoking masonry.

The tragedies of Coventry were part of a protracted series of horrific retaliatory exchanges. Thus is the record of human society. Yet this prayer represents one of those high points in humanity's story, when people of exemplary grace and courage break away from the prevailing current. As mass burials began, the Provost of Coventry, the Very Revd Dick Howard, inscribed the powerful and compassionate words of Jesus on the blackened wall of the sanctuary: 'Father forgive' (*Faith*, November 2007, p. 9).

The seed of a prophetic vocation was planted. On Christmas Day, in a national radio broadcast from the Ruins, Howard urged forgiveness, and committed himself to work with those who had perpetrated the destruction, in order 'to build a kinder, more Christ-like world'.

The litany begins with a verse (Romans 3.23) from what Dr Leon Morris suggests is 'possibly the single most important paragraph ever written'. It is a stark wake-up call to the fact that we are all in the same boat – all in need of forgiveness.

As the prayer progresses, it brings to mind global issues, but simultaneously guides us through a personal examination. Reconciliation begins in us. Gandhi's observation that 'we must be the change we wish to see' is often quoted glibly, but his unique ability to stem conflict was in large measure due to his absolute embodiment of all that he called on others to be and do.

To pray this litany takes courage. It unmasks attitudes that demand we confront them. Here are Dante's 'seven roots of sinfulness'. Here are the vices at the root of every conflict. Whether war in the Middle East, friction at the office, a playground fall-out, or festering congregational dispute – trace back the tendrils of conflict, and here are the origins.

Do not rush into 'Father forgive'. At each stanza, the Spirit's searchlight must be allowed to shine. Then those words come as they should – from a profound and pressing need.

The cover of R. T. Kendall's book *Total Forgiveness* (Hodder & Stoughton, 2003) contains a photograph of Mount Everest. It speaks of the daunting demands of forgiveness, but reminds us, too, of our lofty calling. Only 'total forgiveness' can lance the festering wounds of conflict, and for that we must not only kiss goodbye to revenge, but also pray for blessing for our antagonists.

The closing exhortation reminds us of the imperative place of simple acts of kindness in reconciliation, and also that our unfathomable forgiveness in Christ provides us with security, motivation and inspiration to be far more generous in our own forgiving, doing our part in what Archbishop Tutu called 'drawing out the sting that threatens to poison'.

Steve Aisthorpe
Mission development worker for the Church of Scotland
in the Highlands and Islands.
Church Times, 9 July 2010

NB: Despite the above, evidence suggests that the words 'Father Forgive' were not permanently inscribed on the sanctuary wall until 1948.

What Coventry is saying is that life lived out of faith in the death and resurrection of Jesus is experienced as a tension between death and resurrection *now*, as well as being a journey from death, judgement and hell into heaven as ultimate destiny. To walk from the Ruins into the new Cathedral is not simply to walk from Good Friday into Easter as is often said. It is to make the entire paschal journey of Baptism and Eucharist in which life is always present in death as well as death in life. The font, placed so close to the transparent west end of the new building as to be clearly visible from outside it, and the high altar, whose height, scale and position directly beneath the tapestry give the building such an overwhelming sense of climax, make this spiritual and theological statement unambiguously. Moreover, the very robustness of this theological statement made by the building and its principal focal points

*The Crucifixion: a detail from the lower section of
Graham Sutherland's tapestry.*

make it difficult to see how any liturgical reordering could be undertaken without dramatically subverting the message of the Cathedral, as we shall see.

A second theological issue raised by the building is its management of the tension between transcendence and immanence. Classical theology understands God as transcendent in that the Creator is beyond the categories of the ordinary, the time-bound and the material, beyond empirical knowledge, beyond the capacity of language to speak about other than symbolically or analogically. But it also understands as immanent a God who interpenetrates the cosmos, is actively at work in creation and is known in human experience. The theological task is to hold these insights in relationship with each other, not to collapse faith into the one or the other. Because 'sacred space' is invested with meanings about God, a church building inevitably takes a position on this theological spectrum. Its design, liturgical arrangement and decoration will be experienced as stressing the immanence of a God who has chosen to be intimate with humanity, or the transcendence of a God who is beyond our very imagining. In Christian thought the incarnation is the key to resolving this tension, for if a transcendent God has humbled himself to live immanently among his own creation, a church would strive, in architecture as in life, to achieve balance and hold transcendence and immanence in equilibrium.

However, Coventry seems to me to stand at the 'high' end of that spectrum. In this it reflects the language of the brief which spoke of majesty, eternity and glory. Had it spoken instead of mystery, suffering and self-emptying love, the building might have been very different. This is not a comment on the size of the building but on what it is trying to be. Nikolaus Pevsner points out[6] that although the Cathedral is not large compared to the great medieval cathedrals, it manages to *appear* so. This insight is, I think, the clue. It is as if Spence has cleverly exploited perspectives and created illusions in order to 'expand' the space rather in the tradition of religious iconography emphasizing divine presence by inflating the size of whatever is construed as its container. He chose not to create or suggest an intimate atmosphere out of the same volume. Part of this is no doubt to do with the popular if questionable assumption that a cathedral has to be 'grand'.

The explicit programme of Sutherland's great tapestry reinforces this. Entitled 'Christ in Glory in the Tetramorph'*, it depicts the risen Christ surrounded by the four living creatures of the Apocalypse*.[7] He presides as priest and king over the entire cathedral space, fulfilling the same function as the figure of the risen Christ on the tympanum* at Vézelay in Burgundy, sending his apostles into the world to preach the gospel. Both churches have a transcendent Christocentric understanding of the world and envisage the church building as the articulation of this truth. In both, diminutive human figures are assigned subservient positions at the feet of Christ where they have the important effect of magnifying the physical size, and therefore the transcendent significance, of the risen Lord above.

Because the tapestry is so dominant, one way of reading the Cathedral is to see it as its primary 'text', and the rest of the building as commentary on it. Spence tells us that the tapestry was at the heart of his vision of the Cathedral from the very beginning. Moreover, with the west wall dissolved into a glass screen with no clear boundary between the old Cathedral and the new, the space, instead of being enclosed, flows out across the Ruins and out into the world. We can see the tapestry from the east end of the Ruins. So Christ reigns in glory here too, not simply inside the new church. This makes an important statement about the relationship between

*Graham Sutherland's Christ presides over The Veneration of
the Cross as the clergy and congregation kneel beneath the
red-draped cross during the Good Friday liturgy in 2010.*

sacred and secular: 'the earth is the Lord's', and because all things belong to him,
everything is rendered potentially sacred.

This lack of enclosure or defined boundary is also perpetuated inside the building.
Its thresholds, the liminal points marking the transition between nave and choir,
and choir and sanctuary, are, apart from changes in floor level, indistinctly marked
and ambiguous, as they sometimes are in Gothic 'hall' churches with their even light
and undifferentiated spaces. Despite the choir stalls, the spatial characteristics of the
choir are little different from those of the nave. The absence of screens, of significant

accents to mark thresholds, of much sense of enclosure anywhere, all speak of a building in which everything is exposed to the searching gaze of Christ in Glory. At times it is undoubtedly exhilarating, at times reassuring, at times perhaps oppressive. It can be a relief to find refuge in the only truly intimate space in the whole Cathedral, the Chapel of Christ in Gethsemane, aptly likened by Pevsner to a dark womb-like cave. Only here, and to some extent in the Chapel of Unity, do we seem to glimpse the real possibility of divine immanence in human life.

The Chapel of Unity: daily prayers are held in the Chapel, which is physically linked to the nave and is the responsibility of the Joint Council of all Christian denominations.

We are uncomfortable with a theology whose confident transcendence perhaps comes perilously close to the romantic triumphalism of De Falbe's protagonist. We are more at home now with ideas about the vulnerability of God, his self-emptying for the sake of humanity, the belief that God suffers in and with broken human beings and does not preside serenely above the cosmos untouched by the pain of the world. When I wrote my book on the tapestry, I argued that the wounded hands and feet of the risen Christ were to be understood as the eternal suffering of the Divine in and through his world. I believe that is theologically valid, but I doubt if the tapestry is read by most people in that way. Yet for most people the problem of suffering is the number one issue with which religious faith has to struggle. It is important that somehow contemporary religious architecture demonstrates how this (literally) crucial question is visibly and credibly presented to the world. In the twenty-first century we would be more likely to do this in ways that are in tune with our values of compassion, inclusiveness; perhaps, too, a certain postmodern reticence in recognition of the provisional, fragmented nature of human experience.

It is in these respects that it could be argued that Coventry has dated rather quickly. The past, even the comparatively recent past, is another country: they do theology differently there. This does not make the Cathedral any less fine or deserving of our respect as the carefully worked-out expression of a particular neo-orthodox theological understanding. But it does place it in its time. This had to happen; in my view it is a good thing. It enables us to see it more clearly for what it is and celebrate the undoubted achievement it represents.

The Cathedral as a liturgical space

Theology flows seamlessly into liturgy. Liturgy articulates the theology of a faith community; it learns theology, at least implicitly, from the texts and rituals of the liturgy. One of the key meeting points is ecclesiology, the nature of the Church. The theological brief for the new Cathedral states:

> The doctrine and the worship of the Church of England is liturgically centred on the Eucharist. The Cathedral should be built to enshrine the altar. This should be the ideal of the architect, not to conceive a building and to place in it an altar, but to conceive an altar and to create a building. In the Anglican liturgy it is the people's altar; the altar should gather the people, it should offer access for worship and the interpretation of the Word.[8]

These much-quoted words are critical for our estimate of the Cathedral as a liturgical space. I have already suggested that the building actually *functions* as if it were created round the tapestry rather than the altar: from the nave, this is what first compels our attention. But Spence's spatial skill was such that by placing the tapestry and altar in relationship to each other, he was able to suggest that at the Eucharist, the true president is not the human priest but Christ in Glory, seen above with arms outstretched in welcome, celebration and blessing.

It is well known that Bishop Gorton would have welcomed a cathedral with a central altar, or at least an altar sufficiently forward of the traditional eastward location as to put it in closer relationship to the worshipping community. This would be, he thought, to create a building that offered a genuinely contemporary expression of what it meant to be the Church. It was not to be, and this was probably the most controversial and far-reaching decision made about the building. Writing in 1960, that is, before the Cathedral was even completed, Peter Hammond issued a trenchant critique of the design's claim to be contemporary, either as architecture or (my concern here) as liturgical space. He said:

> The new Cathedral at Coventry has already been hailed as a modern church, wholly of its time. I believe that this is a highly superficial judgment: that it is in fact a building which contributes nothing to the solution of the real problems of church design and perpetuates a conception of a church which owes far more to the romantic movement than to the New Testament or authentic Christian tradition . . . What really matters is whether or not the building embodies a modern understanding of the Christian mystery; whether or not it is informed by a theological programme which takes account of the new insights of biblical theology and patristic and liturgical scholarship.[9]

A few years later, when the principles of church design were strongly influenced by the liturgical movement, just this liturgical scheme was proposed for the new Metropolitan Cathedral at Liverpool. Its central altar with the worshipping community gathered around it is in marked contrast to Coventry's traditional liturgical layout. To that extent, the Coventry building can be said to be (in a well-worn phrase) the last of the medieval cathedrals rather than the first of the new. Liturgical experience at Liverpool may lead some to say: so much the better. Liturgy in the round is an excellent concept, expressing as it does an ecclesiology of *koinonia**, shared participation in holy things, as well as a more immanent understanding of God. But it is difficult to manage effectively, especially in a large space. And it can foster an inward-looking attitude where, not only physically but mentally and spiritually, a congregation can turn its back to the world and end up talking only to itself.

But what of the experience of worship at Coventry?

The architect of Coventry's liturgy was Canon Joseph Poole, Precentor from 1958 to 1977, and a member of the original team to shape the ministry and mission of the new Cathedral. A later successor, Adrian Daffern, described him in a centenary address as 'one of the most innovative liturgists of the twentieth century'.[10] He quotes his saying: 'Liturgy is not something said: it is something done. Liturgy is the total oblation of the creature to the creator. Christian liturgy is the total oblation of the redeemed community to the Father through the Son in the Holy Spirit.' He believed that liturgy was a theatre of the soul, a dramatization, like the building itself, of the convictions of the Christian faith. He would have approved of Aidan Kavanagh's view that liturgical space was for the public transaction of matters of life and death, not for the easy enjoyment of cotton wool comforts.[11] Poole relished the Cathedral as a hard, bracing space, a place of truth where the costly realities of life could be spoken about through word, symbol and ceremony. He believed that liturgy should challenge and exhilarate, its power to console founded on a genuine encounter with God within a community of love and truth rather than based on fantasy or wishful thinking. His work stood alongside that of the Cathedral's drama department, which in a related way also sought to make truth vivid, accessible and experienced.

Liturgy: something done, not simply said. On Maundy Thursday 2007, Bishop Colin Bennetts washes the feet of a member of the congregation.

To him, liturgy was something *done*, not simply said. An entire generation of clergy, choristers, vergers, servers, lesson-readers and congregations were taught as at drama school how to *perform*. Rubrics were specific stage instructions. Amens were not simply to be *said*, they were to be *exclaimed*. Silences after lessons and during prayers were to be *profound*. Responses were to be said *loudly and clearly,* alleluias to be *shouted*. Poole understood that a building like Coventry Cathedral would stretch both participants and congregation to the limit. The Cathedral's acoustic with its long echo was splendid, but it was unforgiving to those, speakers and singers, who failed to articulate. The distances across which ministers performed required simple, strongly coloured vestments (designed by John Piper and executed by Louis Grossé, among the best of their period anywhere). It needed a deep understanding of how liturgy is an 'embodiment' of divine reality, and so called for a clear grammar of movement and gesture that would be in the best sense balletic. The compromised sight-lines at the edges of the nave suggested an approach to liturgy that was processional and that was deployed in all the parts of the building rather than remaining tied to one place. (In this, Poole was reverting to sound medieval precedent in cathedral liturgy, for in the Middle Ages the last thing a nave was intended to be was a static auditorium.)

In the light of Poole's sustained efforts in the 1960s to create ceremonies that would do justice to the new building, Peter Brooke's observations in his groundbreaking book *The Empty Space* are worth recalling:

In Coventry . . . a new Cathedral has been built, according to the best recipe for achieving a noble result. Honest, sincere artists, the 'best', have been grouped together to make a civilized stab at celebrating God and Man and Culture and Life through a collective act. So there is a new building, fine ideas, beautiful glasswork – only the ritual is threadbare. Those Ancient and Modern hymns, charming perhaps in a little country church, those numbers on the wall, those dog-collars and the lessons – they are sadly inadequate here. The new place cries out for a new ceremony, but of course it is the new ceremony that should have come first – it is the ceremony in all its meanings that should have dictated the shape of the place, as it did when all the great mosques and cathedrals and temples were built. Goodwill, sincerity, reverence, belief in culture are not quite enough: the outer form can only take on real authority if the ceremony has real authority – and who today can possibly call the tune?[12]

This, Brooke contrasted with what I take to be his ideal, Artaud's[13] vision of 'holy theatre':

What he wanted in his search for a holiness was absolute: he wanted a theatre that would be a hallowed place; he wanted the theatre served by a band of dedicated actors and directors who would create out of their own natures an unending succession of violent stage images, bringing about such powerful immediate explosions of human matter that no-one would ever again revert to a theatre of anecdote and talk . . . He wanted an audience that would drop all its defences, that would allow itself to be perforated, shocked, startled and raped, so that at the same time it could be filled with a powerful new charge.[14]

What was Brooke getting at? What was the 'new ceremony' he looked for at Coventry? He could not have meant (could he?) a new liturgical *text*? He might as well have asked for a new text of Shakespeare. Brooke's Shakespeare productions such as the legendary *Midsummer Night's Dream* have all wrestled with how old texts can speak afresh to contemporary society. This was precisely Joseph Poole's programme. He wanted to devise liturgy that could be as vivid and life-changing as the best contemporary theatre. And for him, as for Brooke's Shakespeare, the words were nothing on their own. In any case, he had no power to change statutory liturgical texts beyond minor adaptations for the Coventry use. The discipline was to create an alchemy that would transform text into drama, making the words real and concrete through the passionate commitment of those who performed them. The true text of liturgy was not the words at all but in the ceremony-as-performed, word-made-flesh. In so far as this became a reality, it would be truly incarnational.

Perhaps the climax of 50 years of liturgy at Coventry came at the very outset with the service of consecration in 1962. As I write I have before me my much-prized copy of the order of service for the twofold rite celebrated on Friday 25 and Saturday 26 May. It is half an inch thick, and a work of love. It is printed on fine heavy paper in 16-point Bembo with all the rubrics in red. The attention to detail is immaculate. Those who were present at the ceremony say it was an unforgettable experience, particularly the trinitarian invocation at the entrance of the Bishop at the west end of the church. The rubric (so Poolean) says that he 'lifts up both his hands and calls out':

> COME, Father of inexpressible Majesty;
> Come, Lord Jesus, the Father's incomparable Son;
> Come Holy Spirit, most blessed Lord;
> Come, Holy and Adorable Trinity:
> Come to this house.
> Come today, come now, come always.
> Come, Lord, come.

We can imagine long discussions with the printer (Cambridge University Press) about the indentation of those lines of text, which I have preserved as it appears in the order of service.

I do not have the space to discuss the Consecration service in detail, though its shape and texture are every inch an expression of Poole's vision of cathedral liturgy. It is a pity that this splendid document, so clearly designed to be a permanent memorial of the event, does not contain an introduction setting out the aims of the service and the thinking behind it. Perhaps this is evidence that he expected liturgy to speak for itself, for it is after all the Church's primary form of speech. But in another of his early productions, a rationale for liturgy is set out. This is Poole's order of service for *Evensong in Coventry Cathedral* (1963). Once again, the quality of the production is superb. But this time Poole not only offers an explanation of the rite but also provides helpful devotional texts to enable the (perhaps unfamiliar) worshipper to make the most of the experience of cathedral worship. To some, Poole's liturgical aesthetic smacked of elitism, but a section entitled 'To help you to pray for five minutes' reflects his pastoral instinct that worshippers should be supported in their approach to liturgy and that too much should not be asked of people too quickly.

'What is Evensong?' asks Poole. He replies:

Evensong in Coventry Cathedral is a very tiny fragment of something else: it is a fragment of the worship which is offered to God by christian (*sic*) people, every hour of the twenty-four, in every part of the world. When you come to Evensong here, it is as if you were dropping in on a conversation already in progress – a conversation between God and men which began long before you were born, and will go on long after you are dead. So do not be surprised, or disturbed, if there are some things in the conversation which you do not at once understand.

After analysing the shape of the service, he adds a note about the music of Evensong:

Worship without music does not easily soar; and wherever the Church has been concerned to make worship really expressive of truth, music has been used: simple music for the untrained worshipper, more elaborate music for the trained choir. The music of a Cathedral choir is the counterpart of the architecture and the stained glass of the building: it is a finely wrought music, in which the musicians offer on behalf of the people what the people would wish to do themselves, if they had the ability.

The rite itself is prefaced by a poem by John Donne – Poole was perhaps most at home in the Anglican spirituality of the seventeenth century. The text of Evensong is that of the Book of Common Prayer with some Coventry adornments. The lessons are to be followed by silence for reflection, still a Coventry practice. 'Magnificat' is explained as 'the song which Mary sang when she knew that she was to be the mother of Jesus'; Nunc Dimittis as the song of Simeon thanking God 'for allowing him, before he dies, to see the infant Jesus, the long-expected Redeemer'. When it comes to the Creed, choir and people are to join with the Precentor, 'firmly and clearly'. Strict limits are imposed on the intercessions: 'one of the Ministers offers three prayers, to each of which the choir and the people reply: Amen'. There are final responses and a closing hymn. But when choir and ministers have withdrawn, there is further help for worshippers under the heading 'Before you leave'. They are urged:

Do not be in a hurry to go; and do nothing to disturb those who wish to listen to the music played on the organ. Kneel or sit for some moments of private prayer. Thank God for the beauty of the Cathedral; for its music; and for any particular comfort, or challenge, which your visit has afforded you.

And there are some suggested prayers before leaving.

'He made himself of no reputation, and took upon him the Form of a Servant.' The Cathedral's evening service on Christmas Eve was Joseph Poole's inspired creation.

Joseph Poole's legacy was profound. Many of his texts remained in use for decades; some, such as the Litany of Reconciliation, written in 1958, have become classics that are widely anthologized and used across the world. Up to the 1990s, the Sunday morning eucharistic rite was still drawing on his texts, albeit expressed in contemporary language. The legendary Christmas Eve service, 'The Form of a Servant', was Poole's inspired creation for the first Christmas in the new building in 1962, and while it has seen many adaptations since then, the shape of that service with its emphasis on incarnation as a vocation to servanthood remains at its heart. In 1987 I inherited a rite that, unlike most carol services, ended not with the cliché of a blaze of light and the triumphant bellowing out of 'Hark the herald . . .', but with the procession disappearing into the distance in darkness to the accompaniment of

Debussy's *Syrinx* played by a solo flautist, as if to say: incarnation is a profound mystery, and as the philosopher Ludwig Wittgenstein put it, 'in the face of that whereof we cannot speak, we must remain silent'.

This approach to Christmas liturgy was genuinely pioneering. The convergence of its liturgical grammar of movement and stillness, light and dark, word and music, symbol and text with the architectural grammar of the building itself has proved enduring. It exemplified the Coventry style and ethos that Poole described in his introduction to the Sunday morning eucharistic rite:

> The Communion in Coventry Cathedral has music, movement, colour, pageantry – and has at its heart *philadelphia*, that love of the brethren which is the hallmark of the redeemed community.[15]

I think it is true to say that however much its forms have undergone changes in 50 years, the vision of a vibrant liturgy that does justice to the building, engages with human beings and is transformational in its effect has been central to the Cathedral's life throughout that time.

However, the Cathedral also poses distinctive liturgical challenges. My experience as Precentor during the 1980s and 1990s taught me that the building is least effective when used purely as an auditorium. As I have already said, medieval cathedrals were never designed as auditoria in which large numbers of people *sat*, but as processional spaces in which to move around and express the understanding of church as a pilgrim people.[16] Early in the twentieth century Ninian Comper said of the Victorian reordering of the naves of medieval cathedrals:

> The attempt to use the church as if the whole building were a parish church, or one great choir, produces a most uncomfortable strain upon both the ministers and the congregation; while from the point of view of architectural beauty it is absolutely ruinous.[17]

There is, to my mind, an uncomfortable tension in Coventry when it comes to the meaning assigned to the nave. It *looks* precisely like an auditorium; whichever way the seating is configured (and there have been experiments without end with different arrangements facing all points of the compass), sitting still and listening is what the nave looks as though it is primarily for. And this has the effect of making the space feel a static sitting-place, a destination in its own right, rather than a dynamic place of movement that impels the worshipper-as-pilgrim towards the building's focal point. In this, the sense of liturgical climax intended by the high altar and tapestry is perhaps compromised by the nave or, at least, the sea of chairs that fills it.

When we designed the (then) new eucharistic rite for the Cathedral in the late 1980s, we tried to understand the logic of the building in the light of 25 years of liturgical experience. This included building into it as much movement as possible, for example, using the nave for the opening penitential rite so that a sense of journey through the nave towards the choir and sanctuary could be suggested from the outset. We wanted to try to recover something of the key relationship that exists between the theatre as a building and the performance that takes place within it. In his book *Actor, Architecture and Audience,* Iain Mackintosh explores how the architecture of theatre plays a crucial part in 'the prickle on the back of the head, the chill in the stomach, the tears of laughter and the community of celebration'.[18] His thesis is that the place is as much the thing as the play. Since then there have been other attempts to use the liturgical space as creatively as possible for both eucharistic and non-eucharistic worship. Some of these have been genuinely innovative, some not so successful. Much of the challenge has focused on the position of the altar.

I have already mentioned the debate prior to the approval of Spence's design. Inevitably, when church reorderings became *de rigueur* in the 1980s, there were calls to explore a nave altar arrangement at Coventry. I arrived as Precentor at the end of a period of experiment that left a good deal of bad feeling in parts of the Cathedral community at that time. I thought carefully about what recommendation to make to the Cathedral Council about this. It seemed to me then, and still seems now (*pace* Louise Campbell's thoughtful contribution to this volume),[19] that the high altar is so carefully placed in theological and physical relation to the tapestry that to install a permanent altar in any other position risks robbing the tapestry of its eucharistic significance and sense of invitation. This is particularly the case when a robed choir is placed behind a nave altar as a kind of human reredos* which cuts right across Spence's scheme as well as foreshortening the nave perspective on the tapestry. It subverts Spence's defining idea that only from the high altar can the sequence of eastward-orientated nave windows be seen in their entirety, and their 'story' gathered up at the eucharistic act.

Coventry Cathedral is probably the most difficult cathedral in England to reorder, since it is so clearly of one piece. As part of our audit of cathedral worship in the early 1990s, I invited a professor of theatre studies to attend the Sunday Eucharist and comment on it. He startled us by saying that we needed to exploit the high altar and tapestry properly, and that one way to do this would be for the three sacred ministers to face (liturgical) east. (I should point out here that in Spence's building, with its axis set at right angles to the traditional orientation of the old parish church, the high altar is at the geographical north end of the Cathedral.) The human faces of the ministers would not then compete with the face of Christ on the tapestry, and the John Piper vestments would be exposed in front of the altar to their full extent.

This, he argued, was the liturgical equivalent of the theatrical use of the mask, and he believed it would enhance our worship.

Of course this was precisely what Spence intended. The high altar was designed for eastward-facing liturgy, the norm at the time. We did not go down the road suggested by our consultant, but we did learn that the art of liturgy in large performing spaces is about understanding the possibilities and constraints inherent in a given space. We also learned that there is no substitute for working hard and constantly at the performance skills of those who participate in liturgy, both lay and ordained. To move well and stand well, to preside or assist at worship, to 'hold' the sacred in a way that confers dignity and nobility, does not happen without thought and practice as to what it is we are *doing* in liturgy. Add to that the particular challenges that Coventry Cathedral poses because of its long echo. It calls for much rehearsal if liturgy is to rise to the challenge of a great building. In a large space, even a nave altar does not make it easier, nor does it automatically create a sense of genuine *communitas* if it speaks across the message of the building itself. This is what I believe to be a critical issue at Coventry.

The Cathedral as a spiritual focus

Coventry Cathedral, as we have seen, is a complex symbol-system that embodies a powerful community *mythos*. Fundamental is the narrative of its own death and resurrection, ruin and renewal, interpreted in the context of the paschal mystery. Firmly embedded within this is the equally central theme of reconciliation. Basing his message on the Pauline theology that, in the cross, human beings are reconciled to God and therefore to one another, Provost Howard spoke in his Christmas Day broadcast of 1940 of how the new Cathedral would be a sign of reconciliation and of enmity transfigured into friendship. He looked for 'a kinder, more Christchild-like world' of which the words 'Father, forgive', engraved behind the rubble altar with its charred cross, were the symbol.

Other contributions to this book explore how the Cathedral contributed to the national post-war programme of rebuilding relations between Britain and Germany. It did this largely by creating a particular nexus that brought into relationship three ingredients: a unique history (i.e., its *mythos*), an architecture to make it visible, and symbols and ceremonies to re-enact it (for instance, the recitation each Friday at noon of the Litany of Reconciliation in the Ruins, a ritual as simple as it is moving more than seventy years after the Cathedral's destruction). The Cathedral did not simply make speeches about reconciliation, but made it possible. I shall never forget being present when a former Luftwaffe pilot who had taken part in the raids on

Coventry stood before the charred cross at the fiftieth anniversary service of the Blitz in November 1990, alone with his thoughts and memories in that numinous* place. It was as if the Ruins and the altar of reconciliation had become a statement of anamnesis*, holding collective memory that becomes present and life-changing in the life of communities and individual human beings.

The spirituality of the Cathedral has always had a strong social and political dimension. International reconciliation was the best-known expression of this, and the cross of nails in the high-altar cross, replicated and installed in many places across the world, its symbol. But other aspects of the building express the same vision. John Hutton's screen speaks of how sacred and secular are not separate worlds but belong to a single God-given whole. In particular, the suffering world (represented by the Ruins) is visually, and poignantly, linked to the hope of glory (symbolized by the tapestry). The 'hallowing places' created in the Ruins give contemporary expression to the guild chapels of the old parish church through which the life and work of a prosperous medieval town was honoured, celebrated and offered. The Chapel of Unity speaks both of the quest for unity among Christians and beyond that, surely, to the unity of the human family, a key concern in a city whose diversity calls for a particular focus on relationships between communities of different faith and ethnicity. The Chapel of Christ the Servant, a glass cylinder open to the city on all sides, was designated the Chapel of Industry, the spiritual home of the then pioneering work of the Coventry Industrial Mission. For a time, the sacrament was reserved in this chapel as if it were a huge transparent aumbry* visible to the whole of Priory Street.

This raises the interesting question as to the kind of spirituality the Cathedral fosters. It is important not to claim too much here, but it is arguable that the character of a sacred space is bound to influence the spiritual formation of people whose 'place' it is. I have already cited the work of John Inge in this context. The Cathedral's mission in relation to the 'secular' world is, as we have seen, made explicit in its design, particularly the lack of clear boundary marking out where the 'ordinary' ends and the 'sacred' begins. But there may be another design aspect that is relevant here, and that is the paucity of curves anywhere in the main part of the Cathedral. This is a building that is characterized by assertive, thrusting forms that are decidedly male in character. They are grasping and energizing rather than restful and contemplative. Unlike the medieval Gothic cathedrals to which Coventry is so much in debt, here there are almost no feminine groins* or enclosed spaces to soften the straight lines and sharp edges that dominate the architecture.

Only the Chapels of Gethsemane and Unity provide places of intimate enclosure that offer a different spatial experience from that of the open nave. (The shallow arc of the baptistry window and the undulations of the nave window bays perhaps

The Chapel of Christ in Gethsemane is a place of intimate enclosure. Steven Sykes' Angel is seen through Spence's crown of thorns.

suggest it but only to a much smaller extent.) As to the imagery, the exceptions, importantly, are the tapestry whose play on womb-like mandorla* shapes suggests an important insight into Christ as mother; and the boulder-font, a rough-hewn ovoid perhaps hinting at a folk-memory of the great world-egg from which, in many primitive mythologies, all life sprang. This is an apt symbol of birth into the Christian life through the waters of baptism, a shape echoed in the globular sunburst in John Piper's baptistry window behind. But all in all, the insistence on the masculine is striking. A well-known feminist theologian once told me that it was impossible for anyone, especially a woman, to pray with integrity in front of Sutherland's tapestry, and that my defence of the androgynous elements in it was specious.

The Christian spiritual tradition follows classical Greek thought in recognizing as the two complementary aspects of religious life the *active* and the *contemplative*. One way in which this has been symbolized is through the gospel story of Martha (active endeavour) and Mary (contemplative devotion). A more archetypal approach is to identify the active tendency with the male (phallic) principle, and the contemplative with the female. These archetypes function at an unconscious level, and it would be surprising if they did not influence behaviour. It is speculation to suggest a direct connection between the dominance of masculine forms in architecture and a

55

CATHEDRAL PRAISE

Cathedrals should be flagships for the Church and present the best of different kinds of worship. God's concern is the heart not the outward form. He looks for those who will worship him 'in spirit and in truth' (John 4.23). A more informal kind of service using electric guitars, keyboard and drums is increasingly popular and common in our culture. Part of the cathedral vision worked out with the worshipping community and others over many months in 2002 was the commitment to 'grow healthy congregations who worship God in a variety of ways'. It was also apparent that the average age of the main cathedral congregation was getting increasingly older. On the other hand, the Cathedral is next door to the campus of Coventry University.

So it was decided to start such a service. The emphasis was on informality with no robes, no procession and no written liturgy. There would be time (usually 15–20 minutes) given to continuous worship in song led by a band, and to good biblical exposition (usually 20–25 minutes), working in series through books of the Bible. There would also be time for interviews and testimony and prayer, particularly the encouragement to receive prayer ministry with the laying-on of hands after the service.

In 2002 there was no existing later evening service, so the decision was reached to begin the service after Evensong at 6.30 pm. We began in the Chapter House, which held up to 80 people comfortably. The first service was held in late 2002 and about 25 people turned up. Numbers grew and health and safety reasons required the new congregation to move. There is no medium-sized meeting place and so the only site possible was upstairs in the nave.

In order to try and preserve intimacy, Cathedral Praise moved to the back of the nave near the west window. The space was of immediate benefit, but we have struggles in keeping the intimacy and coping with the acoustics. These were never very good in the Cathedral, and it was certainly not designed for electrical instruments.

The congregation is now an established part of cathedral life. Some members have also started coming to the 10.30 am service. It continues to be a popular service for students and younger people as well as some older ones, and an easier stepping point for some. As ever, there are some tensions. Setting up for the service takes time and there is always the danger of a clash between the end of Evensong and preparation for Cathedral Praise. After the service, people like to hang around for quite a while enjoying cake, coffee and fellowship, and the de-rigging also takes time. This too can put stress on the vergers and locking up times.

Overall, I and many others would argue that Cathedral Praise has added enormously to what the Cathedral has to offer.

John Irvine
Dean of Coventry Cathedral

preference for active as opposed to contemplative spirituality, though it seems to me that (and this is no doubt to oversimplify) an emphasis on *doing* rather than *being* has perhaps tended to characterize the Cathedral's life since 1962. There is also anecdotal evidence about how people *behave* when they come into the building. Most walk around; not many choose to sit still or kneel in prayer or stand for long by the votive candles. And this despite the fact that the tapestry offers a visible, icon-like focus for contemplation that is unique in an English cathedral.

And yet . . . I was one of those who, in 1962, queued for what seemed like many hours to see this unlikely phenomenon of a twentieth-century cathedral. My parents were not conventionally religious people, but they were intrigued by what this new building could say to a nation that already recognized the onset of secularization. At the age of 12, it was one of my first conscious religious encounters. I recall how the jet black floor, then a polished mirror, now scuffed into a permanent grey opaqueness by millions of footfalls, reflected both my own image and that of the stained-glass windows and the tapestry. I left my parents and the human chain that snaked slowly clockwise round the building, and slipped guiltily into the centre of the nave where there was stillness and the opportunity to reflect. Despite the hundreds of visitors, I was almost alone near this still centre of a human whirlpool: perhaps for the reasons I have suggested, or perhaps because the authorities did not encourage it.

I imagine that my perceptions of the Cathedral as a place of pilgrimage and prayer were largely formed that day. That day, the theological brief requiring the architect to design a building that would 'thrust' its truth on those who came through its doors was realized in one young visitor. Its impact was overwhelming and unforgettable. This was the more significant because I had no church background whatsoever, and did not bring any religious assumptions to my experience of the Cathedral. This leads me to question the statement that sacred space necessarily only 'works' effectively when there are shared meanings and a common understanding of religious language and iconography. My experience in four cathedrals is that this is not the experience of many twenty-first-century secularized visitors to sacred buildings who, for all their postmodern perspective with its pick 'n' mix approach to religion, are still touched and moved, and even changed, by what they encounter in them.

It is true that the images and texts of the Christian faith are no longer common currency in the way they once were. But this was already becoming the case in 1962. Even then there was already emerging a sense that meanings are not given and fixed for all time. We bring our own readings to texts; in terms of how human beings interact with architecture both through formal rites and informal experiences, a building is a text to be read and understood. This poses real challenges to all whose ministry in cathedrals is committed to helping visitors with little or no direct religious background interpret these great buildings and what they were built to symbolize and proclaim. There is a clear evangelistic task here. But the evidence is that lack of religious background is not any lack of spiritual aspiration or experience, however much many people lack an oral or visual vocabulary with which to speak about it. Spence's aim of creating a numinous environment that would be 'a serious house' (in the language of Coventry-born poet Philip Larkin) was the same as, if more self-conscious than, that of the builders of the great Romanesque and Gothic cathedrals of Europe, the tradition from which he drew so heavily. For all their artlessness, medieval cathedrals demonstrate at every turn evidence of careful design with a clear eye to its effect on the pilgrim. This is not to manipulate spiritual experience, but to create a setting in which encounter with the divine may take place. This is as true of Coventry as it is of Salisbury or Durham.

Rowan Williams has written of religious art:

For the believer, [art] will communicate the Christian gospel, in both its terror and its transforming hope, to the extent that it does what the gospel should, and dispossess us of our impatient hunger for control, for an understanding that will allow us to exploit. For the non-believer, it may be that the dispossessing force of art is the beginning of a way into grasping what believers are talking about when they claim to be 'reading' the whole world as the work of a self-dispossessing love, which we must be caught up in if we are not to die of isolation and starvation. For both, it is a way back to the body: to the time and space we concretely inhabit, sensed as if for the first time.[20]

Coventry Cathedral has stood as an icon of 'self-dispossessing love' for 50 years. Translating that theological truth into a lived liturgical and spiritual experience is a work in progress. In the lifespan of a cathedral, 50 years is no more than a beginning. But like the Big Bang, the initial conditions set directions of travel. When it comes to worship and prayer, as liturgists sometimes say, 'the building always wins in the end'. A key task for the Cathedral's leadership in the next half-century will

Sir Basil Spence's open spaces accommodate contemporary forms of worship as well as traditional Cathedral liturgy.

be how to understand the given grain of the building and work creatively with it in a way that continues to release its spiritual and human potential. There is much to celebrate in what has been begun at Coventry. There is also much to learn by reflecting on its first half-century as this book abundantly illustrates. For the opportunities that lie ahead for this great building and its ministry are, I believe, even greater in the future than they have been in the past.

* Denotes an entry in the Glossary

Notes

1 John De Falbe, *The Glass Night*, The Cuckoo Press, 1995, pp. 126ff.

2 John Inge, *A Christian Theology of Place*, Ashgate, 2003, p. 90.

3 Basil Spence, *Phoenix at Coventry: The Building of a Cathedral*, Geoffrey Bles, 1962, pp. 3–4.

4 R. T. Howard, *Ruined and Rebuilt: The Story of Coventry Cathedral 1939–1962*, Council of Coventry Cathedral, 1962, pp. 18–19.

5 Spence, *Phoenix at Coventry*, p. 6.

6 N. Pevsner, *The Buildings of England: Warwickshire*, Penguin, 1966, pp. 249ff.

7 Michael Sadgrove, *A Picture of Faith: A Meditation on the Imagery of Christ in Glory*, Kevin Mayhew, 1995.

8 Spence, *Phoenix at Coventry*, p. 4.

9 Peter Hammond, *Liturgy and Architecture*, William Clowes & Son Ltd, 1960, pp. 6–7.

10 Adrian Daffern, 'The Legacy of Canon Joseph Poole', *Friends of Coventry Cathedral Newsletter*, September 2009.

11 Aidan Kavanagh, *Elements of Rite: A Handbook of Liturgical Style*, Pueblo Publishing, 1982, pp. 15, 21.

12 Peter Brooke, *The Empty Space*, Penguin, 1967, pp. 50–1.

13 Antonin Artaud (1896–1948), French theatre director promoted 'in the round' performance, and protested against the loss of mystery and the cult of the commonplace and ordinary in the theatre of his day.

14 Brooke, *The Empty Space*, pp. 59–60.

15 Daffern, 'The Legacy of Canon Joseph Poole'.

16 Michael Sadgrove, 'The Theatre of the Soul', in George Demidowicz (ed.), *Coventry's First Cathedral: The Cathedral and Priory of St Mary*, Paul Watkins, 1994, pp. 169ff.

17 G. W. O. Addleshaw and Frederick Etchells, *The Architectural Setting of Anglican Worship: An Inquiry into the Arrangements for Public Worship in the Church of England from the Reformation to the Present Day*, Faber and Faber, 1948, p. 216.

18 Iain MacKintosh, *Actor, Architecture and Audience,* Routledge, 1993, p. 4.

19 Louise Campbell, 'Architecture, War and Peace', ch. 1 in this volume, p. 27.

20 Rowan Williams, 'Art: Taking Time and Making Sense', in *Images of Christ in Art*, exhibition catalogue, 1994, p. 27.

3 MUSIC AND THE ARTS

MEMBERS OF THE CATHEDRAL

Much of this chapter has been contributed by Heather Wallace and the Editor in conversation with others mentioned in the text.

The Christian Church has been both an enthusiastic patron of the arts, and also at times a severe critic, especially of the theatre. The early Fathers of the Church and seventeenth-century English Puritans like William Prynne were equally opposed to what they regarded as the obscenities of the theatre of their day. Neither Orthodox Judaism nor Islam tolerate the representation of living beings or instrumental music in their places of worship, so it cannot be taken for granted that religious people will welcome every kind of artistic endeavour in their sacred spaces. Christian bodies otherwise very diverse have similar problems with the use of music. The Orthodox Church allows the sound only of the human voice in worship and the Free Church of Scotland permitted instrumental music for the first time in 2010. The Reformation in England, as elsewhere, oversaw the wholesale defacing and destruction of wall paintings and images of saints and martyrs in thousands of churches, viewing them as at best distractions from the Word of God and at worst as idolatrous. But by the mid-twentieth century, after the Romantic movement and the revival of Catholic practices in the Church of England, the Church had once again become a patron of the arts. From the outset there was no question that the ruling policy at Coventry, as at other English cathedrals, would be anything other than to welcome and encourage the worship of God in the performance of a wide variety of music and of dance, to embellish the Cathedral with works of stained glass, lettering and sculpture, and to deepen our understanding and enjoyment of God's world through drama and exhibition.

A feast of art, 1962

This whole-hearted embrace of the arts has been evident from the very first days of the new Cathedral. The year of 1962 was a landmark for the arts in Coventry. The consecration of the Cathedral inspired a three-week festival that brought to the city many of the world's greatest performers, covering all aspects of the arts, a one-off festival that could never be repeated. Never before had such a star-studded array been assembled in the Midlands – Covent Garden Opera, the Royal Ballet, Sadler's Wells Opera, the City of Birmingham Symphony Orchestra, the BBC Symphony Orchestra, the Berlin Philharmonic, the Choir of King's College, Cambridge, Sir Malcolm Sargent, Sir John Barbirolli, George Solti, Yehudi Menuhin, Margot Fonteyn, Beryl Grey and many more. In drama there were performances by the Royal Shakespeare Company; in the Ruins the Mystery Plays* were performed by the Theatre Guild of Coventry, and, at the Belgrade, Andre Obey's *Noah* and a Festival commission *Semi Detached* by David Turner. Other commissioned works

Commissioned for the Festival to celebrate the Consecration of St. Michael's Cathedral, Coventry, May 1962

BENJAMIN BRITTEN

WAR REQUIEM

op. 66

*"My subject is War, and the pity of War.
The Poetry is in the pity...
All a poet can do today is warn."*
Wilfred Owen

*Words from the Missa pro Defunctis
and the poems of Wilfred Owen*

★

Vocal Score
by *Imogen Holst*

'War Requiem': vocal score title page.

included Benjamin Britten's *War Requiem* with Peter Pears, Dietrich Fischer-Dieskau and Heather Harper, *The Beatitudes* by Sir Arthur Bliss, and the world premiere of Michael Tippett's *King Priam*. Recitals were given round the diocese by performers such as Denis Matthews, Julian Bream, Isobel Baillie, and Joyce Grenfell. David Lepine, the new Cathedral's first Director of Music, gave the opening recital on the new organ. Everyone's tastes were catered for – music, drama, poetry, pageants, lectures, dancing, exhibitions and sporting events. How could such a once-in-a-lifetime feast be followed up? The daily fare was bound to be at a more modest level and the product of unremitting hard work.

The cathedral choir

Nevertheless there was a long tradition of Anglican musical excellence to follow every day and not just on the great occasions. Anglican church music has long been sustained by cathedral choirs, and Joseph Poole, the new Cathedral's first precentor, made the case for them eloquently in his introduction to the booklet he wrote for Evensong:

> Worship without music does not easily soar; and wherever the Church has been concerned to make worship really expressive of truth, music has been used . . . the music of a cathedral choir is the counterpart of the architecture and the stained glass of the building: it is a finely wrought music, in which the musicians offer on behalf of the people what the people would wish to do themselves, if they had the ability.

It is not of course just ability that is required, but consistent, unrelenting work with generations of children, to arouse, sustain and develop a love of making music in them. Their parents too have been deeply involved, if only in the endless taking and

The Coventry Cathedral Choir directed by Kerry Beaumont on the nave stage at the entrance to the Chapel of Unity.

COVENTRY CATHEDRAL FESTIVAL 1962

In the Foreword to the Festival Programme the Bishop wrote: 'This festival is an attempt by all sections of society to express their gratitude to God for the building of a new cathedral: they are doing so through music, drama, pageant, lectures, dancing, exhibitions and sporting events.' Extraordinary, and extraordinarily successful, efforts were made to draw people in. Some 110,000 school children were involved, collecting pennies and paying for one of the stained-glass windows in the nave, as well as making school banners and models of the new Cathedral and organizing their own events and services.

Thirty-five sports and games organizations took part in the Festival with competitions beginning in 1961. By June 1962, 250,000 people had taken part in fencing, netball, cycling, tennis, shooting, cricket, canoeing, motor sport and bowls, as well as athletics. There were even 1,000 entrants for an angling contest on the Oxford canal.

In Warwick and Leamington Spa there were plays and concerts: *I will Arise*, 'a miracle play for the times'; Christopher Fry's verse drama *The Lady's not for Burning*, performed in the Lord Leycester Hospital to more than eight hundred over four nights; Peter Albery's play *Anne Boleyn*, so successful it was given an extra performance, and Joyce Grenfell with songs and monologues, predictably a sell-out. Middle-class fare for largely middle-class audiences?

At Kenilworth the chief attraction was a Son et Lumière re-enactment of some of the great events associated with the Castle. The papers marvelled at the technology involved: an 'electronic brain' controlling 60 coloured lighting units and stereophonic sound, the wizardry balanced by the 'rich and rolling tones' of the narrator, Jack Warner. More than 25,000 people, many from overseas, came during the 5-week run.

Leamington's final event was 'the Spa's biggest party', designed to give people an opportunity to meet the Bishop and other cathedral clergy informally. More than 2,500 people were in the Jephson Gardens to hear the Bishop say that he did not share the view of those who criticized the Festival for lack of mass appeal. 'We have tried to cater for every man, woman and child with every possible kind of event.'

The Festival had great ambition and excellent organization; and great numbers came. But it is striking that the Festival Programme, a book of 96 pages, devoted only one sentence to events in Nuneaton, Rugby and Stratford-upon-Avon: one a mining district, another a railway junction with large industrial employers, and the third with its own local deity. These substantial towns, none more than 20 miles from the Cathedral, may have felt remote from what was happening in Coventry.

Richard Chamberlaine-Brothers
Editorial Committee Member

fetching to and from the Cathedral. The first ten boys for the choir of the new Cathedral began work in September 1959 under Joseph Poole, and in May 1961 David Lepine was appointed organist and choirmaster, so by May 1962 the choir was well established and consisted of 24 boys and 12 lay clerks. The boys, at that time, were all educated at King Henry VIII School and rehearsed every morning from 8.00 to 8.40 and again on Saturday afternoons. There were 5 separate services connected with the Consecration and in the following weeks 45 special services. The choir was not involved in all of them but the commitment must have been tremendous.

This demanding routine was spiced with overseas tours. These were seen as an important part of the choir's life, a chance to tell the Coventry story, cement relationships and make new friends. The first tour took place in April 1963 when the choir visited Berlin; since then the choir has visited many countries including Germany, Holland, France, Norway, Sweden, Jamaica, and extensively in the USA. Highlights have included a performance of the *War Requiem* in Caen on the fortieth anniversary of D Day (1984), a visit to Venice, Florence, Assisi and Rome, with a performance in St Peter's and an audience with the Pope (1991), and a celebration in New York of the fiftieth anniversary of the United Nations where the choir joined forces with the Dresden Boy's Choir (1995). In the UK a memorable concert at the Albert Hall was followed by performances in Birmingham and Coventry, where the choir took part in Mahler's *Symphony of a Thousand* (1984). Singing the services at other cathedrals during the summer break has been a chance for the choir to experience the more traditional church architecture and to have a fun time away.

Pope John Paul II greeting the Cathedral Choir at a Vatican audience on 23 October 1991. The choir sang 'Tu Es Petrus'.

The year of 1972 was overshadowed by the sudden death at the age of 43 of David Lepine, but the choral tradition established by him has continued. Kerry Beaumont, the present choirmaster, is the seventh to hold the position, and while worship songs have their place in more informal worship, the heritage of music from the last 500 years is still very much part of cathedral worship.

Paul Leddington Wright

Paul Leddington Wright has had the longest continuous association with the Cathedral's music, having been Assistant Director, Director of Music and Consultant with a break of only three years since 1977. He recalls that, as far as the choristers were concerned, the early link with Henry VIII School made the logistics of early morning practices fairly easy, with a single coach providing transport. There was no shortage of willing recruits, and some gifted singers resulted – Paul Daniel, Harvey Brough, Richard Cook and Omar Ebrahim. This arrangement lasted until the end of direct-grant status for schools like Henry VIII led to the decision to offer the opportunity of being a chorister to a much wider range of schools. Later in the 1980s there was a plan that Coventry Preparatory School should become the Cathedral's choir school, but eventually it was decided again that such an elitist opportunity should be open to all boys with the necessary voice and commitment. This did mean severe logistical problems with a fleet of taxis, and after a while the taxi firm declined to continue the arrangement. With rush-hour traffic now even worse and fewer parents (or taxis) willing to make the commitment, rehearsals take place in an evening and on Saturday mornings. Paul regrets the loss of that early morning freshness, though he understands the pressure of clashing commitments. The girls' choir was begun by David Poulter when he was Assistant Director to Paul, and is now well established. From the beginning their choir had a different brief and a wider variety of music to sing. Their age range was also wider. Girls' voices of course continue to mature without breaking like boys, and the hard fact is that girls are much readier to sing than boys, as is shown by the paucity of tenors and basses in events like the BBC's *Songs of Praise*. If boys do not learn to sing while at school, where will our male singers come from?

The International Church Music Festival (ICMF) was an idea in the minds of two Americans from Nashville, Elwyn Raymer and Ed Seabough, who first brought together choirs and musicians from different countries in Portsmouth in 1984 under the batons of David Willcocks and John Rutter. The international reputation of Coventry Cathedral drew them to Coventry in 1985, with the same conductors, and in 1988 with the support of the Lord Mayor and the City Council. Coventry has continued to host the ICMF, most recently in 2010, though expense, and questions of security since 9/11, have meant fewer participants. Paul is now the Artistic Director of the Festival.

New links with the BBC came about with the appointment as Provost of Colin Semper, who had been Head of Religious Programming. His former colleague Roger Hutchings, first at Pebble Mill in Birmingham and later in London, involved the cathedral choir and the St Michael's Singers in the BBC's Choral Evensong and in *Songs of Praise*. Broadcasting achievements perhaps reached their height in 1990, when on Easter Day the Cathedral was broadcasting *Songs of Praise* live, and at the same time appearing in a recording of ITV's *Highway* with Sir Harry Secombe.

Paul Leddington Wright has conducted the Cathedral's St Michael's Singers for over a quarter of a century. Their current Chairman, John Oliver, gives an account of their achievements below.

THE DIRECTOR'S VIEW

When I took over at Coventry in 2006, the cathedral choir comprised 7 boys and 13 girls in one choir, along with the choral clerks. My brief was to build up the choirs, which included the Chamber Choir and the Chapter House Choir. The latter two were later combined into one. In building up the number of choristers, we faced several challenges: there is no choir school and King Henry VIII, the leading independent school in the city, is no longer the main supply route for chorister recruitment. In addition, transport problems relating to pre-school rehearsals had led to the cessation of those rehearsals in the year before my arrival, so that a chronic shortage of practice time made the challenge even greater. Clearly a lot of new recruits had to be found, and a new timetable made manageable for choristers who now had to come from a broad section of the City's schools.

I approached the independent schools, which had once provided most of the choristers, but the results were not encouraging. I needed to cast my net wider, searching state schools for recruits. I contacted all the primary schools in the Coventry area – well over 60 – and most said they would love their children to have this opportunity.

I used a 5-minute spot at school assemblies to put over what singing in a cathedral choir was about, and what they might expect to get out of it: from the exhilaration of performing in public, to working together as a team, and singing some of the greatest vocal music ever written. After a show of hands I left a stock of lively and eye-catching fliers and returned a week later for 3-minute auditions with those who had shown an interest – boys separately from girls as they are sensitive to the jibe that this is not the sort of thing that real boys should be doing. I gave those who seemed to have potential a letter to take to parents setting out what all concerned would be expected to put in, and get out of, being a chorister. Parents can play as big a part in the success of all this as their children. After an extended audition at the Cathedral, those who were successful then joined as probationers.

We achieved our numbers and have kept them, often with some on a waiting list. What seems to get children to stick is to make the whole process a series of steps of achievement, each of which is tested, rewarded and acknowledged. The success of our scheme is that absence and tardiness are discouraged, and commitment, long service, good behaviour and learning about music, the Church and Christian teaching, are encouraged. This way a sense of pride and vocation is gradually built up. Without that the modest choral scholarship of £200 a year would hardly do the trick.

In case that all sounds too deadly serious there must be times when choristers as a group, with or without parents, can let their hair down, lighten up and be venturesome. A summer week at St David's, in every sense a breath of fresh air after the industrial Midlands, barbeques, ceilidhs, prize-givings, and a foreign tour or the prospect of a recording are all an essential part of the life of a chorister.

Kerry Beaumont
Director of Music, Coventry Cathedral

The St Michael's Singers

This choral society (SMS) is a year younger than the Cathedral which is its base. David Lepine formed it in 1963, establishing some key principles which have remained fundamental to SMS: membership is subject to audition (with triennial re-auditions) and carries clear obligations on rehearsal attendance and learning the music, there is a commitment to excellence – the choir's aims and objects have always been defined as 'the study and practice of choral music in order to foster the public knowledge and appreciation of such music, both known and newly composed works, by means of public performance of the highest possible standard'.

The choir was conducted and trained by David Lepine until his sudden death in 1972, then by Robert Weddle (1972–77) and Ian Little (1977–84). Paul Leddington Wright has directed SMS since then – more than 25 years. As well as these conductors, the choir has also enjoyed the support of successive Cathedral Assistant Directors of Music in the role of accompanist. While in these and other ways SMS is closely linked to the Cathedral, it is formally independent. It has its own elected managing committee and is responsible for its own financial affairs.

Over the years, SMS has tackled many of the most challenging works in the traditional choral society repertoire and has also progressively extended its range of activity. In Lepine's time the choir focused almost entirely on an annual pattern of three to four concerts in the Cathedral (including 'Carols for All' at Christmastide). Under Weddle, ventures further afield were added, beginning a warm and most rewarding relationship, lasting more than ten years, with the Orchestre de Chambre de Caen in France. In Lepine's time the choir engaged a greater range of orchestras for its other concerts, and, to help attract a wider audience, started offering local performances in Warwick University's Arts Centre, as well as in the Cathedral. Recordings featuring SMS began to appear from 1983.

The years under Paul Leddington Wright have seen diversification of SMS's singing activities into a variety of musical genres, while still maintaining the values of the British tradition of choral music. Though each season has continued to involve mainstream choral concerts and other live contributions to music and worship in the Cathedral, the choir has also made many hymn recordings on CD and for BBC programmes, both on radio and television, particularly in the weekly Songs of Praise series and, in the last few years, as one of the invited 'stage choirs' in the annual Royal Albert Hall 'Big Sing'. New challenges extending the choir's experience have included concerts sung under different conductors, some of them world-famous names. New works have been commissioned – most recently David Briggs' *Cross of Nails* for the Remembrance concert in 2009.

The choir joined the English Symphony Orchestra in 1999 for the Yehudi Menuhin Memorial Tour of *Messiah* performances, and has continued subsequently to enjoy fruitful collaboration with the ESO. A regular relationship has been maintained with the City of Coventry Youth Orchestra, which gives a joint concert with SMS every Christmas; and there has been a succession of joint events in London and Coventry with the Parliament Choir and South Bank Sinfonia. A number of other guest choirs – some British, some from overseas – have been welcomed in Coventry for performances with SMS. There have been joint performances abroad (Lyon, various German cities, and most recently Prague) and the choir has sung in concerts at many other venues in England, ranging from great cathedrals across the country to parish churches in Coventry and Warwickshire. The International Church Music Festival, hosted by the Cathedral every few years since 1984, has given SMS further opportunities to welcome singers from overseas, sing together with them, and experience different styles of music.

Some particular occasions have been especially thrilling and inspiring. Members who shared in the first Caen trip (1975) will never forget the extraordinary experience of singing Handel's *Messiah* to an overflowing and enthusiastic audience in the great abbey church of St Etienne. There are lasting memories of powerful performances of the *War Requiem*, under Lepine and Weddle early on, and including, in later years, one conducted by Mstislav Rostropovich, and another with a visiting German choir; liturgical presentations of Monteverdi's *Vespers*; Mozart's *Requiem*, sung under Yehudi Menuhin to mark 50 years since the bombing of Dresden; the 150th anniversary performance of Mendelssohn's *Elijah* under Paul Leddington Wright in Symphony Hall, Birmingham; a visit to Israel to record for BBC programmes on Good Friday and Easter Day, 1999; Elgar's *The Kingdom*, under Vernon Handley in Worcester Cathedral; presentations of Bach's *Passions* (St Matthew or St John) as a part of Good Friday worship in the Cathedral; and many other highlights too numerous to mention. Underlying these, together with all the other SMS musical offerings, is a sense of shared continuity and aspiration, resting on the love of choral singing among some 80 people who find it worthwhile, year in year out, to devote substantial leisure time to the disciplines of regular rehearsal, working together on high-quality music to try to rise to that quality, and catch the spirit of each piece, be it a grand oratorio or a simple hymn and, when it comes to performance, trying to communicate something of that spirit and quality to the audience, whether face to face or (through recordings or broadcasts) to people in their homes. An extra and specially enriching dimension comes from doing so much of this work in the unique and inspiring setting of the Cathedral; from the relationship which enables SMS, though separate and independent, to draw on the time and talents of cathedral music staff; and from the real sense of cathedral support and belonging which the choir has enjoyed over nearly 50 years.

Special musical events

A Sacred Concert in 1965. Duke Ellington stood before the Sutherland tapestry and said, 'This music is the most important thing I've ever done or am ever likely to do.' The picture shows the press photo call before he played. © Richard Sadler FRPS.

The absence of a concert hall in Coventry, until the building of the Butterworth Hall at Warwick University, meant that the Cathedral was the venue for many visiting performers in spite of its notoriously difficult acoustics. There was an ongoing programme of recitals, choral works and orchestral concerts. In 1969 two of the world's greatest cellists came to the Cathedral. Paul Tortelier gave a recital of the Bach cello suites and a month later Jacqueline du Pre played the Dvorak cello concerto with the Halle orchestra conducted by Daniel Barenboim. The Berlin Philharmonic Orchestra returned in 1972 with Daniel Barenboim, British Rail offering a £1 return ticket from Euston! The music covered a wide range with visits from Duke Ellington and Johnnie Dankworth, with a work – *Reconciliation* – specially commissioned for jazz quartet and the cathedral choir (1987). There were jazz festivals in the Ruins and in 1997 five cathedral choirs joined with a choir from Nashville Tennessee, a jazz band and brass ensemble to 'Swing with the Saints'.

Following on from the commissions for the Consecration Festival there have been a succession of pieces written especially for the Cathedral's choirs – by Herbert Howells, William Walton, Richard Rodney Bennett, Neil Cox and, more recently, Rupert Jeffcoat and David Briggs.

The group Incantation were commissioned to write a Liberation Mass for the Cathedral's Silver Jubilee in 1987. They sang a concert in the Cathedral and then joined the Cathedral Choir in the new work during the Sunday morning service. © *Edward Ockenden.*

Drama

Worship that engages the worshipper has always had the character of drama. Joseph Poole saw the importance of the theatre to liturgy. The early Mystery Plays* were one of the Church's principal means of communication and education in the Middle Ages. So it was in an attempt to rediscover the role drama could play in the service of the Church that the drama project was established in 1961. Four areas were explored as 'play sites': the open stage in the Ruins – the setting for the Mysteries; the porch between the old and new cathedrals – the setting for the Porch Plays, short simple secular plays performed in the summer months with a single message probing the human situation; the nave theatre, either on the steps of the Chapel of Unity or at the baptistry window; and the Chapter House theatre.

In February 1962 Martyn Colborn, the first drama director, wrote of the theatre spaces in the Cathedral as 'a landmark, in that the estrangement between worship and drama now had a chance of reconciliation'. In his article he wrote that it was important that we got away from 'hay, haloes, beards and bathrobes' and produced plays 'identifiable with everyday problems and situations'. Martyn Colborn was followed by Robert Prior-Pitt, Laura Winnen and Ron Haddon.

Adam and Eve during the 1962 Mystery Plays in the Cathedral Ruins performed by the Theatre Guild of Coventry whose actors remained anonymous. © Richard Sadler FRPS.

The plays were staged by professional performers, solo artists, drama students, local theatre groups, and actors from the Theatre Guild of Coventry. During the holidays, cathedral workshops were organized and young people met and presented their own drama productions, and in conjunction with the Education department a Saturday morning Drama Club was established. The range of plays produced in the early years was amazing, ranging from the simple porch plays performed once or twice a week during the summer to major productions such as *King Lear, Waiting for Godot, West Side Story, Hedda Gabler, Oedipus Rex* and *Godspell*.

An important pilot study was undertaken in 1966 to explore the area of drama in the Church, sponsored by Valparaiso University, Indiana, USA, a Cross of Nails Centre. Led by Professor Van Kussrow of the university's department of drama, ten students came for a summer semester. This project, which became known as COVAL (COventryVALparaiso), developed into a year-long programme in which students took part in a study of Creativity, Communication, Christianity and Community. Based at the Lanchester Polytechnic (now Coventry University), the students became part of the cathedral community and took a full part in the day-to-day work at the Cathedral. With an emphasis on drama the programme's aims were to help students

> investigate the nature and experience of creative expression as related to the Christian concern; the arts as producer and reflector of community; and the interrelationship of intuitive knowledge via artistic expression, humanistic studies, the technological world, the urban environment, theology and man's search for wholeness.

The final production, in May 1972, was *Circus Surreal*, with clowns, animals, dancing, puppets and audience participation, based on the vision of St John as recorded in the book of Revelation, with music composed and directed by Colin Lee, a student at the Coventry School of Music.

Writing about a production of *Prometheus Bound/Unbound* taken from the works of Aeschylus and Shelley in 1971, Dr Kussrow commented:

> The aim was to explore the relevance for today. Is there a place for this sort of play in a Christian cathedral in an industrial city in the late afternoon of the 20th century? . . . the Arts today have rediscovered the validity and power, indeed necessity, of myth and ritual.

We need, in the twenty-first century, in an increasingly secular and harsh environment, to go on exploring ways, through drama and the arts, that will help us grow into the fully human beings that is God's plan for each one of us.

Always open to new ideas and looking for new ways to explore the themes of hope and reconciliation, the Cathedral invited 14 members of the Holy Fools at Passiontide 1985. The Holy Fools are a London-based group of clowns and mime artists, and they explored the seasonal theme, 'The Hope of the Cross'. Starting from St Paul's letter to the church at Corinth, 'We are all fools for Christ's sake' (1 Corinthians 4.10), the group explored various ideas – the clown as a symbol of joy, a symbol of hope, the clown as nonconformist, as vulnerable and as a servant figure, all attributes of Christ.

'This Is The End' was one of a repertoire of 30-minute lunchtime Porch Plays presented during the summer months in 1963–65.

Another unforgettable event from 1985 was *Julian*, a one-woman poetic drama, presented by Roberta Nobleman, celebrating the life of Julian of Norwich, the fourteenth-century anchoress. The fact that over 20 years later it still stays in the mind, long after most sermons have evaporated, points to the powerful message that drama can deliver.

One of the most enduring happenings of the last fifty years, indeed of the last thousand years, has been the Mystery Plays*. Dating back to the twelfth century, they have been part of the City's tradition for centuries. The text of all but two of the pageants (*The Pageant of the Shearmen and Taylors* and *The Pageant of the Weavers*) have been lost, and modern performances have incorporated material from other cycles. But the Coventry Carol has stood the test of time and is known throughout the world. A version, entitled *The Mysteries,* from the ancient play *Ludus Coventriae* (1425), was adapted by E. Martin Browne and performed as part of the Consecration Festival. Rex Satchwell, a long-standing member of the congregation, remembers taking a small part. Other performances followed, and in 1978 the Belgrade Theatre performed the entire sequence with material from the York, Chester and other cycles. Since then there have been regular productions using both amateurs and professionals, keeping alive the link between Church and City and strengthening our grip on our history, the Ruins providing a fitting backcloth.

As with all ministries, the financial restrictions have meant a reduction in outreach over the years and one can only look back with wonder and admiration at the energy and vision of the early years. In the 1990s, productions of *Fiddler on the Roof* and *HMS Pinafore* took place with amateurs from the cathedral congregation and other local churches, produced by John Blackman. Now one of the most popular events of the year is on Christmas Eve when children are encouraged to don 'haloes, beards and bathrobes' as they *Journey to Bethlehem* bringing alive the Christmas story. This in a way brings us full circle.

Exhibitions and other events

The space of the Cathedral and its Ruins has always been a natural vehicle for exhibitions and 'one-offs', from flower festivals, photographic exhibitions and art exhibitions to those imparting information on serious social issues such as AIDS, unemployment and urban renewal. Others have looked back at the people and events that make up our history (recently Anne Frank and Martin Luther King). More popular in their appeal have been such events as *Any Questions*, *Mastermind*, *The Antiques Road Show*, *Flog it* and *Question Time* (all BBC programmes), and even Christian Speed Dating – all fulfilling the object of bringing people into their cathedral.

International weeks held in the past were an important joint venture with the City and, given the numerous 'twinnings' of Coventry, a good way to promote friendships, knowledge and understanding. The Benedictine week of 1990 celebrated the fifteen-hundredth anniversary of St Benedict of Nursia, the patron saint of Europe, and our links with Dresden culminated in the display of the Cross and Orb that went on to top Dresden's Frauenkirche in 2000.

Exhibitions, talks, dance, concerts and personal contact all promote goodwill and understanding and help to fulfil the Cathedral's aims of closer international ties.

Sculpture

Although a great variety of exhibitions have taken place in the new Cathedral, the use of the Ruins for sculpture exhibitions has been sorely limited. The 'Peoples and Cities' conference held in the Cathedral in 1968 inspired the largest single exhibition of modern outdoor British sculpture ever held in the country up to that date. Stephen Verney, the Conference Director, asked the question,

How shall we use our technical skills to build cities that are beautiful, where people can belong and even participate? The answer is that we must do it together – politicians, planners, economists, engineers, industry, the Church and the artist.

The artists featured in the Ruins included Henry Moore, Barbara Hepworth, F. E. McWilliam, David Annesley, Brian Wall and even a joint exhibit by John Lennon and Yoko Ono. The arrival of the *Ecce Homo* statue of Christ by Epstein in 1970 should surely have inspired future exhibitions but they have been few and far between. The silver jubilee of the Consecration was celebrated with exhibitions of the work of John Hutton and Elisabeth Frink, and in 1995 Richard Branson presented the statue *Reconciliation* by Josefina de Vasconcellos. A particularly moving small sculpture exhibition in the Chapel of Christ the Servant was the work of Jean Parker. She called it *Good Grief/Bald Statements*; it was the result of the sculptor's own battle with cancer and dealt with personal loss and the process of grief.

The People and Cities Sculpture Exhibition in the Cathedral Ruins in 1968. 'Large torso' (arch) by Henry Moore was loaned by the Museum of Modern Art, New York. © Cathedral Archives.

77

It seems we have missed out on a great opportunity to continue our recognition of the arts. Peter Ball, a Coventry-born sculptor whose work can be seen in many of our cathedrals, was approached to sculpt a Pietà for the Millennium celebrations but although a maquette* was produced, the piece was never commissioned. It is important that as a repository of many of the great twentieth-century works the Cathedral does not become a museum but encourages new works that can inspire and deepen our faith.

Dance

John Brassington was involved with the St Michael's Dancers from their inception in 1972 until their demise in 2007, and offers an account below of their contribution to the Cathedral's worship.

How can we transform the worship experience, so that it is no longer a 'spectator sport', but becomes a drama in which all participate? Listening to an endless stream of words, some of them prosaic or didactic rather than poetic and inspiring, does not often engage 'our souls and bodies to be a living sacrifice'. Dave Tomlinson of Teamwork Ministries says

> Worship which doesn't incorporate some sort of visual is never really going to touch the average person on the street. Slides and videos are the modern equivalent of stained-glass windows. People are looking for something that will move us up a gear.

On 25 May 1972 a group of dancers appeared in the Cathedral at a celebration of the Eucharist – on the tenth anniversary of the Consecration. Uncertain steps were taken that evening, but, under the direction of Margaret Stevens, we were caught up in a vision and purpose she wanted to share, a vision of a community of Christian people coming alive and moving in patterns of prayer and praise, a purpose that could release the imagination and evoke a response from the inner depths to 'the great things that God has done' (Acts 2.12) . . . is doing . . . will do with us and for us.

Who were these dancers? They were not professionals giving a performance, though some of them had a useful training and experience of dance. They were members of the cathedral community persuaded by Margaret that it was possible for their dance to become worship.

St Michael's Dancers in rehearsal in 1986. 'There's no such thing as a winnable war. It's a lie we don't believe any more' from 'Russians' by Sting. © Edward Ockenden.

As noted earlier in this chapter, in 1971, Van Kussrow, Professor of Drama at Valparaiso University in Indiana, USA, brought some of his students to Coventry to explore ways in which drama and the arts can be an essential part of contemporary worship. He invited Margaret Stevens to lead some sessions on liturgical dance and, such was the enthusiasm of participants, that they asked Peter Spink, Canon Pastor at that time, whether we could have more. It seemed particularly right that a new cathedral should be a place for innovation and bold experiment – and such dance was certainly new to us.

Margaret was asked to tutor us. She began her regular journeys from Reigate in Surrey to Coventry and back home again on a late train, carrying stereo, cassettes, coloured silks and whatever else might be needed. Margaret continued working with the group for more than a year. During that time the group became more stable, with a few people losing their initial enthusiasm, while others realized the serious and disciplined nature of what we were undertaking. When Margaret left us to our own devices, she must have known the risk of failure. Many groups depend on the dynamism and enthusiasm of their leader. When the leader moves on, the group disintegrates. The fact that our Coventry group continued for 30 years is a tribute to the work and the encouragement of Margaret. Her beautiful and innocent smile, her warm hug, encouraged those who were ready to go with her on the creative journey. She valued the contribution each one made, the character and quality of their movement, whatever its limitation.

Some former members of the St Michael's Dancers are now linked with a national network called 'Dance into Worship'. This network was founded in 1991 to encourage the development of movement and dance as a physical expression of worship. John Brassington is presently the chair of the Dance into Worship committee.

The St Michael's Dancers performed more than two hundred dances in the Cathedral and elsewhere over the years between 1972 and 2007. John Brassington has written a full account of the work and development of the St Michael's Dancers, which is included in the book *A Bounty of Passing Moments* by Margaret Stevens.[1] Dance as a visual art needs to be seen and experienced within its liturgical context. Words can never provide an adequate description of movement and how it communicates by 'kinaesthetic identification' with a congregation who may experience within themselves the bodily sensation of the dancer's movement.

This liturgical dance is something fragile, which could so easily sink without trace. It is ephemeral yet the most embodied of art forms, only being made possible by the shapes, movements and intersections of actual physical human bodies. With all our technologies, digital cameras, computer animation, dance notation, the essence of the dance eludes us. It is a costly work of the creative imagination. The choreographer needs the co-operation of others: musicians, designers and makers of costume, liturgists (ordained or lay) and other church officials, even those who move the chairs to create enough space or press the button that plays recorded music at exactly the right moment. Our present leaders have other priorities and have allowed memories of dance as an integral, though not frequent, part of the radical experiment of the 1970s to fade. It may be that such a co-operation might be possible once again at Coventry Cathedral and the St Michael's Dancers might step forward to enrich the worship of this place.

This brief chapter gives some indication of the talent, commitment and hard work of 50 years of music, the performing and the 'stationary' arts at Coventry Cathedral. In an age of austerity the outlook may seem discouraging, with the disappearance of grants and commercial support, but it is difficult to believe that so much skill and ability will not make its mark even in these challenging circumstances.

* Denotes an entry in the Glossary

Note

1   Margaret Stevens, *A Bounty of Passing Moments*, Cairns Publications, 1994.

4 REACHING OUT IN MISSION AND MINISTRY

MARGARET SEDGWICK

Early in 1958, while the Cathedral was taking physical shape, the Bishop of Coventry, Cuthbert Bardsley, invited five men to meet him on the site. He told them he wanted to launch a new kind of cathedral. One of those men was the Rector of St Mary's, Southampton, the Revd H. C. N. Williams, known as 'Bill', whom he had just appointed as the new Provost. Provost Howard, who had watched the old cathedral church of St Michael's burn on the night of 14 November 1940, had retired so that a younger man could build his team. Within six months, those five men had moved to Coventry for an intense period of preparation. The team was entrusted with the formidable task of planning the ministry and mission of a building which, at its Consecration four years later, was to capture the imagination of the world.

'Bill' Williams. Provost of Coventry, 1958–81. © Cathedral Archives.

Provost Williams was born in South Africa in 1914, and his upbringing was to have a profound effect on his work in Coventry. During the South African War (1899–1902) his two parental families had been on opposite sides of the conflict. He was brought up to believe that past bitterness and hostility must be put aside. Reconciliation became central to his understanding of the Christian faith and he believed that Coventry Cathedral, rising again out of the conflicts of war, had a profound message to bring to a divided world.

However, in the period leading up to the Consecration of the Cathedral in 1962, he had a number of other priorities. Appointments to the staff were made in order to design a new ministry based in a new building. The Cathedral was situated in the centre of an industrial city. Cities themselves were being rethought and designed to anticipate the requirements for the future. It was the nature of the city – not just Coventry but cities across the world – and the needs of their citizens, which formed the focus of the mission of the Cathedral for the first 20 years. Central to Provost Williams' thinking was the establishment of a creative relationship between the new Cathedral and its mid-twentieth-century environment. This it could be argued was completely in accordance with its Benedictine foundation. The Benedictines regarded their ministry as being concerned with the whole of life, and not with a 'religious' part of it. 'The Cathedral's principal purpose', he wrote, 'is to establish and sustain the life of a community dedicated no less to the service of God among men than the worship of God in the Church.'

Apart from the normal and pastoral work among the congregation, each member of this remarkable staff team was given a portfolio. The Provost was in charge of planning and administration and had particular responsibility for international and ecumenical work. Educational, youth and adult education projects were the responsibility of Canon Edward Patey who later became Dean of Liverpool. Canon Joseph Poole was Precentor with special duties in the musical and liturgical life of the Cathedral and for the influencing of church music and liturgy in the diocese. Canon Simon Phipps, who was to become Bishop of Horsham and then of Lincoln, was Industrial Chaplain and had responsibility for the services in the Chapel of Christ the Servant. The Revd John Alleyne, Chaplain to the Congregation, had special care for those in shops, the Council House and probation service. The Revd Stephen Verney was Diocesan Missioner and Cathedral Chaplain, becoming a canon residentiary in 1964. He was to become Canon of Windsor and then Bishop of Repton. One of his legacies is his inspiring book *Fire in Coventry*, which tells the story of the lead-up to the Consecration of the Cathedral in 1962 and the response of people in the diocese to be a 'consecrated people', a book that has now been reprinted with an introduction by Christopher Cocksworth, the current Bishop of Coventry.

This team of clergy was soon joined by two lay people who were outstanding in their field: Michael Butterfield and Martyn Colborn headed the Youth and Drama Departments respectively. Michael told me they both joined their first staff meeting together with some trepidation, but were welcomed and valued as equal members of the team.

Provost Williams established a disciplined pattern – a weekly staff meeting, originally starting with Matins but in later years Holy Communion, followed after breakfast together by an hour's intensive Bible study. From studying the relevance of the

INDUSTRIAL MISSION

Simon Phipps was appointed to the Cathedral as its first diocesan Industrial Chaplain in 1958, soon joined by Michael Forrer. They aimed to encourage Christians to recognize the work of God in the world of industry and to offer a Christian ethical critique of its affairs, in consultation with those involved. This was a major contribution towards the strategy of the new Cathedral, taking seriously the relationship between the Church's role as custodian of Christian values and their application in society. Simon Phipps left after ten years to become Bishop of Horsham, having described the role of the chaplains and the Church in *God on Monday* (Hodder & Stoughton, 1966), based on his work in Coventry.

In 1968 the national Industrial Mission Association was formed, followed in 1971 by the establishment of the Coventry Industrial Mission, based in the offices of the Cathedral but an Ecumenical Trust with the Bishop of Coventry, the Roman Catholic Archbishop of Birmingham and the Chairman of the Coventry Free Church Federal Council as trustees. A team of full- and part-time chaplains had evolved, representing Anglican, Baptist, United Reformed, Roman Catholic and Methodist churches.

Regular factory visiting initially formed the basis of every chaplain's work. Relationships were also established with allied organizations – colleges of further and higher education, employers' associations, trade unions and the local authority. It was important to be able to communicate with people at all levels of responsibility in the places of work they visited. Analysis of the daily problems people faced at work was shared with those concerned before any attempt was made at an ethical evaluation. Conclusions were discussed with an invited cross-section of representatives from those same organizations at residential weekend seminars held at William Temple College, Rugby.

The Cathedral often served as the venue for events that highlighted changing employment patterns during the decline of manufacturing engineering in Coventry from the late 1970s. Exhibitions were staged and day conferences held to indicate signs of hope for the future, in consultation with a wide cross-section of local community organizations. Following a visit to Berlin by the new cathedral staff in the early 1960s, a programme of annual educational exchange visits for adult professionals and young workers in Coventry was arranged by the chaplains, along with their opposite numbers in the Kirchlichen Dienst in der Arbeitswelt. For several years, Kennedy House was used as a residential base for the young worker exchanges. This was to last for 20 years until the fall of the Berlin Wall in 1989. Trevor Cooper tells the story in *Who Goes There?*

A Challenge to Humanity (AuthorHouse, 2009). Industrial chaplains also regularly contributed to educational programmes organized by the Cathedral's education department for young people on visits to the Cathedral from various parts of the country and abroad. In 1980 an important seminar on 'Technology and Responsibility' was held at the Cathedral, and in 1981 the 'Peoples March for Jobs', from Liverpool to London, stopped in Coventry for an official reception. Welcoming the marchers in the Cathedral Ruins, Bishop Gibbs reminded them that, like the Sabbath, 'Industry was made for man, not man for Industry', and sent them on their way to London with God's blessing. In 1983 a cathedral service for Warwickshire miners was held on May Day.

The rapid decline, during the 1980s, of Coventry's traditional manufacturing and engineering industries, the rise of unemployment and increased pressure on church finances, led to a reappraisal by the churches of their ministry in the world of work. In Coventry and elsewhere the model of industrial mission pioneered in 1958 was replaced by a different approach. Coventry Industrial Mission was superseded by 'Mission in the World of Work' in 1991 and overseen by the Coventry and Warwickshire Ecumenical Council. This work was itself closed at the end of 2008, and its concerns assumed by a new charity, **WORK**CARE, in 2009.

Industrial Mission in Coventry was one expression of the spirit informing the new Cathedral. For Simon Phipps, it was based on the belief that God is at work in the contemporary concerns of the secular world, including industry: a properly biblical view 'largely ignored by the Church for some hundreds of years'. We hope that the next 50 years will see a continuing Christian concern for the economic, commercial and industrial structures of the world, and those who seek their living there.

Trevor Cooper, industrial chaplain 1967–91
Martin Wright, industrial chaplain 1975–83

Bible to the problems facing them, the staff would then discuss the work of the previous week and make plans for the immediate or long-term future. This pattern continued throughout the time he was Provost. There were monthly meetings held away from Coventry. Once a year, for a substantial part of the week, the staff also met out of the city.

The ministry of the Cathedral grew in the first five years following the Consecration and other departments were established – international youth work, British and local youth work, drama, music and culture, commerce, the law (including a chaplaincy to the police), ecumenical work, public relations, and the pastoral service to the congregation. At one stage there were 18 departments and about 80 staff. All these involved study and training and each member of staff was to be continually informed by the thinking of every other member. Williams claimed that 'what is unique about the Coventry pattern is that all these important areas of ministry are held together in a living relationship in one place'. The Cathedral's policy was to put as much money as possible into the ministry rather than building up capital reserve funds as it was believed that a new building was not likely to be costly to maintain in the first 20 years. Future provosts and deans would have cause to regret this policy.

However, there were tensions between the two main parts of the Cathedral's ministry. Should it be:

the Cathedral of the Diocese of Coventry helping and influencing the work being done in the parishes or should it be the creative centre for enterprises on behalf of the whole Church in Britain and in an increasing number of centres all over the world, making full use of the place of prominence which God, through recent history, has given it?[1]

There was no doubt in Provost Williams' view that the second was the priority aim. The needs covered by the churches of the diocese would be better met if the latter took precedence. It was acknowledged that such a major decision entailed responsibilities and risks with the real possibility of failure.

The Cathedral as a centre of learning

The Education Department headed by Canon Horace Dammers assumed responsibility for adult educational work in October 1965. It provided post-ordination training and adult education courses in conjunction with the Extra-Mural Department of Birmingham University and the Workers' Educational Association, as well as ecumenically based in-service training for clergy. Coventry's young novelist Susan Hill was appointed honorary Cathedral Librarian in 1963 to develop its resources.

Clergy from this country and overseas were keen to seek short-term placements to explore what was seen as a ministry relevant to the needs of the Church and society. One such minister, the Revd H. R. Cho, a Presbyterian minister from South Korea, having spent three months at the Cathedral, wrote:

Coventry Cathedral seems to me to have become a spiritual centre beyond the Diocese and even beyond the Anglican Communion. It is a great ecumenical centre, and shows new vision, new inspiration, a new pattern of the Church, and of church life in modern society, which is of interest for the whole world. It is teaching us how the Church can make a more effective approach to people outside the Church.

The Cathedral Association was formed to promote the study of outstanding contemporary issues, particularly scientific ones. Professor Sir Bernard Lovell was one of the distinguished speakers who addressed some 1,400 people in the Nave on 'Space Exploration: Its Objectives and Implications'. Others well known in their day included the Rt Hon. Richard Crossman, Dr E. F. Schumacher and L'Abbé Michel Quoist. The Bishop, too, was keenly interested in the education work and arranged 'The Bishop's Lectures in the Cathedral 1966' for the diocese. Speakers included the Revd Harry Williams and the Revd David Jenkins (later Bishop of Durham) who like others spoke to a packed Cathedral.

However, Canon Horace Dammers was sensitive to the gaps in the Cathedral's ministry when he wrote: 'We are particularly aware that a great deal of our work does not directly touch the lives of the poor, the hungry, the homeless, the miserable, whom God particularly calls his Church to serve.'

Lay people were very much involved in the Cathedral's ministry whether as paid staff or volunteers or members of the congregation. Many of the last played a full part in the ongoing work of the Cathedral by being associated with the departmental ministries. Their training and development was nurtured and cared for in many ways, not least by a series of lectures given at regular intervals by the Provost, as well as ongoing study programmes on current topics.

Towards the end of the 1960s the congregation embarked on a whole year's programme called 'Study to Serve'. It included lectures, Bible studies, congregation evenings and days, and house parties at different venues, and culminated in a three-day conference at Keele University. At this time there was a general trend at all levels to replace the formal lecture by the seminar, led by an expert but with fuller group participation. Finding it was no longer possible to attract sufficient audiences, it was decided that the Cathedral Association should no longer function as such but give way to an adult education programme, which consisted of three evening lectures by the Provost, lunchtime lectures at the Lanchester Polytechnic (later to be Coventry University), and study sessions arranged by the Department of Extra-Mural Studies, Birmingham University. The areas of study included problems of world poverty and development, and contemporary theology.

Exhibitions also were seen as a means of engaging people in the issues of the day and promoting the visual arts. The modern Cathedral to which so many outstanding twentieth-century artists had contributed great works of art was an ideal venue for exhibitions of modern art. In the summer of 1968 an open-air exhibition of British sculpture was staged in the Ruins as part of an international conference on 'Peoples and Cities'. The exhibits included several works by Barbara Hepworth and Henry Moore. The exhibition was free of charge and 370,000 people passed through the Ruins, many of whom would never have entered an art gallery.

During the years there were exhibitions inside the Cathedral displaying the works of other twentieth-century artists such as Geoffrey Clarke and John Hutton, major contributors to the building, and also displays of modern church vestments. One of these was to mark the tenth anniversary of the Cathedral and was staged by Louis Grossé Ltd, makers of the vestments designed by John Piper. It included the world's first cope in PVC, the creation of Patrick Reyntiens, the stained-glass artist responsible with John Piper for the baptistry window. This exhibition attracted 5,000 people from 30 countries and there was TV, radio and press coverage. David Richardson, a West Midlands Fellow in Creative Photography, requested space for an exhibition showing the variety of communities in Coventry, saying that he was impressed by the Cathedral's informal and unthreatening atmosphere while still retaining its dignity.

Urban issues

But it was urban issues that were central to the Cathedral's ministry in the early years. Between 1960 and 1970 the Industrial Mission arranged more than 30 conferences related to the current situation, as well as setting up many discussion groups in factories, shops and offices, bringing together shop-floor workers and management. Their ministry became a pattern for interdenominational groups throughout the country (see the inserted text). A report given in 1963 by the senior industrial chaplain, Simon Phipps, expressed the view that it was

> a prophetic ministry within Industry itself; an attempt by the Church to make some sort of analysis of the situation of Industry and the salient issues that arise within it, in order to think out what may be the contribution of Christian thought and action to those issues.

The controversial bestseller *The Secular City* by Harvey Cox, published in 1965, was one of the books of the time studied by the staff team. This subjected urban life to the critique of a radical biblical analysis seeing the threats, challenges and potential of modern urban life.

PEOPLE AND CITIES, 1968

In 1968 the People and Cities Conference at Coventry Cathedral brought together 150 delegates from across the world to debate the problems of urbanization, to discuss the social, architectural and integration difficulties of the modern city, and to seek inspiration how best to plan a better social order.

The People and Cities Conference was the brainchild of Canon Stephen Verney. A packed Cathedral heard the opening address of Dr C. A. Doxiadis, Director of the Institute of Ekistics in Athens and one of the founders of this scientific specialty. Other speakers included the Rt Revd Ted Wickham (Chairman of the World Council of Churches Advisory Group for Urban and Industrial Mission), the Revd Harry Daniel (Secretary for Urban and Industrial Mission of the East Asian Christian Council), the UK's leading authority on transport planning, Professor Colin Buchanan (first Professor of Transport at Imperial College of Science and Technology, London) and Richard Hauser (Special Lecturer in Social Education at the University of Nottingham).

Richard Hauser writes:

Within the visible framework of its houses, buildings and streets the community has a fourth dimension which we call the invisible community. It is made up of the people's human relationships; their common links and roots which stem from a common past experience and the common purpose towards which they strive together.

In the past, generations went into producing the values and traditions which created this invisible community and guaranteed its continued survival from each generation to the next; although living in very bad physical conditions, people could still endure the most serious hardship, persecution and deprivation without losing their identity or their faith in better times ahead, because they had human warmth on which to fall back.

The invisible community which took generations to evolve now has to be produced in a matter of a few years.

(*Network*, no. 2, Winter 1968–69, p. 19)

EKISTICS – the science of the relationship between man and his environment.

Conference delegates sought ways of encouraging the growth of this invisible community. During the conference the largest single exhibition of modern outdoor British sculpture filled the Cathedral Ruins and grounds. It featured works by Henry Moore, F. E. McWilliam and Barbara Hepworth as well as by newcomers like David Annesley and Brian Wall.

Stephen Verney commented:

With the planner and the architect the sculptor forms an immediate team, within which he has the responsibility for summing up and expressing the meaning of the city, in buildings and networks, and the human life within it.

Beatle John Lennon and Yoko Ono added their own much-publicized but unauthorized contribution to the exhibition.

Martin Williams
Editorial Committee Member

As part of the Jubilee of the Diocese of Coventry in 1968, under the leadership of the Canon Missioner, Stephen Verney, the Cathedral hosted a major conference, 'People and Cities', attended by 135 men and women from 33 countries. During 1966 and 1967 workshops had been set up in 29 cities around the world, consisting of small groups brought together by a common concern for their city, 'for the problems of the modern city are common to the whole human race, and could plunge us all into catastrophe as the world population doubles'. The workshops were called together in each case by the Christian Church, but the participants were from people of Christian and other faiths, and of none. Each workshop consisted of not more than 12 people – architects, planners, politicians, scientists, teachers, writers, doctors and psychiatrists, and clergy. The outline of study for the workshops was suggested by Dr Constantinos Doxiadis of Athens (1913–75), who was regarded as the most distinguished urban planner in the world at that time. The workshops focused on problems and opportunities, considering such questions as: how could we organize the modern city so that people could easily meet and care for each other?

These reports were sent to Coventry to be compared and analysed. The conference was attended by delegates from the workshops, leaders of the Christian churches, clerical and lay, on their way to the World Council of Churches General Assembly, and leaders or young potential leaders in secular life who were experts in various fields. The conference began with a dinner in St Mary's Hall by invitation of the Lord Mayor, with an opening speech by the Duke of Edinburgh. Each morning began with an exposition of Scripture and there were lectures from planners, and urban and industrial missioners.

Canon Kenyon Wright in 1990.

Towards the end of 1970, the Revd Kenyon Wright came to the Cathedral as Director of Urban Studies. A Scotsman and a Methodist minister, he had been a missionary in India and had set up an urban studies centre in Durgapur. During his 15 years in India his work had become well known in Asia and Europe, especially in the field of training clergy in urban/industrial mission. He said that his time in India had taught him that local problems were inseparable from international ones.

The Centre for Urban Studies was to play a crucial role in the Cathedral's continuing educational work. Kenyon Wright was concerned about what he termed 'the human predicament today'. He said in a lecture given in the 1970s,

The 1960s could be called 'the era of confidence' – it spawned a theology of confirmation which affirmed man's secular control and the possibility of the secular city becoming the place of human joy and harmony. Now we are older, and perhaps, a little wiser.

Not surprisingly, with this focus on urban ministry over the years, there were industrial exhibitions. In 1972 all the major car manufacturing companies agreed to co-operate in presenting in pictures and products the history of Coventry's motor industry from the early beginnings. It also attempted to illustrate the human problems involved in the design and manufacturing of cars. The Church's concern for good industrial relations, the right use of human resources and Christian values in industry were underlined. Cars from Coventry's Transport Museum were regularly

Links with the local motor industry: a 'Grey Fergie' looks on from the back of the nave during the Massey Ferguson 50th anniversary celebrations in November 1996.

displayed beside John Hutton's great west screen as examples of the fruits of local industry – articles created by human beings with skills given by God.

The Centre of Studies

By the mid-1970s a pattern of continuing education at every level was beginning to emerge very much along the lines envisaged by Provost Williams when he wrote:

> The Cathedral, therefore, in the true Benedictine tradition, looks at the whole community in categories which cannot conceivably be comprehended within the geographical boundaries of a parish. Team ministries of this sort are vital if the great centres of Christian influence which Cathedrals have always been either actually or potentially are to be relevant to the communities in which their work is set.[2]

There had been discussion for a number of years about the creation of a 'college' which would be the principal teaching and learning instrument of the ministry of reconciliation. Provost Williams believed that a damaging characteristic of the age was its high degree of specialization resulting in a lack of coherent strategic thinking, and that there was a need for 'horizontal' communication between various specializations. This, he felt, should be the concern of religion.

> Religion in this sense is not one little circle among many other circles . . . economics, sociology etc. Religion is the circle which one draws round the whole of life, and then works for a creative dialogue between all the special circles within it.

In 1973 the Centre of Studies was established in partnership with the then Lanchester Polytechnic (now Coventry University), and opened on 4 June 1974 by Dr Donald Coggan, soon to be Archbishop of Canterbury. It was intended to meet the needs of short- and long-term fee-paying visitors who wished to absorb the ethos of the cathedral ministries by adopting a formal approach to their studies. This development was believed to be fulfilling a long tradition of leadership in learning by the cathedrals of Western Europe as well as bringing together the many specialist programmes which had been built up over the preceding 15 years.

Provost Williams' decision to focus on establishing the Cathedral as a creative centre for enterprises on behalf of the Church was praised in an article by Clifford Longley, the Religious Affairs Correspondent of *The Times* and a distinguished Roman Catholic writer. Reporting on the opening of the Centre he wrote:

> The theme of 'Reconciliation' which began as a simple expression of the desire to heal old wounds of the Second World War, has been taken into the heady realms of social and political theory . . . Coventry, above all English cathedrals, has responded to the growing gulf between religion and everyday life by immersing itself in the issues around it. Industrialists and trade unionists, leaders of education and the academic world, local government and police have all been drawn into the process, stimulated by the Cathedral's staff, of probing the hidden basic questions about man in society.[3]

Clergy, lay leaders and those who wished to take time off from their full-time studies could take advantage of a four-month semester from February to May, but it was open to other people for a shorter time. The courses were experiential and interdisciplinary, thus emphasizing the interdependence of different disciplines in an age of specialization. There was a basic course in communication provided by the new Media Centre at the Lanchester Polytechnic.

These attracted many local clergy of all denominations as well as people from farther afield and laypeople in the area. Many students came from Cross of Nails

Centres where Provost Williams had lectured, and they expressed appreciation of what they experienced. One student from Eckerd College in Florida wrote in the college magazine: 'Have you ever been to a Hindu wedding? Studied at an International School? Made a movie? Skied in the Scottish Highlands? Played darts in an English pub?' Another participant commented: 'The impression that lingers longest is an image of the many persons whose lives interacted with mine and who taught me, mostly in unspoken words, all the rough and smooth edges of reconciliation, resurrection, liturgy and love.'

With urban theology at its height, the Centre set up a Diploma in Urban Studies for theological students and ministers from developing countries and attracted many from India and Africa who not only benefited from the cathedral community, but also, while living in various parts of the city, learned a great deal about European culture. They, in their turn, gave much to the Cathedral. The programme used the expertise of the cathedral staff, especially the international ministry team, and participants were encouraged to regard themselves as part of the cathedral staff. Due to changes at the Lanchester Polytechnic, the Media Centre course was lost, but other colloquia were inserted in its place. During the following years, hundreds of students, clergy, including bishops and deans from all over the world, took advantage of the extensive programmes on offer or had a course specially arranged depending on their interest. Groups of clergy came from the troublespots in Northern Ireland several years running, and thought through the trauma of their situation in the relaxed atmosphere of the Cathedral.

In 1974, discussions also took place on training for the congregation. It was noted that there was a great hunger for theological training and knowledge – something more than addresses in Holy Week and a few lectures in September. On Canon Joseph Poole's retirement in 1977, Dr Stephen Smalley was appointed Precentor. He and his wife Susan organized a number of study programmes. One on 'Lay Ministry and the Church of the Future' gave people an early insight into the future roles of the laity. For the fifteen-hundredth anniversary of the birth of St Benedict in 1980, a very full programme based on the *Rule of St Benedict* was arranged for the cathedral community and the diocese.

The 1970s were the hey-day of the Cathedral as a major centre of learning. Thousands of students passed through its doors. Other cathedrals and institutions were keen to learn from the Coventry experience. But the Cathedral had to face the problem of its limited finances as visitors decreased. The Cathedral had few endowments and by the recession of the early 1980s its financial situation looked threatening.

Changes in the 1980s

In February 1980, the senior staff held a day conference to consider what the ministry of reconciliation might mean in the 1980s. The changing patterns and developments in theology and ministry were carefully studied. It was observed that in the 1960s there had been a concentration on the nature of God, his transcendence and immanence, and the world set the agenda. The mood had changed in the 1970s and there was theological speculation about the person of Christ, the questioning of traditional formulations, confusion about the relationship between the Jesus of history and the Christ of faith, and new analysis of the cultural context of the New Testament. With Christian influence being seen as marginal in society, all of this might indicate a failure of confidence in ministry and a withdrawal from social commitment. In fact, there was renewed interest in 'relevant spirituality' and liturgy. They wondered if the 1980s would be marked by a coming together of these emphases in a balance between faith and belief, worship and service and action. Cathedral people began to ask whether there was too great an emphasis on the international ministries or on the community-based ministries. With issues such as increasing unemployment in the city, was there enough flexibility to respond to the new challenges?

In 1981, Provost Williams retired and Canon Kenyon Wright moved to be General Secretary of the Scottish Churches Council. By this time the Cathedral was finding it increasingly difficult to keep up the momentum of experiment. People were drifting away from the Church and Coventry was no longer the boom city it had been.

Nevertheless, a very full programme of studies continued through 1981 and the number of clergy on sabbatical leave had increased, requiring more individually tailored programmes. One seminarian wrote: 'This is an opportunity for ordinands to bridge the gulf between cultures and to broaden their vision of the Church's work in the world.'

In September 1982, Canon Colin Semper was installed as Provost. He came from being Head of Religious Programmes for BBC Radio, and saw the Cathedral as a marketplace for ideas and communication. He wanted to build a 'bridge of faith' between cathedral and diocese. He also inherited a cash crisis, which meant the Cathedral could no longer offer such a comprehensive programme of studies, nor could it cater for so many students. One way of increasing income was converting the Cathedral undercroft into a visitors' centre. Financing such a project was difficult, and he faced much criticism, but the scheme was cautiously welcomed by the City and County, as well as by the English Tourist Board. GEC and others provided financial backing to begin the project, which was completed by the summer of 1983. There was a historical display in sound and light about the major incidents in the history of Coventry, including a bombed house with sound effects, a Treasury exhibition and an audio-visual show outlining the life of Coventry over the centuries, culminating in the destruction of city and cathedral in 1940. It was the first of its kind to be placed in a cathedral and therefore attracted much attention.

Community relations

Post-war Coventry, with its many industries and opportunities for growth, attracted immigrants from the Indian subcontinent and the West Indies. Their welfare became the focus of attention for the churches in the region. In 1963 Peter Berry had been appointed Bishop's Chaplain for Community Relations, one of the first such appointments in the Church of England, with special responsibility for new immigrant workers from India, Pakistan and the Caribbean. In 1966 he was invited to use the office facilities and be part of the team at the Cathedral, later becoming a residentiary canon and then Vice-Provost before leaving to be Dean of Birmingham Cathedral. This was a pioneer ministry and another example of responses to changes in our cities. He wrestled with the question of how to honour the Sikh, Muslim and Hindu communities without prejudicing the integrity of the Christian faith.

In 1982 he was the co-ordinator for a week-long Coventry Festival of Peace. The festival organizers included representatives of the City Council, churches and voluntary organizations, as well as the Cathedral. The programme connected local concern for industrial, racial and social peace with wider international issues of suspicion and fear between East and West. Canon Peter Berry said at the time: 'Coventry faces an unprecedented threat to its own peace. Growing unemployment divides our city into those with work and those without; growing prejudice and intolerance divide our city along racial lines.' It was a controversial event and an editorial in the *Coventry Evening Telegraph* prompted letters from both Canon Berry and Provost Semper. The latter made it clear that the Cathedral would not become a platform for one political party. The task of the Cathedral was to provide a platform for many views that should be openly discussed.

In 1987 the Cathedral hosted part of an exhibition of local Coventry artists shown in many parts of the multicultural city. One exhibit presented a difficult problem for a Christian place of worship. This was a sculpture by a young Indian artist, Anil Varia, entitled *Meditating on Vishnu*, representing a devotee on a bed of nails before the many-armed Hindu god Vishnu. Dr Christopher Lamb, who had taken over Canon Berry's work as Diocesan Adviser for Community Relations, recognized that such a sculpture in a Christian church would be offensive to some, and wrote an explanatory notice that this was not an object of worship taken from a Hindu temple but a work of imagination:

We may not at first appreciate the style. We may want to argue with the ideas. But sometimes what is initially strange may bring us a more powerful and vivid understanding of God, his care for us, and what it takes to offer our lives to him.

Debate and display

'Today's Work for Tomorrow's World': a nave exhibition in 1986 demonstrating the fruits of the City's industry – a real festival of creation.

The Cathedral throughout the 1980s continued to be a natural forum for debate and display. Particularly controversial was 'Today's Work for Tomorrow's World', organized by the Coventry Industrial Mission as part of the 1986 'Festival of Creation' when the City was still deeply affected by the manufacturing recession. It was an exhibition of hope for the City, opened during the Sunday service by Howard Stableforth, presenter of the BBC's *Tomorrow's World*. It brought together over 50 exhibitors ranging from large employers, trade unions, colleges and university to smaller local initiatives like worker co-operatives. The Senior Industrial Chaplain, the Revd Trevor Cooper, and his URC colleague the Revd Dick Wolff organized a lunchtime public meeting on 'Alternative Futures for Employment'. 'Despite the crucifying experience of the last 10 years, there is plenty of evidence of new life waiting to break through,' commented Provost Semper. However, he felt on reflection that insufficient explanation had been given as to why industry, trade unions, local government, education, politics and 'alternative futures' had come together. Had this been done, people would have more easily seen what were intended to be the implications for a kind of urban industrial harvest festival. After all, to speak and work for another resurrection of the City was exactly what the Cathedral should be doing. However, much thought had gone into the design of the exhibition which was not without its own humour. Who, one wonders, decided that the political parties should all exhibit together in the Chapel of Unity?

Another controversial exhibition was by Amnesty International. In the cathedral magazine *Network*, Provost Colin Semper made clear his editorial policy on exhibitions in which he said he asked himself simple questions: 'For example, will this display speak of the Kingdom of God – or what we know of it – hidden in the folds of ordinary lives or of that transformation of society which Jesus both was and came to point to?' He acknowledged the exhibition was shocking, but said that that was as it should be. The torture of our fellow human beings was a denial of peace, justice, freedom from oppression and care – the marks of the Kingdom of God.

The Cathedral's work with schools

The Education Department was run on a part-time basis until January 1964 when Rosalind Lake was appointed as Cathedral Education Officer in the team led by Canon Patey; she left the following year when she married. However, she saw the importance of contact with local authorities and religious education teachers. In July 1965 Horace Dammers was installed as Residentiary Canon, becoming the Cathedral's Education Officer and taking over the work begun by Canon Edward Patey. He took from the Prologue to the Rule of St Benedict the words 'The School of the Lord's Service' to describe the aims of the department – to develop a centre for Christian education and discipline rooted in the ministry of Coventry Cathedral. He was assisted by 36 speakers for the department who gave introductory talks to parties that visited the Cathedral. Some of these were prepared to travel all over the country to speak and show films about the Cathedral's ministry. Others were ready to give talks in French, German or Spanish. One specialized in parties of deaf people. The ministry of these speakers was regarded as a lay ministry of outstanding importance. It transformed the visits of thousands every year from simple tourism to opportunities for inspiration from the Christian symbolism of the buildings and the variety of the Cathedral's ministry.

School visits are a regular feature of cathedral life during term time. The Schools Team prepares material for teachers and children and provides sympathetic guiding around the building.

A special course for primary and special schools was established, which became known as 'The Cathedral Belongs to Us'. Whole classes, mainly of 10-year-olds, attended a course of three or four sessions at the Cathedral during school hours. The Cathedral was seen as a gigantic visual aid for the teaching of Christian truth and for acquiring a sense of belonging, a sense of 'our Cathedral'. In the first annual report of the Education Department between October 1965 and September 1966, 364 schools from all over Britain had visited the Cathedral. Canon Dammers wrote: 'There is a real sense in which our work among the visitors, particularly those from schools, is missionary work.'

As a young teacher working in the south of England and a subscriber to the publication *Learning for Living*, I remember reading with great interest the article written in 1969 by Canon Dammers, by then Director of Studies, entitled 'Coventry Cathedral: An Opportunity for Christian Education', in which he described the work being done by the Education Department for school pupils. At the end of his paper, Canon Dammers made a summary of certain theological presuppositions for their work:

> First, God is the God of love incarnate. He wills his church to love our neighbours, not least the up- and coming generation; to care for them and to show them how to care for each other in happy community living. Secondly, God is the God of all kinds of goodness. Like the leaven in the lump, his Church must concern herself with good government, with cities that are good to live in, with goodness in personal relationships, with the good life in general. Thirdly, God is the God of beauty who delights in his creation and in man's pro-creation of beauty in the visual arts, music, drama, architecture. He desires in us sensitivity to beauty, and to ugliness for that matter. And fourthly, God is the God of truth who leads us into all truth and desires us to follow the truth wherever it leads us. He wants us to encourage the young to grapple with ultimate questions and ourselves to combine an open mind with commitment to the truth as we already are seeking it. I suppose that this is a kind of Christian humanism. Amen. So be it.[4]

The Schools Team has throughout the years managed to adapt to changes in the curriculum and modes of delivery. When finances were especially tight in the 1980s, it was fortunate that the Manpower Services Commission was established, providing short-term opportunities for the unemployed. The Cathedral maintained a seven-year relationship with the MSC. Each year Connie Downes, who headed the Education Department, and the manager of the agency, Jack Carpenter, well known to Connie as a churchwarden at Holy Trinity, had to go before 20 men and women of various trade unions and the City where they were questioned at length. Connie felt that it was ironic that these meetings took place adjacent to St Mary's Hall which had been the headquarters of the city craft guilds in the Middle Ages with their own chapels in the old Cathedral. However, on the whole, the links with the Manpower Services Commission staff were excellent. As the number of Asian children coming on the schools' programme increased, a tutor was appointed from the Asian community who produced leaflets in Gujerati and Hindi.

The last year when funding was available was 1988, but the existing programmes continued and radio and television featured the Cathedral's work. During the summer of 1989 a representative from *The Times Educational Supplement* looked very thoroughly into the programme. In the October 1989 *TES*, under the heading 'Alternative Services', David Self looked at the educational role of cathedrals and gave a comprehensive account of those who were involved in this type of ministry.

Pupils from church schools throughout Coventry Diocese taking part in the Reconciliation Arts Festival in July 2006.

On Coventry he wrote: 'Without doubt, Coventry's Education Service is one of the best organised. It has to be: it plays host to 10,000 school children each year.'

Following a suggestion made at a deans and provosts conference, a conference for cathedral visit and education officers was arranged at the National Society Religious Education Development Centre in London. Connie and one of the tutors, Mavis Weitzel, were asked to make a presentation on the Cathedral's work. It became obvious that Coventry was well ahead in the educational field, and the first to use people from the Job Creation Scheme to produce work packs. Many representatives from cathedrals came to visit Coventry to find out about the education programme and to experience the Visitors Centre as tourism became more important.

In the 1990s the education team, under the leadership of Tina Mead, took on the responsibility of programmes for school parties staying at Kennedy House. These came to Coventry to visit mosques, temples and places of worship for many faiths, including the Christian denominations not always present in the areas in which they lived. Many of these young people had the opportunity to go into the 'Cathedral by Night' when it was quiet and dark and very different from the way it was in the daytime. A former member of the education team, Chris Rose, recalls that this always had a profound effect on young people, and teachers found it unlocked a door to spirituality in young people that no other activity had done. Christingle services for Coventry schools were introduced at this time, and over 1,000 children attended them each year. These have continued to be a great success.

The story of Coventry and its cathedral in the Second World War has always attracted many school parties. A member of the Schools Team, Winston Collier, and his son Andrew began to build up a collection of artefacts that lent themselves to hands-on activities and eventually the old International Centre in the Ruins became a museum illustrating different aspects of wartime Britain, open to the public as well as schools.

Today the Schools Team, under the leadership of Emma Griffiths, is passionate about providing an excellent educational and spiritual experience for each visitor. Schools are offered a practical service that enables them to fulfil their needs in following a changing and varied curriculum. They work closely with other city-centre education providers to co-ordinate their programmes, and the team leader is a member of a number of bodies including the Diocesan Board of Education. All these partnerships provide opportunities for teachers and pupils to have as broad and up-to-date a professional experience as possible.

Taking children out of the classroom is a worrying prospect especially in a litigious climate, and to do so to a place of worship is especially daunting where there may be religious sensitivities. However, the team believes that for staff, pupils and parents they can provide a secure access point for discovering the Cathedral. Approximately 14,000 school-aged students are welcomed each year on guided tours and workshops covering a variety of subjects including art, architecture, history, religious studies, mathematics and citizenship. Resource packs are available for use in schools and activity packs for use on a visit.

Following a Key Stage 1 visit from a Church of England school in the diocese, a parent governor for the School Spirituality Development Project expressed appreciation of the creative activities which she felt brought Christian symbols to life. Several parents had mentioned to her that their children returned home and taught them some information they had not known, and had noted the central idea of reconciliation.

A secondary school pupil wrote:

In the original cathedral I was so overwhelmed with emotion that I felt like crying. To think how through all of this devastation had come such peace and unity I could not believe it . . . The thing that made me feel most touched was the statue of Reconciliation, which I found very moving. I have now made it my mission in life to go to each place where these statues are; Hiroshima in Japan, Belfast in Northern Ireland and Berlin in Germany as I found this the most touching part to me of the whole day!!

A teacher from another secondary school wrote: 'The staff and students came away with an appreciation of the power of forgiveness and love and with a little more places of calm in their lives, which is all good.'

In the twenty-first century there has been a significant development in bringing the work with schools into the ministry of reconciliation. A member of the Schools Team moved into the International Centre for Reconciliation to take responsibility for educational projects. A project entitled 'Exploring Hate, Understanding Power, and Valuing Life' was developed with schools, aiming at Key Stage 2 and Key Stage 3 students in citizenship classes. This provided an opportunity for young people to consider the root causes of hatred and hostility, sharing in a range of thoughts and emotions, helping them to reflect on their own priorities and beliefs, while trying to encourage a sense of self and civic worth, finally exploring the sanctity of life with reference to world religions and particularly to the story of peace and reconciliation at Coventry. A police spokesman commented:

This project is excellent, as it teaches the children about the cause for so much violence, bullying, hate crime and anti-social behaviour. By helping the children understand this emotion, they will be able to deal with their own emotions in a more positive way and so make them better young people.

The department also worked in conjunction with the chaplaincy at Rainsbrook Secure Training Centre on a programme of study for young offenders – entitled 'From Despair to Trust' – tackling key questions about the importance of identity and the possibilities of renewal, both individually and collectively, in their lives.

Youth conferences have been held at the Cathedral with representatives from different countries, local churches and the cathedral community. A number of schools have themselves become Cross of Nails Centres, which has helped them cement their particular school ethos.

Over the last 50 years, work with schools has probably been the most consistently successful area of ministry, appreciated by schools in the City and beyond. Staff have been quick to respond to changes in education and have developed excellent partnerships with other providers in the City. The Cathedral's message of reconciliation has remained the main focus and inspiration since the schools work began after the opening of the new Cathedral.

Kennedy House

In 1961 the Cathedral, with the assistance of the Dulverton Trust, appointed Michael Butterfield as Youth Officer to develop a varied programme of work with young people in Coventry and Warwickshire and further afield. His task was to develop youth work within the congregational life of the new Cathedral, including work of an interdenominational character centred on the Chapel of Unity. He was to involve young people of the city, county and beyond in the experimental thought and work of the Cathedral, especially in the field of industrial relationships, social service, music and drama, and to take the best possible advantage of the opportunities for international contact. It was also seen as essential that he should be available for the promotion of work among young people within the diocese as a whole. An open Youth Fellowship at the Cathedral catering for the 13–16 age group had been in existence for some time. A new group of young people, chiefly in the 17–25 age bracket, was gathered into the '62 Group' in October 1961. Its purpose was to involve young people in the developing life of the Cathedral and in responsible action in the community. A member of the group in today's cathedral congregation told me of the many and varied opportunities for worshipping, studying and socializing. As a member of the group she attended the Consecration Service. The moment that brought a lump to her throat (and the memory still does) was when Basil Spence, on his own, walked the length of the Ruins to greet the Queen, and all the people broke into spontaneous applause.

The 62 Group was invaluable in the development of the Cathedral Youth Project and its members were active in welcoming groups of young people from this country and overseas and in interpreting the Cathedral to them. During the Consecration Festival in 1962 an International Youth Assembly was held, involving 70 young people from the dioceses throughout Britain and 80 from 20 overseas countries who shared in a week of lectures, discussion, Bible study and worship. After the Consecration tremendous interest was shown by youth organizations throughout the country and it became clear that if the potential of the new Cathedral was going to be realized a residential centre was essential. Therefore in 1962 a beginning was made with some temporary accommodation, using builders' huts in the cathedral grounds. Between September 1962 and November 1964, the hostel welcomed over 2,500 young people from Great Britain and overseas. On New Year's Day 1963 a three-day programme of cathedral workshops began for fifth and sixth forms, involving 130 students from 22 schools in the diocese in a programme of drama, music and art. Because of the tremendous demand on space for lectures and visiting groups, the ground on which the hostel stood was going to have to be used for an extension to the cathedral plant. This meant that the temporary youth hostel would have to be moved and a new hostel built.

So it was that Kennedy House came into being. It was a residential centre for young people, primarily those who wished to visit the Cathedral and take part in courses organized by the Youth Department. It was designed by Sir Basil Spence and comprised four dormitories each housing ten people with two single rooms for leaders. It had a common room, reading and writing room and a kitchen.

The name 'Kennedy House' was suggested by Provost Bill Williams. He regarded the centre as an integral part of the ministry of the Cathedral and felt that without it, the youth programme would collapse. Kennedy House was officially opened on 24 April 1965 by Herr Willi Brandt before an invited audience of 300 people, including the German Ambassador and 50 American deans. The Dean of Washington read out a message from Jacqueline Kennedy:

Dear Provost Williams,

I was deeply touched to learn of the ceremonies on April 24th dedicating the new youth center at Coventry Cathedral as 'Kennedy House'.

President Kennedy often spoke of youth as being our greatest resource . . . and, because of his great hopes for the younger generation, I know that he would have been most interested in the work you are doing at Coventry. This is a most fitting tribute and one which the President would have appreciated. My thoughts will be with you, Mayor Brandt and all those present during the ceremonies.

Sincerely,

Jacqueline Kennedy

From the opening of Kennedy House in April 1965 to March 1966 approximately 1,665 young people from 58 different groups made use of the accommodation for lectures and conferences. The duration of their stay was from one night to a month. Groups had come from all parts of the British Isles, from Tipperary to Wallsend and from Keswick to the Isle of Wight. They came from church youth groups and local education authority groups, from schools and colleges. Groups came from Germany, Denmark, Czechoslovakia and the USA. Individual young people had come from most European countries, from Asia, America and Australia.

The expansion of the residential programme was only made possible by the very ready co-operation of members of the congregation willing to give hospitality and by the University of Warwick who made it possible to use one of their residential hostels for a number of courses.

Courses at Kennedy House reflected the main focus of the Cathedral – that of the City and the place of the cathedral in a secular world. The most significant of the residential courses was the Service and Study Programme. It was designed to involve a group of 15 young people from a country overseas with a similar number from the British Isles, in a fortnight of study and service to the Cathedral. Some of these became significant religious or secular leaders in their own countries, including an American bishop and the American Ambassador to Nigeria.

At the end of each fortnight every member of the groups was given a form to record their comments about the programme. These made clear the impact that living in an international and ecumenical community made on the young men and women who came from so many different churches and different countries. For the first time they were able to see people of other nations as real people and not as stereotypes. It was also apparent that through the programme the young people deepened their own understanding of the Christian faith and the task of the Church. Reports contained comments such as:

'I've learned to like Americans.'
'I found that my father's anti-German prejudices had rubbed off on to me – I've tried to erase them – they still linger on but are much milder.'
'I've learned that the God I thought didn't exist doesn't; but there's another one!'

Many letters of appreciation were received from groups in this country. A diocesan youth group wrote: 'What impresses me most . . . is the perpetual sense of "outwardness", and its real place in the life of the city and beyond.' At Kennedy House in the 1970s over 2,000 students from all over the world were coming annually to take part in study programmes and service projects. In addition, individuals came from many nations for special study and training in leadership, in social and industrial and urban problems. Special care was given to leadership training for potential leaders from the developing nations. Service projects included many local enterprises in the context of immigration problems and underprivileged areas, as well as an agricultural project in Lefkas, Greece, and the rebuilding of the Deaconesses' Hospital in Dresden.

But already by 1980 there were signs that Kennedy House was not attracting the numbers, despite the optimistic decision only two years before to add extra dormitory accommodation in Bardsley House. Some groups were using it as a cheap hotel and stating a preference for organizing their own programme. There was also concern about the state of the building. The roof structure was very weak and one area had to be closed because it was unsound and a public danger.

One of the major problems in the running of the House was the lack of continuity of staffing and the reliance on volunteers. Too often, inexperienced people took on a job that they held only for a short period, and despite their enthusiasm this had an adverse effect on the continuing success of the centre. However, even with the employment of a caterer and a reduction in the number of volunteers, bookings were down and questions were being asked: 'Why and for whom does Kennedy House exist and what can it uniquely offer?'

Despite a new committee drawn from the Cathedral, Diocesan Education Committee and the Local Education Committee, and the complete refurbishment of the building with substantial financial support from the City Council, Kennedy House continued to run at a loss and it became clear in the early 1990s that there was insufficient money to pay a full-time residential warden. The number of domestic groups and schools had decreased mainly because there was less need to provide opportunities to visit temples and mosques when more of these were being built across the country. Despite this, when the City produced plans for redevelopment of the area, the Cathedral agreed to its demolition on condition that it was replaced in a slightly different location. Even at this time there was reluctance to face up to the fact that a residential youth centre as first established in the 1960s was no longer viable. It finally closed in March 1999.

Opportunities for young people from this country and abroad continue to be provided on an occasional basis, accommodation being found either in private homes or Coventry University. The original vision of bringing young people together still remains as an integral part of the ministry of reconciliation, but whether there will be another building remains to be seen. Plans for the future need to be put into the context of a 50-year-old cathedral building which is still unique, and a ministry of reconciliation which is still relevant, but which will not attract the vast numbers who came in the 1960s to see a new cathedral. However, the importance of Kennedy House in the story of the new Cathedral cannot be overestimated.

Cathedral youth work

During the 1960s the Cathedral Youth Club thrived, opening on average three evenings per week and membership was at the fixed maximum of 150 with a whole range of activities. The Cathedral conducted what was probably the only open youth work in the centre of the city. Activities included a series of discussions under the heading 'The Things that Divide Us' and representatives of the club attended the Coventry Council of Youth. The Cathedral Youth Club's own beat group, The Rippers, were placed fourth in the National Beat and Folk Festival sponsored by Christian Aid in

*On the Cathedral steps Cilla Black cuts the tape to start a 48-hour
sponsored fast by young people to raise money for Christian Aid
in 1969.*

1965, and 150 members of the club took part in a rally in Trafalgar Square. Young
adults were also catered for and a student group for those at university and college
met in each vacation at the home of Canon Verney.

Michael Butterfield was keen to expand the open youth work of the Cathedral
but this was prevented by inadequate premises. New possibilities emerged when a
former bakery was purchased by the Cathedral, and the City Council and the government Department of Education and Science supported its conversion into a youth
centre. In 1970 Bardsley House began functioning and was used by a number of
youth clubs throughout the week.

By the 1980s there was no money for a youth officer, but there was an active
Young People's Fellowship run by Jane Williams and Sheila Leddington Wright,

COVENTRY UNITED

In 1995 the Methodist Association of Youth Clubs (MAYC) for the first time invited an ecumenical youth group to join 15,000 members at its annual London Weekend. The group was Coventry United – 50 young Coventry people aged 14 to 23 years, who took part and performed in the Royal Albert Hall before capacity audiences. The inspiration for the group came from Sheila Leddington Wright, Liam Quinn and Jane Williams, cathedral organizers of activities for young people.

The group devised a dance programme to fit the Royal Albert Hall. The only places big enough for rehearsals were the Centre AT7 gym in Bell Green, Coventry, and the cathedral nave cleared of chairs. Their Sunday evening rehearsals aimed for a completely professional presentation.

The London dress rehearsal was Saturday morning. After a Hyde Park picnic it was time for the shows. The young members tell their own story. Emma Wright says:

> With an explosion of light and sound the dancers converged on the arena. Immediately, I sensed that the audience liked it. The months that we had spent practising and preparing for the Show were coming together.
>
> The audience response amazed me. The atmosphere was overwhelming and made our item complete. As our item came to an end, the audience screamed appreciation – it was clear that they had enjoyed our performance.
>
> In the finale involving all 800 performers we sang *The Circle of Life* using British sign language. I found this quite emotional, and I know that members of the audience found it moving, particularly those who were deaf.

That night the group slept on St Barnabas Church crypt floor (the parish priest was John Irvine), a 20-minute walk from the Royal Albert Hall. Next morning they joined 15,000 young people in worship at Battersea Park, which included pop music, dancers, videos, gospel groups and speakers. The congregation showed the same noisy exuberance as the previous day – quite different from Sunday morning Cathedral worship!

Later, members spoke about their experiences from the cathedral pulpit:

> The whole worship meant a lot to me, some parts were light-hearted, some made me think hard. One part moved me to tears. The whole weekend was a very special experience.
>
> Liz Watts

The culmination of the rehearsals resulted in an amazing weekend which enabled me to feel accepted as a person and experience something special. I think this whole experience will always be one of the highlights of my life.

Rosamund Chester

When I performed at the Royal Albert Hall I experienced something that I find difficult to express. All I can say is that it left me with a greater understanding.

Gary Watson

Martin Williams
Editorial Committee Member

two members of the cathedral community. The aims were to encourage, support and develop the members in the growth and development of their Christian lives, to encourage them to take a full and active part in the life of the Cathedral and to enable each person to feel an equal and valued member. The group took responsibility

Archbishop of York Dr John Sentamu commissioning youth workers at a 2005 gathering in the Cathedral of Youth For Christ, a national Christian charity founded by Billy Graham.

for two Sunday services a year, including the sermon, and had the courage to invite the congregation to complete a questionnaire assessing the service. The leaders maintained contact with those at university and college and encouraged members of the congregation to do the same. In the mid-1990s Coventry United was formed, an ecumenical youth group of which the Cathedral's WHY ('Worship Helps You') group was part, which enabled young people to experience fellowship and support within an ecumenical social arena. A good proportion of members were ex-choristers.

When the leaders retired, as happens in churches, there was a period when there were few activities for young people. The appointment of a Youth Minister in 2002 meant this whole area of ministry was revitalized and took a totally new direction with particular attention given to disadvantaged and disaffected youngsters who had little if any connection with the Church. There is now a Youth Team led by Keith Parr, which works in co-operation with other city churches providing activities and support in often challenging circumstances. There are about 500 members, ranging from 11-year-olds to the mid-20s, 97 per cent of whom are unchurched. Some, however, are becoming engaged with the cathedral community and involved in Cathedral Praise, the informal act of worship on Sunday evenings. Emphasis is placed on the importance of leaders gaining qualifications in youth work.

A youth group from the Cathedral visited a hospital for the mentally handicapped in Chelmsley Wood in 1990. © Jane Williams.

The Ministry of Reconciliation yesterday and today

The Ministry of Reconciliation at Coventry is most closely associated in people's minds with international affairs, covered elsewhere in this book, but reconciliation has been a theme running through all the Cathedral's activities. Unsurprisingly, every provost and dean has defined it somewhat differently according to his own theological and ecclesiological standpoint. Each identified people, clergy and lay, to work with him on what were and are his particular priorities.

Trevor Beeson, in his book *The Deans*, describes Provost Williams as 'one of the two most significant figures in the twentieth-century history of the cathedrals, the other being Frank Bennett of Chester in the 1920s'.[5] He certainly pioneered a ministry that influenced other cathedrals and attracted staff and volunteers who were excited by his vision of the Church in the twentieth century. He ensured the Cathedral engaged with contemporary and often controversial issues. He travelled abroad, preaching and lecturing, particularly in Germany and the United States. 'If the Christian church', he said, 'cannot speak sense to a world divided by nationality, by history, by politics, by race, by colour, then all we read of the claims of the Bible about unity and reconciliation is hypocrisy or worse.'

In the early 1960s he said that the Ministry of Reconciliation was defined by Kennedy House, the International Centre in the Ruins, the post of a youth officer, a cathedral congregation opening their homes to foreign students, and research and experimental work on reconciliation. One of the greatest of Provost Williams' legacies was the establishment of the Cross of Nails Centres. In 1973 Canon Kenyon Wright, the first appointed Director of International Reconciliation, suggested these centres should form the Community of the Cross of Nails (CCN) which would be a worldwide body united in prayer, discipline and commitment. Williams embraced the idea with enthusiasm. The relationship between Coventry and the CCN has changed over the years and the work of reconciliation has been redefined, but Coventry would not be known across the world for its ministry without those initial links.

Yet his Ministry of Reconciliation seemed to be more readily understood abroad than at home. He received the *Bundesverdienstkreuz*, the Order of Merit of the Federal Republic of Germany, and he was awarded an honorary doctorate by the University of Valparaiso in Indiana. In Great Britain neither church nor state awarded him any honour. This may have been due to his self-imposed isolation from local and national church structures. He felt neither church nor state were taking account of the changes in society. He questioned the parochial system as the only way to exercise ministry. Although it is not uncommon in dioceses for parishes to feel dis-engaged from the mother Church, he believed there was a historical explanation for this. In the Civil War, Coventry took the liberal, radical side of the Parliamentar-ians, while Warwickshire supported the conservative Royalists. So he felt the tension between City and County was largely a hangover of historical prejudice rather than anything to do with the Church. Be that as it may, it was not only rural parishes that felt isolation; some in the City also expressed the view that the Cathedral had little or no impact on their activities. This was a great pity given the great impetus towards the Consecration given across the region by Bishop Bardsley and groups of clergy and laity.

Bishop John Gibbs. © Cathedral Archives.

After Provost Williams retired in 1981, Bishop John Gibbs felt the Cathedral needed a new direction with less emphasis on the war. He appointed Colin Semper with this in mind. The new Provost found a very different city from that known by his predecessor. At its Consecration the Cathedral was a symbol of a city that was successful. In the first half of the 1980s it was a city in recession, with high unem-ployment and severe loss of jobs in manufacturing industry. He recognized that parishes, especially those in the south of the diocese, felt remote from the Cathedral, and strove to work more closely with these, as well as with the City Council. He believed this should be a servant cathedral. During his five years he was a constant visitor at the Council House and he became a well-known visitor in the factories. He wrote in a letter:

This 'Super Church' lurches from crisis to crisis, but can do some glorious things. It is an infuriating place but has the habit of being like a shaggy dog and shaking itself to produce moments of glory. The trouble is that we have been so triumphalist and now must learn to serve the City and the Diocese more closely.

Despite having to deal with a very difficult financial situation, Colin Semper achieved a great deal in five years and his experience of the media was a crucial factor in the establishment of the Visitors Centre.

When his successor as Provost, John Petty, arrived in 1988 from the parish of St John the Evangelist, Hurst in Manchester he brought with him another dimension to the ministry of reconciliation, that of healing, in which he saw many people recover wonderfully from cancer and other diseases. His healing gifts attracted enormous interest, and publicity which he did not seek. People came from all over the country and from overseas for this ministry. In 1989 there was an important exhibition of paintings by Diana Constance, entitled 'AIDS', accompanied by a seminar, the aim of which was to promote a feeling of understanding and compassion to those afflicted, and to create a greater awareness of the dangers of the illness. An editorial in the Coventry *Evening Telegraph* commented:

The Provost was brave after London councils, running scared of public criticism, withdrew their support. But this is one of the big issues of our time and no church concerned about people should be frightened to tackle it. Thankfully the Cathedral wasn't.

In January 1996 the Cathedral Development Trust funded a Healing Centre with individual counselling rooms and a quiet chapel in the Cathedral Offices in Priory Row. However, lack of funds meant this work had to be discontinued and with Provost Petty's departure other priorities took over. John Petty continued the work of his predecessor in improving links with the City and the parishes, at the same time entering enthusiastically into the international ministry, but with decreasing resources, which he did his utmost to remedy.

With the arrival in September 2001 of Dean John Irvine, a man from the evangelical tradition and Vicar of St Barnabas, Kensington, more time and resources were directed to evangelism, and there was a major shift in emphasis from the transformation of society to the transformation of individuals. In one sense this was a revival of one of the aims and objectives of the Christian Service Centre, a building in the original concept which never materialized because of shortage of funds. There were plans at that time for research and pioneer work in new methods of evangelism and an encouragement of the formation of Christian associations, groups and cells of every kind and size both in the Christian congregation and outside, fostering growth, co-ordinating their activities and training leaders. Now this has become a priority for the Cathedral's outreach mission but seen from a very different theological perspective from that of the Dean's predecessors.

The Dean led a re-examination of the priorities of the Cathedral's ministry and in 2004 the Cathedral Vision was approved following extensive consultation. This emphasized that because of its history Coventry Cathedral has a special responsibility to take the message of reconciliation across the world. However, there were financial problems in continuing the high-profile work that had been led in the Middle East by Canon Andrew White, and in Africa by Canon Justin Welby. In 2006 these forced the Chapter to discuss the purpose and definition of the international ministry of reconciliation. It was agreed that the ministry must begin with the Coventry story, be symbolized by the Cross of Nails, be based on the Coventry Litany of Reconciliation, be underpinned by prayer and be Christ-centred.

Canon Justin Welby prepared a revised form of the Coventry Discipline first devised by Provost Williams, which could be used in a variety of contexts by Cross of Nails Centres across the world. It reflected the view that more emphasis should be given to reconciliation within the cathedral community itself, and within the communities of the city and diocese, at the same time nurturing and supporting the CCN centres worldwide. When Canon Welby was appointed Dean of Liverpool in 2007, Dr David Porter, a lay theologian with a great deal of experience of reconciliation work in Northern Ireland, was appointed as the Director for Reconciliation Ministry. International links continue to be important, but more initiatives at local level are being introduced, especially engaging with young people on issues of justice and reconciliation.

Dwindling resources over the years inevitably put a brake on the Cathedral's outreach ministry begun in the heady days of the 1960s, which attracted so many people, including myself, to become part of the cathedral community. Some areas quite rightly moved out of the Cathedral. Inter-ethnic and interfaith relations became the responsibility of the diocese alone, and industrial mission was newly managed by a trust working with ecumenical partners. Successive bishops of Coventry have always seen the ministry of reconciliation, and in particular its international dimension, as an integral part of the work of the diocese as a whole, even though it is still seen by many in the parishes as the work of the Cathedral. What is particularly exciting as the Cathedral celebrates its Golden Jubilee is that the Department for Reconciliation is now reclaiming some of the priorities of the 1960s, engaging in a different world with issues of justice, forgiveness and reconciliation, while the Schools and Youth Teams seek to help young people understand these too.

Archbishop John Habgood made a perceptive comment in a 1987 sermon at the Cathedral commemorating its Silver Jubilee: 'You have shown us what it is to fly and to run, but perhaps you have yet to learn what it is to walk.' Another 25 years on it is interesting to ask whether we have learned what it is to walk. Financial restrictions have certainly forced us to slow down, and be more reluctant to take risks. We can never recapture the excitement of the world as experienced 50 years ago, nor can we afford a multiplicity of specialist departments, but that does not mean we can forget our story as a cathedral ruined and rebuilt, and what has been understood by a succession of provosts and deans, canons, staff and congregation, namely that 'God reconciled us to himself through Christ and has given us the ministry of reconciliation' (1 Corinthians 5.19).

* Denotes an entry in the Glossary

Notes

1 H. C. N. Williams, *Coventry Cathedral Review*, January 1965.
2 H. C. N. Williams, *Coventry Cathedral in Action*, Religious Education Press, 1968.
3 *The Times*, 5 June 1974.
4 Horace Dammers, 'Coventry Cathedral: An Opportunity for Christian Education', *Learning for Living*, March 1969.
5 Trevor Beeson, *The Deans: Cathedral Life, Yesterday, Today and Tomorrow*, SCM Press, 2004.

5 THE CITY AND THE CATHEDRAL – VIEWS BOTH WAYS!

RICHARD FARNELL

A prologue: origins

Where do conversations about the City Council begin when those schooled in the Cathedral's post-war narrative sit down together? Without exception they start with recollections about the conflicts created by councillors' opposition to the building of the new Cathedral. The story is well rehearsed in the memoirs of protagonists and in the reflections of local academics.[1] The City Council Planning Committee had the view that 'the Cathedral should be rebuilt in stone on its old site, an exact replica of the medieval church of St Michael', although Alderman George Hodgkinson, the committee's vice-chairman at that stage, observed that there was 'a growing feeling among the citizens that the ruins ought to be retained as a monument to man's indiscretions between 1939 and 1945'.

Sir Basil Spence's concept for the new Cathedral, incorporating the ruins of the old, was successful in the 1951 competition. It was a design concept welcomed wholeheartedly by the City Architect, Donald Gibson, by George Hodgkinson and by many other aldermen and councillors. At least, they applauded at the select luncheon party to celebrate the decision. But in early 1954 the City Council, led by Alderman Sidney Stringer, announced that while they were supportive of the principle to build a new cathedral, they felt that construction should not commence for at least ten years. There were other priorities for the City, including the provision of homes, schools and services to meet the needs of Coventry's residents. Bishop Gorton and Provost Howard had for years maintained that they too shared that opinion, but that getting started on the project would not be a diversion from these priorities. Different materials and different skills were needed for constructing a stone-built cathedral. Despite council opposition a licence was granted on 4 May 1954 for £985,000 to build a new cathedral at Coventry.

In making his decision David Eccles, the government minister, wrote to the Lord Mayor in the following terms:

> The Cathedral is not a building which concerns Coventry and Coventry alone. The echo of the bombs that destroyed your city was heard round the world. We cannot tell how many people are waiting in this country and abroad for this church to rise and prove that English traditions live again after the blitz. The threat of far worse destruction is with us today, demoralising and corrupting our thoughts. We have never had a greater need for acts of faith.

In the following decades this viewpoint was to become a foundation upon which the story of the Cathedral was constructed and, according to George Hodgkinson, nobody who voted against the starting date rejected the invitation to the opening ceremony in 1962.

How might one understand the behaviour of the local politicians in Coventry at this time? Nationally, a Labour government was elected in 1945 in the immediate aftermath of victory. It was widely accepted that as the nation organized for war, it should now organize for peace. This meant state intervention in many areas of public life. Means of production and communication were nationalized. A regulatory system of Town and Country Planning was introduced. Health and education services were developed. The economy, targeted at rebuilding the infrastructure of the nation and meeting the needs of those returning from the war, would be controlled by the government.

Locally in Coventry the implications of this approach were far reaching. The Labour Council was determined to act quickly and comprehensively, guided by the concepts and plans presented by the City Architect as early as 1941. Almost immediately after 1945, Coventry's manufacturing industries began to prosper. Skilled workers were needed. Returning war veterans and new migrants took the opportunities Coventry industries provided. This created issues for the Council, which found itself in the awkward position of constantly having to satisfy an increasing and unpredictable demand for its services with wholly inadequate resources. Uncertainties were compounded by the election of a Conservative government in 1951, headed by Winston Churchill.

Though branded as a 'socialist city', mass support for Labour had never existed in Coventry. The Conservative share of the local working-class vote was fairly substantial. Commentators have suggested that prevailing currents within the party made for significant difficulties in the public presentation of policy, especially between 1953 and 1955.

> The local party leadership found itself staggering from one political crisis to the next, including altercations with the Cathedral in 1954. In each case, what was damaging to Labour was not so much its final position on the issue itself, but rather the argument and the dogmatic assertion which inevitably seemed to be a feature of the decision making process.[2]

In addition, socialist self-identity, developed through working-class engagement in manufacturing industry, projected an identity on to the Cathedral as the 'Establishment', with its Oxbridge-educated leaders and the perceived ethos of the Church of England as the 'Tory Party at prayer'.

Understanding the City and the Cathedral

This is a well-known story of relationships between the Cathedral and the City Council during those formative years. Three elements were important to this relationship: the prosperous working-class City, the confident yet unsettled politics of the City and the 'much more than local' significance of the new cathedral project. How did these relationships develop in subsequent years? Tracing them is far from straightforward. The structures of local government have changed, as have organizational approaches and management. The political complexion of the Council has shifted more regularly than many people would have predicted in the 1950s.

A superficial look at the Cathedral might suggest that it has experienced a more settled pattern of life. The forms of worship are broadly similar in the twenty-first century to those introduced in the 1960s. Over this 50-year period there have only been three provosts and two deans, four leaders in total. (John Petty was appointed as Provost and became Dean, as part of new nomenclature in the Church of England, just a few weeks before retirement.) Yet closer inspection shows that turbulence has also characterized the Cathedral's experience. The place of the Christian faith in UK society, the role of the Church of England, the nature and purpose of cathedrals and the attempt to develop theologies that are true to historic faith and relevant to contemporary life, have all introduced questions, tensions and challenges.

The fortunes of the city over the last 50 years add an extra dimension to this complexity. Much has changed in the city; it has seen both prosperity and poverty. People migrated to Coventry; others avoided the place. These social, economic and environmental changes have had their consequences for the Cathedral as well as the public authorities.

Colour Gallery

1   Ecumenical landmark. In July 1967 Archbishop Cardinale, the Apostolic Delegate, was guided around the Cathedral by Bishop Cuthbert Bardsley and Provost Williams before attending a service. This was the first visit by the Pope's official representative to an Anglican Cathedral since the Reformation. © David Fletcher.

✠

2&3   In 2001 the Cathedral nave was so badly damaged by smoke from a fire that started in the undercroft that every surface in the building had to be cleaned. Fire officers were already familiar with the building from its use in training exercises. © Edward Ockenden.

Christmas in Coventry

4   On Christmas Eve Canon Joseph Poole, Precentor, pauses with the Coventry Cathedral Choir procession in front of the Cathedral Christmas tree. © Robert Weddle.

5   In 1962 Basil Spence commissioned and donated to the Cathedral a Christmas and Epiphany Crib created by Alma Ramsey-Hosking. The crib was restored in 2007 by her daughter, Sarah.

6   *Journey to Bethlehem* is a Christmas Eve service for children that takes them around the nave travelling from the Inn to the Shepherds and finally to the Stable.

7   On Christmas Eve at the *Form of a Servant* the choirs gather around the Christmas tree.

John Piper vestments

8–13   John Piper was commissioned to design six seasonal sets of robes for use in the new Cathedral: 8 Celebration Gold; 9 Passiontide Red; 10 Lenten Sackcloth; 11 Advent Blue; 12 Trinity Green; 13 Holy Spirit Red.

✠

14   St Michael's Dancers use liturgical dance in a service of welcome to the Holy Spirit at Pentecost.

Congregation activities

15   Parachute games at a Cathedral community weekend at the Diocesan Retreat House in 1986. Away days and retreats are regular features of congregation life.

16   In 1998 congregation members cleared the nave of chairs so that supporters could pay to do aerobics as part of *Heart to Heart* – an event to raise funds for outreach work in Sibiu, Romania.

17   Each year a group from the congregation spends a week in retreat on Lindisfarne (Holy Island). It is not usually hot enough for Bible study to take place on the beach as happened in 1990.

18   *Moving Forward* was the title of a day of youth activities in the Ruins to celebrate the new Cathedral's 40th anniversary in 2002. The CREW, Coventry's own team of cheerleaders, demonstrated their talents.

19   *Coventry United*, an ecumenical group of Coventry young people organized by Sheila Leddington Wright and Jane Williams. They devised and performed a dramatic musical piece before an audience of 10,000 at the Methodist Association of Youth Clubs Annual Weekend in the Royal Albert Hall in May 1995.

✠

20   The Blessing at a Diocesan Ordination.

✠

21   The first ordination of women in Coventry Cathedral on 23 April 1994. Thirty-five candidates were ordained in the presence of Bishop Maria Jepsen (Bishop of Hamburg, the first woman Lutheran bishop) and Bishop Penny Jamieson (Bishop of Dunedin, New Zealand) who was the first woman in the Anglican communion to be elected bishop. © Lawrence Mortimer.

Cathedral concerts

22   The International Church Music Festival brings together church choirs and musicians from all over the world. Seen from outside the building through the west screen with its reflections of the Ruins, Sir David Willcocks conducted the closing concert in June 2000.

23   Before Christmas each year the St Michael's Singers (founded in 1963) present *Carols for All*. Paul Leddington Wright conducted the concert in 2010. © Craig Wilson.

Prayers in the Cathedral ruins

24   The Litany of Reconciliation is said each Friday at noon at the altar in the Cathedral Ruins. At the same time each week this action is repeated across the worldwide network of more than 160 member centres of the Community of the Cross of Nails.

25   The statue 'Reconciliation' by Josefina de Vasconcellos was unveiled in the Cathedral Ruins in 1995 and was the focal point of the Remembrance Day service in 1996.

✠

26   Prayers at Epstein's statue of St Michael during the Patronal Festival in 2008.

✠

27   Local scouts abseiling down the Cathedral walls alongside the statue of St Michael in the rain raising sponsored gifts for the Church Urban Fund in 1986.

✠

28   The Millennium Chapel displaying the Stalingrad Madonna behind its altar was dedicated in 2000. The glass walls record the names of supporters of the Cathedral Development Trust as well as the names of people in whose memory gifts were made. It is the only additional chapel since 1962.

✠

29   In 1995 Queen Elizabeth distributed the Royal Maundy in Coventry Cathedral. © Tom McIlroy.

✠

30   The joint congregations of the Cathedral and of Holy Trinity Church pause for Bible readings in Priory Gardens during their Palm Sunday procession in 2006.

✠

31   *HMS Pinafore* in the Cathedral Lecture Hall is one of several musical shows that have drawn on hidden talents within the Cathedral community.

Baptism

32   A baptism at the Cathedral font, which is made from a boulder taken from a hillside near Bethlehem.

33   Baptism by full immersion in the Cathedral Ruins.

34   The congregation is sprinkled with water as a reminder of their baptism at a Lent service around the Chi-Rho in the nave floor.

✠

35   Easter Liturgy 2010: in the early hours of Easter morning the Bishop prepares the light of resurrection to be carried into the new Cathedral from the darkness of the Cathedral Ruins.

✠

36   At his Installation Service in 2001 Dean John Irvine knelt before a young chorister for the presentation of a Coventry Cross of Nails.

✠

37   On 14 November 2010 three thousand Coventrians filled the Ruins for prayers on the 70th anniversary of the Coventry Blitz. Special floodlighting created a ceiling of light.

1

2   3

4

5

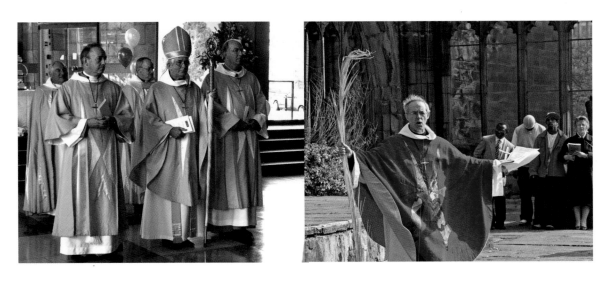

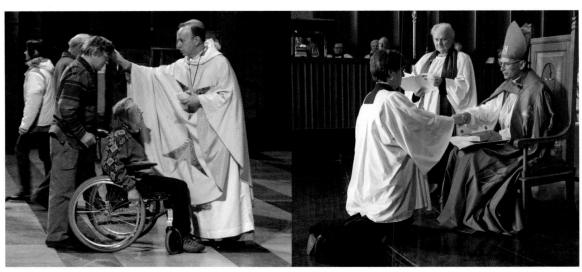

14

15

16

17

18

19

20

21

22

23

24

25

26

27

28

29

30

31

32

33

34

36

37

AN EXTRAORDINARY VISION

Between 8 and 20 October 1945, over 48,000 people visited an extraordinary exhibition at the Drill Hall. 'Coventry of the Future' went well beyond reconstruction of the city centre; sections on transport, industry, housing, public services, amenities and central redevelopment presented a forward-looking vision of where and how Coventry's entire population might live, work and play. Within the residential zones, each neighbourhood of approximately 10,000 inhabitants would have its own health clinic, branch library, community centre, schools, parks, allotments and even swimming pool.

The plans had been in gestation since 1938 when the City Council appointed a dynamic 29-year-old, Donald Gibson, to the newly created post of City Architect. The population of Coventry had tripled from 70,000 in 1901, to over 200,000 by the 1930s, imposing severe strains on housing, public health, education and general amenities; the narrow, crooked medieval streets at the centre were said to be congested and lacking in open spaces, with little room for the motor car. But by 1945, the war had given Gibson a blank canvas.

The exhibition told how a central area, within an inner ring road, would accommodate all the city's cultural, civic and commercial life. Europe's first traffic-free shopping precinct opened onto a new Broadgate, with fountains, flowers and Lady Godiva statue, and was aligned to an uninterrupted vista of the cathedral spire. St Mary's Hall, Holy Trinity Church and the cathedral spire, described as 'a group worthy of fine display', were set in a large area of open parkland, extending into Pool Meadow, where the relocation of the bus station to a transport hub at the railway station, made room for a lake, bandstand and cafés.

Donald Gibson left Coventry in 1955. His vision might have been idealistic and implementation inevitably involved compromise, but his core ideas survived. While many Coventrians mourned the loss of their medieval heritage, Gibson's vision had given the city a new identity and a sense of place. During the closing decades of the twentieth century, private developers were invited to modernize Coventry's central areas, said to be 'tired' and no longer meeting the needs of contemporary retail. Identity and sense of place had given way to shopping malls and infill developments that mutilated Broadgate, cluttered the Precinct and obscured Donald Gibson's precious vistas.

The Phoenix Initiative, completed in 2004, marked a welcome return to self-confidence, vision and civic identity. Aimed at regenerating a difficult corner of Coventry, public art combined with architecture and urban design to create a series of spaces cascading from the cathedral quarter to the Transport Museum.

> The realization, however, was not without its critics. Basil Spence's Kennedy House was demolished and Sainsbury's reluctance to relocate forced a reduction in size of Priory Place and the planned open vista to the cathedral spire was lost.
>
> In echoes of the 1945 Drill Hall exhibition, September 2008 saw the launch of a public consultation on a 15-year masterplan, for the complete reshaping of the city centre.
>
> *John Willis*
> *Editorial Committee Member*

Yet another dimension is the extent to which the role and activities of both the City Council and the Cathedral have been in flux over the years. Services once provided by local authorities have been given to other public or semi-public bodies. Providing water and sewerage services, social housing, bus transport, health services and policing are just some examples. In recent times it has been realized that effective action to promote the well-being of people and communities can only happen with a commitment to partnership working between public, private and voluntary sector agencies. Some activities initiated by the Cathedral are now seen to be more appropriately undertaken by the Diocese of Coventry, others are undertaken together. The bishops, diocese and cathedral are part of the Church of England, and have differing yet flexible roles.

With these factors in mind, and in the knowledge that a lot has happened in 50 years, the approach to analysing relationships between the City and the Cathedral in this chapter is selective of incidents, events and statements. What follows is organized around 'views both ways', first from the City Council and then the Cathedral.

Before these views are presented, markers are needed to help clarify the analysis. How has the City of Coventry changed since the 1950s? What about the changing nature of religion in our society and the role of cathedrals? How have attitudes changed to the role that faith plays in politics and policy-making?

Coventry: a city in transition

The people of Coventry have lived through turbulent times since 1945. To appreciate the volatility of the City's fortunes it is helpful to sketch aspects of Coventry's earlier story. Despite a prosperous medieval past, Coventry saw little of the growth that the Industrial Revolution brought to other cities such as its near neighbours,

Birmingham and Leicester. Watch-making, sewing-machine and bicycle production laid foundations for twentieth-century industrial manufacture, but there was little administrative, governmental or cultural provision in the city. The population of Coventry in 1901 was only 70,000.

Yet by the outbreak of the First World War there were 20 motor-vehicle manufacturers in the city, which built nearly 30 per cent of the cars produced nationally.[3] By 1922 there were 96 such firms. In the 1930s the City's total labour force was about 100,000 people, 38 per cent of whom were employed in the motor-car industry. Coventry's businesses responded enthusiastically in the late 1930s to the need for aircraft and aero-engines with the growing threat of war. A programme of 'shadow' or duplicate factory construction on the fringes of the city was implemented. By this time Coventry was a city of migrants, coming from Scotland, Ireland, Wales and the north-east of England.

It was a 'workers' city'. The inter-war period had been a struggle for the Council to deal with this growth in population and the pressure for development. The medieval centre had hardly coped; some new roads had been built and the A45 constructed to the south of the city to relieve congestion. And then came the war and 14 November 1940! Every aspect of life in Coventry was affected fundamentally by the war. Economically the war increased reliance upon motor vehicles, aircraft, electrical and mechanical engineering, sectors that immediately after the end of the war returned to a level of domestic production that was to grow significantly over the following 20 years. In these years Coventry continued to produce about 20 per cent of Britain's output of motor vehicles, assembling the more fashionable vehicles from component parts made in Birmingham and Wolverhampton. A warning was articulated in *The Times*, 31 March 1959, commenting that Coventry's long-term prosperity would remain vulnerable as long as the City was so heavily dependent on the motor industry; 'our prosperity, impressive though it is, could vanish into thin air almost overnight', said one union official.

Employment opportunities in Coventry at this time were almost unlimited. Wages for skilled craftsmen and semi-skilled manual workers were high in comparison to other places. By the 1951 census the population was over 250,000. *The Observer* Magazine of 14 November 1965 talked about Coventry as having 'no very rich and no very poor, with a peculiar class structure based more on money than accent or background – this is a workers' city'. It identified 36 working men's clubs with over 50,000 members and commented that 'the Bridge Restaurant in the city centre has table lamps and looks intimate and expensive from the outside, but men in pullovers march in without being intimidated'!

These were the boom years for the City. The economy was flourishing, people were migrating to the city and the City Council had plans for everything, especially the rebuilding of the city centre, the provision of council housing on new large estates on the city fringe, schools, health centres and roads, in particular the new 'Inner Ring Road' around the centre. Despite the saga of the Cathedral and the Council in the early 1950s, these were the decades when the new Cathedral was conceived and born, to be celebrated by all in 1962.

But where were the middle-class professionals, bureaucrats and managers who ran Coventry? The conventional explanation is that they were choosing to live outside the City in Warwickshire, to the south in Kenilworth, Leamington Spa, Warwick and Stratford-upon-Avon. While they might earn their living in Coventry, their consumption was centred on the shops of Leamington and the cultural resources of Stratford and Birmingham. Despite the innovations of the pedestrian precinct, the retail profile of the City reflected its predominant residents' interests and purchasing power.

Almost imperceptibly, Coventry's fortunes began to change. Towards the end of the 1960s the structural difficulties with its economy and its reliance on manufacturing employment began to surface. A series of Lord Mayor's conferences were held in 1968 to investigate the City's difficulties and future prospects: 'Attention focused on the problems of motor and aircraft manufacture, the adverse impact of government regional policies and the relative absence of both the new science based and service industries.' During the previous 20 years, 15 major companies had come to own Coventry's industry. Most were national or multinational and almost without exception did not have their headquarters in Coventry. Between 1975 and 1982 these companies removed 55,000 jobs from their books in Coventry. The boom city of 30 post-war years became the clinically depressed city of the next 20.

In the mid-1980s over 45 per cent of Coventry jobs were in manufacturing, many more than in other comparable places. The City Council struggled to respond to these issues by encouraging inward investment. Many new firms did migrate to Coventry, technological, science-based, distribution and service industries. Warwick University Science Park, Coventry University Technology Park, business and distribution centres near the motorways provided stimulus to these developments. The employment structure of Coventry became more balanced, with 12.5 per cent in manufacturing jobs by 2007, similar to the national economy as a whole. The City has been in a process of renewal for the last decade and a half, with property development projects in the centre, including the Phoenix Initiative, and through the use of 'brown field' sites made available following the closure of manufacturing industries.

This is not the whole story. There are other markers in the life of the City that help in understanding relationships with the Cathedral. As well as being a workers' city, Coventry is also a migrants' city. Migration to the city in search of work has been a characteristic for well over 100 years. Manufacturing industries relied on labour coming to and settling in the city. In 1982, out of a population of 310,000, the Lord Mayor's Committee on Racial Harmony identified 34,000 as British-born internal migrants, from Ireland, Scotland and Wales, and 5,000 from Eastern Europe, including people from Ukraine and Poland. A further 25,000 were classed as people born in other parts of the world, particularly of New Commonwealth and Pakistani origin, arriving in Britain following the government's invitation to come and work.

The Lord Mayor's report showed that most of the migrants from the New Commonwealth were living in Hillfields and Foleshill to the north of the city centre, areas with cheaper terraced houses available for rent or purchase. These new Coventry residents provided their own places of worship and meeting space for their community's needs by adapting existing property and, later, building new gurdwaras, temples and mosques. Coventry has become a more global city in recent decades with the arrival of asylum-seekers and refugees from different parts of the world and with residents from other European Union countries coming to live and work in Britain. Like many other cities, Coventry has become host to Muslim refugees from Somalia and Roman Catholic economic migrants from Poland and other Eastern European countries.

In the 1950s and 1960s Coventry embarked on a large programme of council house building to meet the needs of its growing population. Estates were started in Willenhall, Bell Green, Wood End, Stoke Aldermoor, Tile Hill and Cheylesmore. These rented homes for workers were welcomed; long waiting lists encouraged a sense of achievement when tenancies were signed. Twenty-five years later, in the face of all-party commitment to home ownership, council housing, or as it became branded 'social housing', was seen as the residual form of tenure, the last resort for those unable to afford to buy their own. Despite all the efforts of the City Council and housing associations, the city is more spatially segregated. Those who are poor, because of unemployment, disability or old age, have few options about where they live.

In summary, a prosperous working-class city went into severe depression and has been attempting to rediscover itself ever since. It has become a city of many peoples and many communities where religion is important to identity and behaviour. It has also become a more socially and economically divided city where poverty and disadvantage are common experiences.

Faith, theology and the Cathedral

Since the 1950s much has changed not just in Coventry, but also in the place of the Christian faith in British society. This may be seen in the attitudes of ordinary people towards faith and spirituality, in the place that the Church and its cathedrals hold in contemporary life and, indeed, in the way that Christian theologians have thought about the Kingdom of God. As with the narrative about the City, these observations provide further markers for later discussion.

Sociologists of religion like Grace Davie provide valuable insights into the changing face of religion in Western society. Post-war, attempts were made to reconstruct patterns of pre-war life and the place of the Church within it.[4] This nostalgia came to an end in the upheavals of the 1960s. How could religion and the Church survive? Secularization was inevitable. Human reason and autonomy would prosper without being hindered by practices, traditions and thinking derived from the Church and the Christian faith. These debates, taking for granted the incompatibility of urbanization and religion, provided basic assumptions for Harvey Cox[5] in his book *The Secular City*. Cox embraced the processes of secularization, arguing that the secular city sets the agenda for the Church. These ideas resonated with thinking about industrial mission developed in the 1950s by Ted Wickham, the post-war pioneer of mission to the industrial working classes. These ideas were to be influential in Coventry in the 1960s.

Over the following decades this conceptualization of Christian mission and the sociological assumptions on which it was based have been subject to many critiques, from both theologians and sociologists. Elaine Graham and Stephen Lowe[6] provide a clear summary of the theology in their book on public theology and the urban church. For them the debate is crystallized in the 'twin Christian vocations of citizenship and discipleship'. These vocations provide a necessary tension, which avoids either endorsing the status quo or losing the ability to relate effectively in the public square. 'It is rather about being in the world but not of the world: of affirming the goodness of creation while anticipating its further and ultimate transformation.'

Recent years have seen a growing challenge to the notion that the modernization of societies brings inevitable secularization. In many places the Christian faith is growing strongly alongside modern, technologically developed societies, whether in the Americas, Africa or Asia. With an eye to this global reality Grace Davie has provided valuable insights into religion in Britain, especially changes in the nation's Christian heritage. Two particular insights are relevant here. She shows that since 1945 a decline in churchgoing in Britain was matched by a decline in active membership of all political and social organizations, and that what we are seeing in Britain is not so much a decline in belief but a change in the way belief is expressed. As

The Cathedral in its role as public utility fulfils a need of people to acknowledge significant events, such as the death of Diana, Princess of Wales. Flowers were placed spontaneously in the Ruins in September 1997.

she says, 'believing without belonging' is a phenomenon that seems to be a general symptom of late modernity.

Her second thesis, developed in relation to studies of religion in modern Europe, identifies 'an instinctive adherence to religion in Europe, accompanied by the notion that churches operate vicariously: they are there to perform functions and social roles on behalf of us all'. Churches have a role as 'public utilities', which are brought into use when there is a public need to acknowledge socially significant events, such as the death of a celebrity, and which only come to wider attention when no longer available.

Another, not unrelated, debate has particular importance when considering the relationship of religion and politics in Britain. Over the twentieth century certain assumptions about this relationship became widely accepted, based on the notion that 'religion is, and should be, a private affair'. The public square is deemed to be a neutral space where explicit appeal to religious and/or moral values is regarded as illegitimate. Such secular liberal views are the subject of considerable controversy in the new century,[7] but they are ubiquitous in government organizations especially at local level. It is because of the acceptance of such views that there continues to be suspicion and unease about relating to faith-based agencies, including churches, especially when issues of funding are being discussed. In a way that was probably untrue in the 1950s and 1960s, the officials of the 2000s are often illiterate about Christianity and religion in general.

In the light of these markers, how does the story of Coventry and its cathedral unfold, from the perspective of the City, first of all, and then from that of the Cathedral?

The Cathedral's identity in the city: from icon to 'public utility'

There is no doubt that for the vast majority of the citizens of Coventry, and indeed its politicians, the newly consecrated Coventry Cathedral was an icon. It symbolized the recovery of the city from its wartime desecration and, along with the city-centre pedestrian precinct, it was 'the phoenix* rising from the ashes'. Despite the initial controversies between the Council and the Cathedral, by the 1960s, if not long before, the Cathedral was perhaps the pre-eminent expression of 'boom time' Coventry. There was confidence in the air, from prosperous businesses, effective local government and mission-driven Cathedral.

Reconciling nations: in November 1990 the Queen Mother and the President of Germany attended a service of remembrance to mark the 50th anniversary of the Coventry blitz. © Edward Ockenden.

In 1961 the Lord Mayor's New Year's message stated:

The act of faith of those who, when the future of the country was still in balance, decided that there would be a new Cathedral; the confidence of those who resolved to build a new City; this I feel is what Coventry now represents. A faith in the future of our country and City. I believe that Coventry Cathedral symbolises this faith, and as it approaches its completed form, I feel that its very presence helps to strengthen our resolve to go forward to produce a better City and a happier community.

The 'faith' mentioned by the Lord Mayor is, of course, faith in the country and the City, but the Cathedral symbolizes it!

In 1960 Council House Prayers were started. Each Monday morning, before the working day commenced, those who wished could meet in the Council Chamber for prayer. The Provost welcomed this unique 'Civic and Christian fellowship as a great adventure, releasing the Holy Spirit in our work-a-day world'. Monday morning prayers continued well into the 1970s.

On 4 June 1961 Canon Edward Patey preached at a Civic Service in the undercroft, with members and officers of the Council in attendance. The following extracts from the sermon give an indication of a cathedral perspective, and one might assume that a measure of agreement was forthcoming from the congregation.

CIVIC SERVICE
SUNDAY 4 JUNE 1961
EXTRACTS FROM CANON EDWARD PATEY'S SERMON

The welcome visit to this Cathedral Church this morning of the Lord Mayor, Aldermen and Councillors of the City of Coventry, together with its principal officers, raises inevitably and rightly this simple question: 'What is, and what must be, the relationship between the life of the City and the life of this Cathedral now rising up within it?'

This much is certain. Should the Church or the Council claim to have all the answers cut and dried now, then there will be no relevant message for the future.

> May the Cathedral rather be seen as a laboratory of relationships put here by God to be offered humbly and willingly to the whole community. Not for its own purpose or power or prestige, but simply because it is called to serve God by serving its fellow citizens.
>
> New kinds of relationship are possible here and now between man and man because of a new kind of relationship established between man and God by Jesus Christ. The plain truth is this, that there is not one single item which could be found on any agenda of any committee or sub-committee within the Council which is not rooted firmly and squarely there, there in the very things for which this Cathedral stands.

The City Council, both members and senior officers, were willing participants in this 'laboratory of relationships' before, during and after the excitement of the consecration year and through the 1960s.

Participation was not limited to the Council as such, but embraced others from the public life of the City. Coventry Council of Social Service gathered for a cathedral service on 9 July 1962. A 'nurses' service' was held on 19 April 1963. A Tuesday lunchtime service was inaugurated in 1959, which 'covered every part of the City's life through the involvement of representatives from across the City: a managing director of a great industry, a Chairman of a Council Committee, a policeman, a school boy, a solicitor, a banker, a member of the fire service, of public transport, a representative of one or other of the trade unions and so on'. The Council's mid-1960s Development Plan Review, mentioned above, raised awareness of the changing nature of Coventry's residents. People from the Caribbean, Pakistan and India were arriving in the city and the Bishop, Cuthbert Bardsley, appointed a Chaplain for Overseas People to aid reconciliation in race relations. In 1966, Canon Peter Berry became Chaplain for Community Relations as part of the cathedral team.

Of special importance, an international conference celebrated the Diocesan Jubilee in June 1968, focusing on 'How people meet and care for one another in a modern City'. On a Sunday afternoon three years earlier, 50 people responded to a joint invitation from the Bishop and Lord Mayor to meet in St Mary's Guildhall to explore the theme of urbanization.[8] The range of attendance is significant to an understanding of the Council's view of the Bishop and Cathedral. Apart from the Lord Mayor, six councillors, the Town Clerk, Sir Charles Barrett, the City Architect and Planning Officer, Terence Gregory, and his deputy, Basil Rossiter, the Director of Education, Walter Chinn, and the Children's Officer, Mary Barnes, were there, as well as people from industry, the unions and commerce. The Council was a willing participant in the Diocesan Jubilee.

This conference was an important marker in the development of the international role of the Cathedral, a role embraced strategically as is discussed below. In the 1970s the more local, City-based focus of Canon Peter Berry's community relations work was added to by the creation of the Cathedral's Centre for Urban Studies in 1971. Under the leadership of the Revd Kenyon Wright and Father Ron Darwin, the Centre announced five programmes, which, in addition to work on worship and liturgy, urban ministry training and international links, would respond to planning policy proposals that were being developed by the Council for the City as a whole in the Structure Plan, and for the neighbourhood of Foleshill in the District Plan for that area. The Foleshill Area Churches Team (FACT) would work with local residents in the development of their communities and the facilities they needed.

The Home Front Memorial was unveiled in the presence of the Queen, Prince Philip, the Archbishop of Canterbury, the Prime Minister and leaders of all political parties on 3 March 2000. © Tom McIlroy.

BONDS OF FRIENDSHIP
From Stalingrad to Jinan

Coventry is twinned with no fewer than 26 towns across the globe and is proud to be known as a city that embraces internationalism, peace and reconciliation. It is a story, however, that has its beginnings during the darkest days of the Second World War.

In the autumn of 1941, a few months after the launch of Operation Barbarossa, Hitler's devastating attack on the Soviet Union, the women of Coventry cabled the people of Stalingrad with the message, 'From this city, scarred and ravaged by the arch enemy of civilisation, our hearts go out to you, who now face slaughter and suffering even more fearful.' It was followed by a book bearing over 6,000 signatures. The Battle of Stalingrad, still 12 months in the future, is today remembered as one of the cruellest encounters of the war. Despite communications remaining difficult, the message from Coventry became the first of a series of exchanges, as well as a £20,000 donation for medical aid. In June 1944, the Town Clerk wrote on behalf of the people of Coventry proposing a 'Bond of Friendship' between the two cities.

The mood among the war-ravaged cities of Europe was epitomized in 1946 when Coventry came together with Stalingrad, Warsaw, Caen and Arnhem for a joint Christmas Day broadcast on the theme 'Don't let this happen again'. The following year, Coventry formalized a second friendship link, significantly within Germany itself. Mr Gwillym Williams, helping to clear the rubble in the heavily bombed city of Kiel, was inspired by what he saw as a common experience with his home city of Coventry. He encouraged an exchange of letters, resulting in an invitation to Coventry's Mayor, George Briggs, Trades Secretary, Wilfred Spencer, and Provost Howard to visit Kiel.

From the mid 1950s, Coventry's twinning programme was extended beyond the kinship of wartime experience. Internationalism took on a wider meaning, and by the end of 1962, the year in which Coventry Cathedral was consecrated, 20 of the 26 twinning links had already been established. After 1983, when the promotion of trade was the reason behind Coventry's twinning with the Chinese city of Jinan, no further links were formed.

Coventry's Twin Towns and Cities

1944   Volgograd (formerly Stalingrad, Russia)
1947   Kiel (Germany), Lidice (Czech Republic)

1955   Saint-Etienne (France)

1956   Parkes (Australia)

1957   Caen (France), Belgrade (Serbia and Montenegro), Graz (Austria),
        Sarajevo (Bosnia and Herzegovina), Warsaw (Poland)

1958   Arnhem (The Netherlands), Cork (Eire)

1959   Dresden (Germany), Ostrava (Czech Republic)

1960   Bologna (Italy)

1962   Coventry (Connecticut, USA), Dunaujvaros (Hungary),
        Galati (Romania), Kecskemet (Hungary), Kingston (Jamaica)

1963   Granby (Canada), Windsor (Canada)

1971   Coventry (Rhode Island, USA)

1972   Cornwall (Canada), Coventry (New York, USA)

1983   Jinan (China)

For a fuller account of Coventry's early 'Bonds of Friendship' and twin towns see the first four chapters of Dr W. E. Rose's excellent *Sent from Coventry: A Mission of International Reconciliation*, London: Wolff, 1980.

John Willis
Editorial Committee Member

Collaboration with the City Council was maintained through their 'Twin Cities' programme, where the early emphasis was on twinning with places that shared the desire for reconciliation following the war, such as the links with Dresden. Yet a growing distance between the City and the Cathedral was revealed in the announcement in 1979 that one of the Cathedral's prime tasks was to renew liaison with the City of Coventry.

Drifting apart and coming together

Why did relationships cool? Undoubtedly, there were issues on both sides. For the Cathedral, the international ministry became more central. This demanded frequent visits abroad for senior staff. Resources were not as plentiful as they had been, and while the Cathedral was still a popular destination for tourists, they no longer came in their millions as in the early 1960s. Donations and the income generated through the bookshop and café were slipping.

For the Council, the 1970s were also a decade of change. In the early part, a new Chief Executive, J. D. Hender, introduced a radical system of corporate management and following the recommendations of the Seebohm Committee, Coventry employed its first Director of Social Services, Tom White. Restructuring to improve management and deliver better services was a good basis for confident reaching out to other stakeholders in the City, including the Cathedral. Such confidence was to be challenged over the next few years. In 1974, Coventry City Council became a second-tier local authority with strategic responsibilities being taken by the newly formed West Midlands County Council. The Chief Executive moved to this new authority. Party political control of the Council was becoming more volatile. Problems for the City's manufacturing economy began to bite following the recession of 1973/74 with unemployment rising steeply in 1975/76, and exponentially at the end of the decade. The general election of 1979 brought in the Thatcher government with all that was to mean for policy in relation to local government. Power and resources were to be diverted from the public sector and especially from those local authorities under Labour Party control.

Coventry's world had changed radically in a decade. The boom-town confidence and excitement, demonstrating a willingness to experiment and take risks, gave way to a clinical depression where anxiety and an inability to make decisions became the norm. This appears to have been true for both the City Council and the Cathedral. In the early years of the new Cathedral a unity of interest was apparent. This unity could cope with the 'establishment egos' of the cathedral leadership and the 'political egos' of the socialist Council. From the perspective of the City Council, the Cathedral served at least two purposes; it provided a focus, a symbol and, indeed, an icon of the renewed City; it served a number of civic functions where its size and celebrity status provided appropriate space and, more significantly, prestige on the national and international stage. The City Council took great pride in the existence of the Cathedral. When times grew more difficult each institution had to fight harder for its corner. Divergent interests gained a higher salience and egos were not so easily mollified. However, this is not to argue that council members' and officers' views of the Cathedral lost a sense of its civic and iconic place in the City.

In relation to policy agendas, the Archbishops' Commission on Urban Priority Areas, *Faith in the City*, reported in December 1985. Senior figures in the Conservative government attempted to brand it Marxist for its challenge to the fundamental injustice that poverty and disadvantage brought to so many of the nation's citizens. Councillors welcomed the report and in the following September a conference was called, by the Leader, Peter Lister, and the Bishop, Simon Barrington-Ward, at the then Henley College to discuss the relevance of the report to Coventry.

The FITC Consultation drew together an amazing variety of people from the Council, statutory and voluntary agencies. It was a real sign of potential partnership between the statutory bodies and voluntary agencies, including the Church.[9]

In April 1987, proposals were accepted by the Leader and the Bishop to establish a series of 'neighbourhood forums' in the Urban Priority Areas, where the 'powerlessness' experienced by local people was the key notion undergirding the proposal. A 'central group' of leading figures from the City, its industry, unions, public agencies and the Church would have the 'power to get things done' on behalf of the forums. While momentum for these proposals was subsequently lost, cathedral involvement, alongside other church agencies, should not be overlooked.

The Blitz commemoration took place in 1990, 50 years after the bombing of the city and the destruction of the medieval St Michael's Cathedral. For some observers this represented the City and the Cathedral at their closest, with the Cathedral for that moment at the centre of the City's life. A year of preparation resulted in a three-fold commemoration, with remembrance in the morning at the communal graves in the London Road Cemetery, a service of reconciliation at the Cathedral in the afternoon attended by the Queen Mother and the President of West Germany, and a celebration of reconciliation and multicultural Coventry in the evening in Broadgate.

Another example was the initiation of the Provost's breakfast meetings, following John Petty's visit to Chester Cathedral in 1992, where something similar was already happening. The breakfasts, held in St Mary's Guildhall, were for leaders of the City and were initially co-chaired by the City Council chief executive, Iain Roxburgh. Five times a year on a Wednesday morning, between 7.30 and 8.30, a topical speaker gave way to networking opportunities. Despite tensions and difficulties caused by development proposals involving the City Council and the Cathedral, these breakfasts continued for the rest of the decade.

The late 1980s saw some improvement in Coventry's economy before it was pushed down again by the recession of the early 1990s. It was around this time that the search for a renewed identity for the City, for a turn in the City's story from one of decline to growth, began to be discussed. The Unitary Development Plan for the City, adopted in 1993, aimed 'to strengthen and diversify the economic base of the City, to maximise the benefits for its people and, above all, to create and protect jobs'.[10]

One of the major regeneration projects of the time was the Phoenix Initiative, planning for which commenced in the mid-1990s, with construction beginning in 1999. Located in the city centre, proposals were developed to create a visual and pedestrian link between Hill Top, adjacent to the Cathedral and Holy Trinity Church, and the Coventry Motor Transport Museum. New public squares, gardens and water features were designed and the foundations of the original cathedral priory of St Mary revealed to make clear Coventry's three-cathedral history. From the perspective of the City Council the negotiations with the Cathedral over land and design were complicated. It has been suggested that there was an initial view in the Cathedral that the proposals were too adventurous and risked failure. Discussions did not get off to an auspicious start when the Council approached the Bishop first, rather than the Provost. Nevertheless, as happens in most complex property development, the requirements of the sponsoring investors had considerably more influence than the Cathedral and, maybe, even the Council.

Architectural lighting provided another point of contact between Cathedral authorities and the Council in the 1990s. Although the Cathedral was partially illuminated already, a city-centre-wide scheme to install more architecturally sympathetic lighting was promoted by the Council. The Cathedral agreed to the proposals, including the old cathedral Ruins. The Council paid for the work, but was somewhat disappointed to have notifications of potential claims for compensation because of the damage to historic stonework.

When land, property or business interests are at stake, or even issues of health and safety, professional relationships can come under pressure. An example, humorous in hindsight, concerns the millennium celebrations in the city centre. A French high-wire specialist was contracted to traverse the gap between the Holy Trinity and cathedral spires on millennium eve. When he arrived a few days before to prepare for the 'walk', it became clear for the first time that he did not intend to use a safety wire. There was talk of abandoning the spectacle. Negotiations were intense. Eventually the artiste agreed to use a safety wire. With the Provost waiting in the cathedral spire to provide a welcome, the 'daredevil' paused half-way across the divide and, removing the safety wire, completed the tightrope walk without it. It is understood that the Provost was not amused.

Such stories illustrate the robust nature of the dealings between the City and the Cathedral. When legitimate interests are complicated and personalities do not necessarily gel, this is to be expected. But equally one should not assume that professional disagreements prevented the development of strong personal friendships.

In more recent times, the Council has taken steps to project images of the City which have resonance with the Cathedral's core commitments to forgiveness and reconciliation. The Lord Mayor's Peace Month, subsequently reduced to a week, provided the opportunity for the Council and the Cathedral to jointly sponsor the Coventry Peace Prize. The logo 'Coventry, City of Peace and Reconciliation' filled the welcome signs on main roads into the city from 2005. An 'International Spire of Peace' was proposed in response to the Big Lottery Living Landmark competition, creating a fourth spire in the city centre. The bid was promoted by the Council and CVOne, the city-centre company, and could have incorporated an International Centre for Peace and Reconciliation. Options for the location of the 'spire' included Hill Top, next to the Cathedral, and Swanswell Pool, to the north-east of the city centre. The bid failed.

The City has been attempting to reinvent itself for over 20 years after a period of corporate anxiety and low self-esteem. Over this time relationships between the Council and the Cathedral have not been as close as in the 1960s and 1970s. There has been a drifting apart, punctuated by events, commemorations and celebrations where aspirations have coincided and where each has valued the input of the other. A certain 'instrumentality' has become characteristic of the relationship, as much and maybe more than a set of shared values.

Yet from the City's perspective, this icon has contributed many practical, well-recognized benefits. It draws tourists, although fewer now than in previous decades. The Cathedral provides a public service in other ways, too. To use Grace Davie's term, it is regarded as a 'public utility' by the Council and many Coventry citizens. It is a space that can accommodate a lot of people, ideal for mayor-making, the Annual General Meeting of the City Council, and for university graduation ceremonies. Over the years it has consistently responded to significant events in the life of the City, nation and world with speed, good organization and dignity, to deliver services, ceremonies and events that give expression to deeply held public emotions. Whether what is called for is remembering the Blitz, celebrating the origins of a church-initiated housing association, praying after the terrorist attacks on the World Trade Center in New York, or providing an opportunity for shared grief at the deaths of servicemen in Afghanistan, the Cathedral demonstrates the ability to deliver.

The Cathedral has always been a public utility, although much less a civic institution than it was. Its role as a Coventry icon continues but with less widespread appeal and acceptance in a more diverse, fragmented and turbulent Coventry.

Cathedral agendas: from local to global to survival

In 1961, Bill Williams commented:

Industrially the City of Coventry has within it all the characteristics of our contemporary industrial situation. It is probably one of the most highly concentrated centres of industry in Europe. And set right in the centre of this City is the new Cathedral, not insulated against the commerce, administration and industry by a cathedral close, but entirely exposed to the contact which it is constantly trying to encourage.[11]

He amplified his view of the role of cathedrals two years after the Consecration when he argued that no creative work could be done by the Cathedral until it had established a relationship with the community in which it sits. The remoteness of cathedrals in the twentieth century, he suggested, produced an image of massive irrelevance. The Cathedral was not a place to which people go, but a place from which activity goes out; a base for an outgoing operation into as many categories of activity in the community as possible.

Three initiatives during the 1960s are illustrative of this approach. First, the work of the ecumenically governed Industrial Mission, under the leadership of Canon Simon Phipps, had been established. By 1964 three full-time and five part-time chaplains were employed, visiting factories such as Standard, Hawker Siddeley Aviation, Coventry Precision, Bristol Siddeley Engines, Jaguar and Massey-Ferguson. Residential weekend courses related industrial issues to Christian faith, often held at

Industrial Chaplain Michael Forrer at the Rolls-Royce factory near Coventry in 1967. © Rolls-Royce.

Peter Berry engaging with a member of the immigrant community in Hillfields in 1966. © Sunday Mercury.

the William Temple College in Rugby. The interest was in the structures of power and processes of decision-making in industry rather than the pastoral support of individuals.

Second, the impact of immigration from new Commonwealth countries was recognized both by the diocese and the City Council. While responses might have been relatively slow, the appointment of Peter Berry as Bishop's Chaplain for Community Relations focused on the life and experience of migrants, initially the men to be followed by their families. The Community Relations Councils set up in Coventry, Leamington, Rugby and Nuneaton were developments facilitated in part by Peter Berry.

Third, the Cathedral participated fully in the creation of the Bishop's Council for Social Responsibility in 1965. The Council, chaired by Lord March, met for the first time on 24 November 1965.

The Council, said a 1972 review, was to be a 'thinking group', not directly under-taking new social projects, although these might be stimulated by the Council. From the outset it was understood that the Council had not been established 'merely to serve the Church, but to serve the whole community more effectively.'

The membership of the Council was broad, including, Councillor Peter Lister, Dr Richard Finlayson (a medical practitioner), Tony Robbins (a senior probation officer), Dorothy Parncutt (a head-teacher) and Canons Stephen Verney, Simon Phipps and Peter Berry. Race relations, mental health, physical handicap, unattached young people, young mothers and industrial relations are examples of the topics investigated. A 'Day Centre for the Mentally Ill' was created at Queens Road Baptist Church as a result of the Council's deliberations and a willingness of churches and statutory agencies to work together.

Bill Williams talked about the basis for the experiment being 'the conception of a secular cathedral, with a community of men working and worshipping in close fel-lowship, undertaking specific tasks in the community around it'. Williams' secular cathedral was some distance from that of Harvey Cox in *The Secular City*, referred to above. For the Provost, there was little or no suggestion that the secular city alone would set the agenda for the Cathedral, rather that the Church's mission as the body of Christ should involve both being separate from the world and yet deeply involved in the world.

Nearly three years after the Consecration, the Provost reflected on the scale of the Cathedral's activity in youth, education, music, drama and pastoral work, with over 1 million visitors a year, 12 ministerial staff, 10 full-time secretaries and a total administration department of 27. In the light of all this activity he realized that choices would have to be made about cathedral priorities. Was the diocese the prior-ity or should the Cathedral be

> the creative centre for enterprises on behalf of the whole church in Britain and in an increasing number of centres all over the world, making full use of the place of prominence which God, through recent history, has given it? To pay no heed to the opportunities for experiment, which the world links of the Ministry of the Cathedral give us, would mean that the benefit to the diocese would be infinitely less and would progressively diminish.[12]

The direction was clear because of the overwhelming international interest and celebrity status that had been accorded Coventry Cathedral in its first few years. It was an icon not just for Coventry, but for the nation and beyond.

Over the next ten years the international ministry was to develop in many imagin-ative and productive ways. Highlights include:

- the 'People and Cities Conference' in 1968
- engagement in debates about the European Common Market and a worship service, 'Vision of Europe', in 1973
- a conference on 'Ecology and Christian Responsibility' in 1975 at Sewanee, Tennessee
- the nuclear issue prompted the creation in the mid-1970s of an international organization, the Christian Peace Conference, based in Prague with Canon Kenyon Wright its vice-president.

These events, activities and the global networking created through the Community of the Cross of Nails, established more formally as a 'community' in 1973, did indeed provide positive feedback to the City and the diocese. The celebration of the International Year of the Child in 1979 was chaired by the Lord Mayor, Harry Richards. Coventry hosted a United Nations Youth Assembly with participants from Europe and America, as well as Coventry. Local school children participated in providing a Land Rover for Calcutta. Coventry '80 was a celebration of life 40 years on from the Blitz under the title, 'Pride in our Past, Faith in our Future'.

Cathedral life in the 1970s was characterized by internal reorganization to clarify strategy and to focus on implementation. The Centre for Urban Studies was followed by the Centre for Studies (1974) aiming to work out a 'theology of reconciliation'; the Centre for Social and International Reconciliation (1977) had a name change to the Centre for International Reconciliation two years later, when the Department of Social Ministry was formed. The latter, led by Peter Berry, had four priorities, all of which revealed considerable unease about the Cathedral's relationships with the local authorities. There was a need for greater involvement in strategic long-term issues with the West Midlands County Council, in urban and rural affairs with Warwickshire County Council and local county district councils, and, in particular, 'renewed liaison with Coventry City Council especially in planning and social services', as mentioned earlier. Through the 1970s Peter Berry continued with the community relations work, but largely as a one-man band. By 1979 it still needed to be higher on the agenda. Industrial mission work continued but without much interest in local race relations.

By the time Bill Williams retired and Kenyon Wright moved to Scotland in 1981 there was a widespread view that 'the international dimensions of this ministry made it difficult for the Cathedral to relate effectively to its immediate City and diocesan communities, both of which complained of being neglected'.[13]

The 1970s saw an increasing set of problems for the City. Manufacturing jobs were lost, with a once-confident local council feeling battered and unsure where to turn. During that same period, the Cathedral also began to exhibit uncertainty

BOOM TOWN TO GHOST TOWN?

In the early 1950s designs for the new Cathedral were taking shape and Coventry was booming. Workers flocked to the city from all over Britain, attracted by high wages on the car assembly lines. Humber, Hillman, Singer, Sunbeam, Jaguar, Daimler, Standard-Triumph and Morris all had factories in Coventry, as did London Taxis (Carbodies), Alvis, Lanchester and Massey-Ferguson tractors. But by 2005 there remained only London Taxis, Jaguar's research and development and Peugeot's spare parts and commercial centres – all the rest had gone.

At the Coventry Transport Museum, the City's story is told through the rise and fall of motor car production. The 1950s, 1960s and 1970s carry the label 'Boomtown', while the years from 1980 to 2010 take their title 'Ghost Town?' from the 1981 hit record by the Coventry band 'The Specials' – said to reflect the demise of their native city.

The museum tells us that between 1950 and 1970, 35–40 per cent of working people in Coventry were involved with the motor industry, producing 23 per cent of the UK output. During the 1960s and 1970s, demand for cars increased, but so did the competition, particularly from Japan and Europe, forcing a programme of local rationalizations. Jaguar acquired Daimler before merging with the British Motor Corporation; Standard Triumph became part of Leyland Motors; Alvis ceased car production, but continued making military vehicles, and Chrysler took control of Rootes (Humber, Hillman, Singer and Sunbeam). In 1978, Chrysler, facing severe financial difficulties in the USA, sold their European operations to Peugeot. Associated with all these changes came cost reduction, wage restraint and redundancies, leading to industrial tension and strikes. By 1979 Coventry factories produced only 11.4 per cent of total British output. The 1980s and subsequent decades saw a devastating series of factory closures: Standard Triumph (1980), Morris Engines (1989), Massey Ferguson (2002) and Peugeot (2005). Jaguar, bought by Ford in 1989, retained the Coventry Browns Lane factory for a further 16 years before closing it in 2004. Coventry's position as the capital of the British motor industry had been consigned to history.

Yet at the museum, 'Ghost Town?' carries a question mark. Remnants of the motor industry still survive, but they are not the whole story. Since the Middle Ages, as Coventry's thriving industries have gone into decline, prospering new ones have taken their place. Woollen industries gave way in turn to silk weaving, watch-making, cycles, motor cars, aeroplanes and telecoms. Coventry is again undergoing such a transition, with a swing to new technologies and service industries.

John Willis
Editorial Committee Member

about how it should express its message of reconciliation, especially locally. The international ministry had blossomed but the more local ministry needed to be reinvented on a regular basis. Financial, staffing and organizational issues, together with a vastly changed social and economic context, began to eat at the mission and ministry of the Cathedral.

Survival was the central issue for both the City and the Cathedral. The City was at rock bottom, with the Cathedral not far behind. Hopeful anticipation was in short supply. In 1982 the Cathedral's plight was signalled by one of the first tasks of the new Provost, Colin Semper. He signed off the sale of the Provost's House, a mansion in Davenport Road reportedly more elegant than the Bishop's House up the road. At about the same time the editor of the Coventry *Evening Telegraph* is understood to have called the Cathedral 'that Independent Empire'. Apart from Peter Berry's community relations work there appeared little direct contact with Coventry City Council and none with the local authorities of Warwickshire. When Peter moved from Coventry to become the Provost of Birmingham Cathedral, the personally sympathetic *Evening Telegraph* announced that 'our friendship broker has gone'.

If the 1980s was a time of survival for both the City and the Cathedral, a sense of determination to bring about improvements began to germinate in the 1990s. The City was trying to 'reinvent itself', to diversify its economic base and to improve its image, especially in the city centre. One aspect of this was continuing co-operation to mark important historical events, celebrating significant achievement or commemorating painful experience. Many of these had an international dimension, but others had a more national and even local flavour.

Fifty years after the bombing, the commemoration in 1990 was a sophisticated royal occasion, as mentioned previously. The Rugby World Cup of 1991 saw Peter Rossborough, former England rugby player, punting a rugby ball into the cathedral Ruins from the Unity Lawn with Councillor Dave Edwards in attendance. Joe Clifford, Lord Mayor in 1995, participated in the unveiling of a sculpture in the Cathedral funded by Richard Branson, to focus attention on reconciliation with Japan; another cast of the sculpture was unveiled in Hiroshima. National attention was given to the funeral, in February 1995, of Jill Phipps, who had died protesting about the air freighting of live veal calves from Coventry Airport to the continent. The centenary of the first car produced in Coventry was in the following year. An event to mark this was initiated by the City Council and took years to plan. There were protests in the old Cathedral by 'Friends of the Earth', but it was the nude protest in the new Cathedral during the service that grabbed the headlines across the globe. Ten years on from the launch of the Church Urban Fund in the Cathedral, another service celebrated its achievements in 1998. After the colourful processions

Provost John Petty, Bishop Simon Barrington-Ward and Terry Mitchell undertaking a sponsored cycle ride around the diocese raising money for the Church Urban Fund in 1989.

at the end of the service, young people from Foleshill proceeded to show their skills at rollerblading, from one end of the cathedral nave to the other. More locally, Touchstone Housing Association, a successor to Coventry Churches Housing Association, and the Extra Care Charitable Trust held services to mark significant stages in their developments. The prestige of the big, formal occasion was a welcome characteristic of this time and served to keep the Cathedral in the public eye, bringing healing and celebration where it could.

Relationships with the City Council took a turn for the better with the appointment of Chris Burch as Canon Precentor. Almost immediately on his arrival in 1995, he was appointed to chair the Coventry Anti-poverty Forum, a partnership between the City Council and the voluntary sector. Led by Councillor John Fletcher, the Coventry City Forum grew in subsequent years, Canon Burch chairing the Tackling Poverty Programme Delivery Group. This provided a platform to contribute greater awareness of poverty in the city, but also to enable change. *Faith in the City*, the challenging 1985 report of the Archbishops' Commission on Urban Priority Areas, was not forgotten in the Cathedral, or by the City Council for that matter. A group was established to support those engaged in urban ministry and mission with Chris Burch as Chaplain to UPAs.

Even in the mid-1990s there was a certain arrogance in the stance of the Cathedral towards the City and its Council. It has been suggested that this could be perceived in 'the way the City was talked about', in slightly disparaging tones. An anonymous source suggests that the Cathedral was somewhat 'up itself' and not a little 'self-regarding'. Maybe a similar attitude was perceived in the diocese. The Cathedral was independent and proud of its roots, even of its reconciliation theology. That there were some cathedral staff committed to the struggle against poverty provided a welcome breach in this sense of superiority.

The Cathedral's participation in a Church Action on Poverty 'Pilgrimage from Iona to London' in October 1999 also helped to shift attitudes. The march came through Coventry. Speeches were made on the steps of the Cathedral by the Lord Mayor, among others, and hospitality provided. Catherine Kendall[14] researched a comparative study of poverty in Coventry in the 1930s and 1990s. Poverty and gross inequality was still very evident after 60 years. The report was commended by both the Bishop, Colin Bennetts, and by John Fletcher, Leader of the City Council.

Both the City and the Cathedral tried to reinvent themselves in the early 2000s. For a while, the City was more prosperous, public resources were available and investors came to the City, before the recession of 2008–10 cast a shadow. Significantly, the Cathedral has never really emerged from financial stringency. The struggle to maintain fabric and basic ministry has taken energy and commitment from many people. Nevertheless, steps have been taken to improve relationships with the City Council at a personal level. Mayor-making is an annual event in the Cathedral. The current Dean, John Irvine, sits on the Board of CVOne, the City Centre Company. Youth work in the city centre has been initiated. A community forum has developed from relationships with the police and a new Director for Reconciliation, David Porter, appointed with a remit to work more locally, as well as internationally.

A postscript: challenges and futures

How might the history of relationships between the City and the Cathedral be portrayed without falling into caricature? When the new Cathedral was built, consecrated and inhabited in the late 1950s and early 1960s its iconic significance for the City and the nation was clear to all. The socialist leaders of the City Council were eventually as keen to celebrate as were the establishment figures of the Cathedral and the Church of England. The reputation of Coventry and its cathedral transcended the local and the national to become global. But as boom City turned to bust, so the Cathedral began to struggle with its priorities and their resourcing. As the City became clinically depressed the Cathedral looked away, choosing to maintain its identity and self-confidence through its international links and its grand worship events. Although a simplification, it seems as though the relationship became much more instrumental over the years, with the Cathedral asking, 'What can we get out

Civic links: David Burbidge chairs a meeting of the Coventry Cathedral Development Trust in the Lord Mayor's Parlour in 1997.

of the City Council?' and the Council asking, 'How might we use the Cathedral to aid the renewal of the City and as a location for solemn events, enacted with appropriate gravitas?'

The city has changed, as has society. While Coventry has been a migrants' city for over 100 years it is now, like others, part of a diverse, ethnically mixed and multifaith world, where rapid change and global communication are the norm. Yet it is an unequal city, fractured along lines of poverty and wealth, prosperity and disadvantage, access to centres of power and a debilitating sense of powerlessness. This unequal city sits within an unequal diocese. The south has little to do with the north, or so it seems. For at least three decades, Warwickshire County Council has developed strategies to mitigate these inequalities, but without being able to fulfil its aspirations. If the Cathedral can be criticized for looking to the local interests of neither the City nor the County, then it is also relevant to note that for many in the south of the county, Coventry is not their city and braving the inner ring road is attempted only in emergencies or for really special occasions, some of them at the Cathedral.

Attitudes to the Christian faith, to the Church and its cathedrals have also changed dramatically over the 50 years. In the post-war period a public obligation to the

Church as an institution was still acknowledged among those with a degree of standing and influence. A civic role for cathedrals was widely accepted by government and business. These roles now feel dated. Two generations on, consumer society in all its diversity and inequality gives little time to considering cathedrals and churches. The 1970s and 1980s saw a growing acceptance of the notion that faith is a private matter and that religion has no place in the public square of politics and policy-making. While still widely espoused in some circles, the last 20 years have witnessed a growing challenge to these sentiments. 'God is Back' says the editor of *The Economist*, as he assesses how a global rise of faith is changing the world.[15] At philosophical, social and political levels the debate about faith at the public table is now engaged.

Where does this leave Coventry Cathedral as its leaders ponder its calling from God, 50 years after the Consecration? The issues of how the Cathedral relates to the City, its Council and its people, are central to finding purpose and direction. Perhaps the time is ripe for the development of priorities for mission and ministry that acknowledge the profound personal, societal and cosmic dimensions of a 'Kingdom of God' theology. Could this provide a renewed sense of the importance of relating to the multifaceted city that is Coventry and the county that is Warwickshire? It is not insignificant that theologians from various mainstream traditions, catholics, liberals, evangelicals and charismatics, are all traversing this terrain at the current time.[16]

To what extent can the Cathedral be an expression of, indeed an icon of, the Gospel of Jesus Christ to the people of the City and County, especially those whom our society counts less valuable: the poor, the marginalized, the powerless, the strangers and the outsiders?

Acknowledgement

Research for this chapter was made possible by the willingness of many people with insight into the history of the City of Coventry, its Council and the Cathedral to undergo lengthy interviews. I am grateful for their candid co-operation, but they bear no responsibility for my judgements!

* Denotes an entry in the Glossary

Notes

1 See, for example: George Hodgkinson, *Sent to Coventry*, London: Robert Maxwell & Co., 1970; Basil Spence, *Phoenix at Coventry*, London: Geoffrey Bles, 1962; R. T. Howard, *Ruined and Rebuilt*, Coventry: Coventry Cathedral, 1962; Kenneth Richardson and Elizabeth Harris, *Twentieth-Century Coventry*, Coventry: City of Coventry, 1972.

2 For an excellent analysis of Labour Party politics in Coventry, see N. Tiratsoo, *Reconstruction, Affluence and Labour Politics: Coventry 1945–1960*, London: Routledge, 1990.

3 Full and informative economic histories of Coventry are provided in David Thoms and Tom Donnelly, *The Coventry Motor Industry: Birth to Renaissance*, Aldershot: Ashgate, 2000; Bill Lancaster and Tony Mason (eds), *Life and Labour in a Twentieth-Century City: The Experience of Coventry*, Coventry: Cryfield Press, 1987.

4 For an overview of the discipline, see Grace Davie, *The Sociology of Religion*, London: Sage, 2007.

5 Harvey Cox, *The Secular City*, Harmondsworth: Penguin, 1968.

6 Elaine Graham and Stephen Lowe, *What Makes a Good City? Public Theology and the Urban Church*, London: Darton, Longman & Todd, 2009.

7 The legitimacy of faith perspectives in public and political debate is creating a considerable literature, of which the following are examples: Adam Dinham, Robert Furbey and Vivien Lowndes (eds), *Faith in the Public Realm*, Bristol: Polity Press, 2009; Nick Spencer, *'Doing God': A Future for Faith in the Public Square*, London: Theos, 2006; Michael J. Sandel, *Justice: What's the Right Thing to Do?*, London: Allen Lane, 2009.

8 Stephen Verney, *People and Cities*, London: Fontana, 1969, p. 26.

9 Richard Farnell, *Faith in the City and Local Politics*, London: General Synod office of the Church of England, 1988.

10 City of Coventry, *Coventry into the 21st Century: The Unitary Development Plan 1988–2001*, 2003.

11 H. C. N. Williams, *A Vision of Duty: Sermons Preached in Coventry Cathedral*, London: Hodder & Stoughton, 1963.

12 H. C. N. Williams, 'Coventry Cathedral Policy and Organisations', *Coventry Cathedral Review*, January 1965, vol. 5, no. 2.

13 Trevor Beeson, 'The Very Reverend H. N. C. 'Bill' Williams – Obituary', *Daily Telegraph*, 11 April 1990.

14 Catherine Kendall, *Living with Poverty: Coventry in the 1930s and 1990s*, Coventry: Steering Group to mark the visit to Coventry of Church Action on Poverty's Pilgrimage against Poverty, 5 October 1999.

15 John Micklethwait and Adam Wooldridge, *God is Back*, London: Allen Lane, 2009.

16 See, for example, Graham and Lowe, *What Makes a Good City?*; Graham Cray, *Disciples and Citzens: A Vision for Distinctive Living*, Nottingham: InterVarsity Press, 2007; Nick Spencer and Jonathan Chaplin (eds), *God and Government*, London: SPCK, 2009.

6 THE ARCHANGEL MICHAEL TAKES WING

PAUL OESTREICHER

> 'Truly, I tell you, no prophet is taken seriously in his own country.'
>
> Luke 4.24

In the great firmament of the stars our globe is unbelievably small. As the Archangel Michael's wings enfold us on God's mission of justice and peace, on every Friday at noon, perhaps in summer sunshine, perhaps as a bitter wind blows sleet across the old cathedral Ruins, a small group of humans from near and far gather to pray. Others in distant places, in Havana, Cape Town, Dresden, are praying the same Litany of Reconciliation in Spanish, Afrikaans, German. In that prayer they face up to the deadly sins of the human family with which the Archangel is engaged in spiritual warfare. But not and never as an avenging angel.

The Coventry Litany echoes seven times the words inscribed behind the altar, 'Father Forgive', forgive, as Jesus forgave his killers, forgive the killers not only of a thousand people in wartime Coventry, but of the millions – each one infinitely loved – murdered in the mindless cruelty of war. Forgive both the killers and the killed, for none are innocent, all bound together in the human condition. Place names become symbols of our complicity and our corporate inability to put love into action. Coventry is one such alongside Dresden and Hiroshima and Warsaw and Stalingrad, alongside My Lai and countless erased and forgotten villages the world over, for they are no more, known by name only to the survivors.

With God's love in his heart and with an enlightened, courageous mind, Provost Howard launched Coventry Cathedral's ministry of international reconciliation at Christmas 1940, less than six weeks after the destruction of his Cathedral. He could not then, in the midst of war, have foreseen the consequences of his counter-cultural refusal to embrace the retaliation that was the way of the world. In the traditional Empire Broadcast of the BBC these were his words:

What we want to tell the world is this: that with Christ born again in our hearts today, we are trying, hard as it may be, to banish all thoughts of revenge . . . We are going to try to make a kinder, simpler, a more Christ-Child-like sort of world in the days beyond this strife.

That unpopular, prophetic declaration must be seen as the motto of everything the cathedral community has done since then to try to achieve that objective. It is a story of light and darkness, far too rich, complex and many-sided to be adequately told in one chapter of this jubilee volume. These personal reflections of one of the actors in the story cannot possibly do it justice. With a broad brush I shall do my best to give a personal overview of what became of Provost Howard's vision. My selected highlights will have to stand for the whole. Two German books have already ventured to tell the story much more fully. Oliver Schuegraf's *Forgive One Another, As God Has Forgiven You* may soon be available in English.

Provost R. T. Howard led the Cathedral through the Second World War and the initial stages of building the new Cathedral. He is shown presenting an original cross of nails to a visiting delegation in 1941. © Cathedral Archives.

Art, poetry and music can give such dreams ultimate symbolic expression. Wilfred Owen's poignant insight that 'I am the enemy you killed, my friend', is immortalized in the incomparable *War Requiem*, inseparable from the birth of the new Cathedral, and Benjamin Britten's greatest gift to a world of music that breaks down all frontiers.

Jesus was thrown out of his home-town synagogue. Unpopular though Howard's message was, he did not fare as badly. Some heard the message and acted on it. They set about learning German and, when it was permitted, invited German prisoners of war into their homes. Not much more than a year after the end of the Second World War they formed the Coventry German Circle. It still exists. At Christmas 1946 the BBC Empire Service came back to Coventry for an exchange of greetings between children in Coventry and Hamburg, where the Provost had established links of friendship with a Catholic parish. In Hamburg Allied bombing had killed not 1,000, but 40,000. Once again Howard spoke on the BBC: 'If only we could cast out bitterness and hatred and begin again, then I believe that our children – yours and ours – may live together in peace.'

Dr Will Rose, the historian of those early years, wrote in his book *Sent from Coventry*:

> That Coventry Cathedral was chosen for such a broadcast at that time was an acknowledgement that in the eyes of people everywhere it had acquired a special significance as a symbol of all those towns which had suffered heavily . . . and also that it stood, in a material and in a moral sense, for resurrection after crucifixion – a theme which runs like a refrain through Provost Howard's utterances. Coventry had become a special case.[1]

The words 'in the eyes of people everywhere' no longer apply today, but in 1940 these broadcasts on what later became the BBC's World Service were beamed to those abroad. At home, Coventry attracted huge numbers of visitors all through the 1960s. But it was the architecture – and with it the story of rebirth – that drew them. For only a few shared the insight that this cathedral had broken in a unique way with British and Anglican insularity and passionately embraced internationalism. And some of that few didn't much like it: 'Surely that is not what a Cathedral is really for!' In Germany, on the other hand, but also to some extent in the United States and later in South Africa, Coventry early achieved the iconic status it still has there today.

Taking Jesus at his word ('. . . but I tell you, love your enemies'), it was inevitable that Germany should be at the heart of the Provost's vision. It was a vision shared, despite popular feeling, by leading members of the mainly socialist City Council. In the devastated German seaport of Kiel, the 'Branch Officer for Building', Gwillym Williams, a Coventrian who was part of the British military occupation force, was committed to helping the people of Kiel to rebuild. Why not, he thought, in partnership with his home city? The Mayor of Kiel did not need persuading. His Coventry counterpart George Briggs and Provost Howard accepted an invitation to visit Kiel and were received with enthusiasm. Within a short time, a Society of the Friends of Coventry in Kiel had a membership of around 800. This friendship link two years after the war's end became a formal partnership a year later in the first Anglo-German city twinning. In this, both the Cathedral and the Council House were running ahead of public opinion. Nevertheless, a Society of the Friends of Kiel failed to get off the ground in Coventry.

When Provost Howard addressed a large meeting of Lutheran and Catholic Christians and presented the church in Kiel with Germany's first Cross of Nails, he probably did not realize that he had launched a movement and had sown the seeds of what became the Community of the Cross of Nails (CCN), committing its members in many countries to reconciling the unreconciled. The CCN would eventually be one of the pillars of what became the Cathedral's Centre for International Reconciliation (CIR).

Dick Howard was a man of quiet dignity, deep faith and undoubted courage. When he held up the Cross of the Nails taken from his ruined Cathedral in the midst of people who until very recently had obediently served Hitler's tyranny, this was more than going the extra mile. It was a refusal to stand in judgement on those who at that time showed no sign of penitence. His friendship was unconditional. That, for him, was enough. Reconciliation was perhaps an idea for later. His was a Mandela-like refusal to humiliate the guilty losers of history. 'Were we not guilty too', he asked himself, 'when we did nothing to help those Germans who in the '30s did have the courage to resist?' The first concentration camps, people often forget, were built for those German resisters.

By 1958 the essentially modest Provost felt his work was done. His prophetic voice had borne fruit. The world had begun to see Coventry with a cathedral at its heart as a symbol of new life growing out of ruins, a phoenix* from the ashes. The arguments had been won. Basil Spence's new Cathedral of St Michael would be built. The Archangel would fly, fly globally. It was time for new leadership.

Bill Williams, not an Englishman but born and educated in South Africa, would come from a successful ministry in Southampton to launch the new Cathedral on the world. He had caught the vision and was big enough – in many senses – to breathe life into it. The worldwide potential of his cathedral and of his own role energized him. This was an undoubted blessing, but also a mixed blessing. In the years to come it was inevitable that many who did not 'fly' with the vision wondered how much

Coventry as a city, Coventry as a diocese of the Church of England, really engaged him. Pedestrians have a price to pay for high-fliers.

Hardly installed, Provost Williams was invited to London to meet Professor Theodor Heuss during the first state visit of a German President. He was presented with 50,000 Deutschmarks to meet the costs of the windows in the planned Chapel of Unity. He had stepped into controversy. Though much of the reporting was restrained, friendship with Germany was no easy venture. One national paper declared, 'Provost of Coventry accepts blood money'. He rose to the challenge, fully realizing that Coventry could become a key player in Anglo-German relations. He wrote both to the Mayor of Berlin, the future Chancellor Willy Brandt, and to Berlin's Bishop Dibelius asking to be given a chance to explain Coventry's mission to the German people. The invitation came. Arriving four months later at Tempelhof Airport, received by both Church and State and holding aloft the Cross of Nails he declared, 'As you made Coventry a symbol of destruction, so now, join with us and make it a symbol of reconciliation.'

The German response was hands-on and unexpected. Dr Lothar Kreyssig, a lawyer who had bravely resisted Hitler and, unlike most opponents, had survived, formed an organization to enable young Germans to go as volunteers to countries that had suffered in Hitler's war of aggression and to help where help was accepted and needed. It was called *Aktion Sühnezeichen* (Action to Expiate), offering to make good in penitence what Germans had inflicted on other nations. It was, in effect, to be a German peace corps, so later the word *Friedensdienste* (Services to Peace) was added to the title. In English, inaccurately translated, it became Action for Reconciliation and Services to Peace (ARSP).

ARSP chose Coventry as its first major engagement. In 1960 a team of young Germans came to live and work in Coventry for six months. Their task was to turn the ruined vestries of the bombed Cathedral into a new International Centre. The young people lived with Coventry families. It was a significant example of the building of friendships as well as an impressive story of physical reconstruction. Bishop Dibelius came from Berlin to open the Centre in 1961. I was privileged to be invited to preside in German at the Eucharist to farewell the volunteers.

From then on, ARSP became an integral part of the Cathedral's life. Its volunteers in Britain were organized from an office with a German secretary at the Cathedral. Two volunteers staffed the International Centre for many years, ran a soup kitchen for the less privileged and for passing tourists, and told their stories. For ARSP's headquarters in Berlin, Coventry remained a focal point of reference until almost the end of the century when a new cathedral management ill-advisedly cut the links, hopefully not for good. ARSP moved to London. It remains a major ecumenical player in Germany, and has a presence in many countries, now jointly run with a

Polish component. In July 2011 ARSP celebrated its first half-century in England and chose to do so in Coventry Cathedral.

Within weeks of the Consecration of the new Cathedral, Provost Williams formally launched the International Ministry at one of the large-scale liturgical events that were to put this new national icon on the map. The context, significantly, was an international youth assembly, the first of many. I have vivid memories of the occasion. As a BBC radio producer, I directed the broadcast of the event. The sermon left a deep impression. It was nothing less than a manifesto on a large canvas against which it is not unfair to judge all that followed. That probably had to fall short of the dream. It did, but not by much. It was, controversially, not everyone's dream.

Here is how the sermon ended:

> We offer this Cathedral to the world as a place of meeting, to learn more of each other, to learn more of Jesus Christ and so to learn more of true peace . . . We pray that the Church in every nation may be set free from restraint – from restraints imposed from without by those who misunderstand its purpose and from within by Christian leaders who are imprisoned in ecclesiastical traditions which they have not the faith to discard. We pray that the Church may be free to lead the mind and spirit of the young to a world community in which all are members one of another because we are all members of Jesus Christ.

So, without restraints and with money pouring in from huge tourist numbers, Bill Williams got to work. He had the capacity to work, though not always comfortably, with colleagues of unusual ability, canons whom Bishop Cuthbert Bardsley had appointed. They were a formidable team, each of whom went on to make a significant career in the Church. Bill had the self-confidence not to feel threatened by them. He trusted them, each in his own speciality. But he was the undisputed International Director. Germany, and soon thereafter the United States, consumed his energy. International he was, but, distrustful of all ecclesial structures, Bill was not much interested in the organized ecumenical movement, either within Britain or abroad. He would be ecumenical in his own way, recognizable, but only just, as part of the Church of England.

Visible action was the order of the day. A tractor was bought for the Greek island of Lefkas where the harvests had failed. A Coventry House was built to put up international volunteers at the Corrymeela Community in Northern Ireland, bringing young Protestants and young Catholics together with young people from around the world. Founded by the Revd Ray Davey, Corrymeela resonated with Bill Williams. He was willing to spend a good deal of money to identify with this kind of peace-

Mary McAleese, President of the Republic of Ireland, opening the rebuilt Coventry House, Corrymeela, Northern Ireland in April 2009. Inset with the President is John Stroyan, Bishop of Warwick.

making nearer home. Ray Davey, as a prisoner of war, had seen Dresden burning. That turned him into a remarkable peacemaker. There will be much more to be said about the Dresden that had shaken Ray Davey so deeply.

From early on, the Provost planned to build a residential youth centre for the young people he hoped to bring from afar. It took time and effort and co-operation from the City. John F. Kennedy House was finally opened by Willy Brandt in 1965. What foresight! The two names Brandt and Kennedy ensured that the key foreign players, the USA and Germany, were aboard. Basil Spence designed it – a slightly upmarket youth hostel. A series of gifted youth leaders assured its success for some 15 years as a meeting place for young people. Specially popular among them was Fr John McGuire, a brilliant and charming American Dominican friar, who went on to become a professor in Rome and New York. A succession of Americans enriched the cathedral staff in various capacities for periods until the late 1980s. German pastors were to come later. Both the international and the ecumenical life of the Cathedral, but above all its mission to youth, was greatly enhanced by JFK House.

Herr Willy Brandt opening John F. Kennedy House youth hostel in April 1965. © Cathedral Archives.

By the 1990s, however, it showed signs of wear, the money to employ adequate staff was running out, and so was the capacity to find subsidies for youth travel. Finally the house was pulled down as part of a major redevelopment of the northern sector of the city centre. This was Coventry's millennium project, known as the Phoenix Initiative. Under the adjacent Holy Trinity Church hall and JFK House were found the remains of Coventry's first Cathedral, and the archaeological dig threw new light on Coventry's past. The City Council offered to build a new centre but the Cathedral opted for a state-of-the-art office building instead. A wise decision?

What about South Africa, Bill's homeland, in the international mix? The ecumenical movement throughout the world, in solidarity with the country's oppressed majority, along with many significant Anglicans worldwide, had put the anti-apartheid struggle at the heart of Christian witness. Not so Bill's cathedral. He had presented a Cross of Nails to the Wilgespruit Fellowship Centre in Roodeport, but when it joined the radical opposition, sailing close to illegality, the Cross remained, but nothing more was heard from Coventry. The Provost, not a joiner anyway, could not bring himself – so it seemed – to go against his own deep roots in white South Africa and join the Anti-Apartheid Movement, any more than he could bless apartheid. So there was something close to silence. Not until many years later, when white rule was on its last legs, did South Africa become a significant part of the Cathedral's ministry.

On his pioneering visit to Berlin the Provost was asked what he thought about Dresden. He did not immediately understand the question. But soon after, he understood only too well and determined not to let this sleeping dog lie. When he had internalized the devastation wrought by the RAF, he determined that expiation must work both ways. Young Germans had helped rebuild the Cathedral. Young Britons must do the same for Dresden. By 1959 the socialist City Council of Coventry had, to head-shaking in some places including Kiel, made Dresden its 'other' German twin city, 'other' because it was in communist-ruled East Germany. The Cold War was at its height. The City, without the Cathedral's involvement, had chosen to leap the Iron Curtain. I think Provost Howard would gladly have shared in that decision. Provost Williams, a liberal Christian with essentially conservative values, found working hand in hand with a left-wing council – or maybe with any council – instinctively difficult. In fact Council–Cathedral relationships have always been on a roller-coaster, depending very much on personalities at any given moment. Essentially secular councillors inevitably had problems with being upstaged by a world-famous cathedral and by a determined go-it-alone Provost.

But Dresden now presented a challenge to which Bill Williams rose. He achieved the near impossible. With the help of Coventry's left-wing Labour MP Dick Crossman and the tacit approval of the British government he went to East Berlin to confer with Secretary of State for Religious Affairs, Hans Seigewasser, seeking his government's permission to send a team of young Britons to Dresden to help rebuild the Lutheran Deaconess Hospital which Allied bombs had destroyed. Never before had this suspicious and closed society allowed a group of young people from the West to live and work and even travel freely for up to half a year in the German Democratic Republic. How did the Provost of Coventry 'convert' the Communist leadership? It was a long, highly complex diplomatic process. One of those young volunteers many years later turned the story into a doctoral thesis, which, while not wholly accurate, provides a fascinating account.[2]

The Provost was determined that this should be a church-to-church operation and not something sponsored – though necessarily permitted – by a Communist

A party of 30 young people led by Martin Turner and John Alleyne went to Dresden in March 1965 to help clear rubble at the Lutheran Deaconess Hospital that had been bombed by the Allies. © Cathedral Archives.

government. Who would take responsibility at the East German end? The Lutheran Bishop of Saxony was not acceptable to the government. But, person to person, the Provost got on well with the Secretary of State who agreed to let ARSP in the GDR (its West German branch had sent the German volunteers to Coventry) act as the hosting body. That was not quite enough. It took a word in the ear of Walter Ulbricht, Communist Party chief, from his advisor on matters religious, Dr Hans-Joachim Seidowsky, a senior Stasi* officer. He persuaded his boss that to permit this enterprise would be good for the country's reputation abroad. That, at any rate, is the nearest to the truth I can get. I wish it were true that I had an influential role in the process, as Merrylin Thomas suggests.

At any rate, the Revd Martin Turner and his idealistic young team made a huge success of this enterprise. They have not been forgotten in Dresden to this day. They were ambassadors of the best kind, making friendships that have been passed to following generations. The Deaconess Hospital remains one of the most significant of Germany's Cross of Nails Centres and Sr Edith Haufe, who helped to look after the young Britons, lives on to tell the story.

For a decade Bill Williams travelled frequently to Germany with the message of forgiveness, presenting Crosses of Nails and making many feel embraced by the love that went out from Coventry. He did the same in America, which he loved, where he was cherished – perhaps more than at home – and where too he created a network around this unique Cross with its moving story. Many friends in the USA were liberal American Christians involved in the civil rights movement, very much part of 'middle America' and not far from the Washington establishment. That grand Anglican shrine, the National Cathedral, had to have and to cherish its Cross of Nails. But there were also those closer to the edge, building bridges to Cuba and Nicaragua. That was un-American. The spectrum of Coventry's friends – from right to left – was wide, both in Germany and in America. Bill Williams brought no ideological baggage. Sign up to what you think 'reconciliation' means, and you are welcome. In Germany it could be the chapel on an Air Force base and equally well a church committed to the peace movement, like the parish of the Twelve Apostles in the East Berlin suburb of Pankow with its remarkable pastor Werner Krätschell. The parish's Peace Group was a constant thorn in the flesh of the Communist government. All this reflected an all-embracing liberal Cathedral.

Until 1973 Bill Williams, never without keen and mainly young helpers, made the international running alone. With a rich programme of international cultural weeks with significant speakers from abroad, he tried to keep the cathedral community involved. However, neither then nor thereafter was that easy. In 1973 Kenyon Wright was appointed the first International Director. The task was too demanding for the Provost alone. Kenyon Wright, until then Director of Urban Ministry at the

Cathedral, had more than the necessary qualifications. For 15 years he had worked as a Methodist missionary in Indian Bengal, and founded the Ecumenical Social and Industrial Institute in the new industrial town of Durgapur. This became the national training centre for urban-industrial ministries in India. From 1963 he had had close links with Coventry through Simon Phipps and Stephen Verney, who had proposed his appointment to be his successor as Director of Urban Ministry. By virtue of his incorporation into the united Church of North India nothing stood in the way of his being made a Canon of Coventry Cathedral.

Until then, what I have been prematurely calling the CCN and the CIR had little formal structure. The new Director, working alongside the Provost, thought and acted more systematically. The visionary Provost had more or less allowed things to happen spontaneously. His charisma and authority seemed to suffice. Canon Wright was a much more radical theologian and systematic thinker. He gave shape to what already existed. There was an attempt to bring all the ministries of outreach together and to relate these formally to the Joint Council of the Chapel of Unity, as the expression of the Christian Service Centre which was planned beside that chapel but never built. For two years this was the Centre for Social and International Reconciliation (CSIR) before it became simply the Centre for International Reconciliation (CIR).

Kenyon's much more socialist vision, formed by his Third World experience, was in marked contrast to that of Bill Williams. Such diversity seemed natural in a place marked by liberality. Such tensions as there were never severely ruffled the surface. By the time he returned to Scotland in 1981, the International Ministry had been given the shape that survived under my later leadership more or less to the end of the century. Some aspects worked. Others did not. A great deal continued to hang on the personality of whoever was in charge.

The new Director knew the value of symbols and built on that Coventry tradition. He took groups to Auschwitz and Hiroshima. He had no hesitation in crossing the Iron Curtain and making friends with the alleged enemy. He was determined that those around the world who had understood the Coventry story and wanted to be part of it should constitute a definable link. He had the vision of a worldwide interrelated network that would be Coventry's ministry of reconciliation, each in its own place and in its own way. There would be no rule book but simply Coventry's heart-beat, enshrined in a history, a prayer and a cross. CCN centres would inevitably differ widely in their degree of commitment. Some would naturally fade away as new ones joined.

The German centres, though still engaged with the East–West confrontation, were transformed by a new emphasis on North–South issues under the title 'One Europe, One World'. Bill Williams had written to Kenyon, saying, 'Your present attention to Europe's responsibility for the Third World must be the dominant theme for the

THE ARCHANGEL MICHAEL TAKES WING

next phase.' This also led to the work with the newly formed Bangladesh, and to the Europa-Calcutta Consortium, chaired by Canon Wright, which drew together agencies in Germany, the Netherlands, Denmark, Canada and the UK in a co-ordinated project for that city, supported by the World Bank. In the International Year of the Child in 1979, a competition in all the Coventry schools led to the sending of a medically equipped Land Rover to Calcutta. Another fruit of this concern was One World Week, pioneered in Coventry in 1977. It has since become a national event in October each year.

The CCN ran a series of major international conferences, mainly in the States and Germany, on key topics, most of which were subsequently published as books. One of the most important of these was 'Ecology and Christian Responsibility', held in 1975 in Sewanee, USA. It was prophetic in its warnings and its theological interpretation of an ecological crisis that is now inescapable.

In 1976, links were established with Israel/Palestine, developing in two centres. Neve Shalom ('Oasis of Peace'), was an interfaith village in the south of Israel. Shfar-Am was an Arab village in the north, where the CCN group there were helped to build a 'House of Hope' as a meeting place for Jew, Muslim, Christian and Druze. Kenyon's frequent visits to the Holy Land led to an invitation to speak in the Great Mosque in Damascus, and he was also able to meet Yasser Arafat in Tunis.

A long-cherished hope of Provost Williams, shared by Canon Wright, was that there might be a Common Discipline, a simple rule of life akin to those in the third orders of many religious communities. Benedictine principles were at the heart of various drafts of this Common Discipline, for it was a great Benedictine Abbey that long ago made Coventry such a significant Christian centre. The discipline would be lived out in Coventry by the cathedral community and by those who looked to it for inspiration. It was an aspiration that, in my judgement, never took root and flourished, either at home or abroad. In that sense the CCN did not become a religious community as commonly understood. It could only be a network of Christian friends, with differing theologies and a variety of social and political allegiances, all somehow wishing to be peacemakers.

In 1973 the Provost announced the formation of the Order of Companions, an idea proposed by Kenyon Wright. Women and men who – again mainly in America and Germany – had worked for the Cathedral's ideals were in this way to be specially honoured. Six people were initially ceremonially invested with a purple mantle, much like the knights of an order of chivalry. Over the years many others have followed. In every case the honour was well deserved, latterly a stole replacing the more regal mantle, but Canon Wright's hope that the companions might meet regularly to give wise counsel to the Cathedral, that they might become a council of reference for the CCN, never happened. Not too far from that was the unspoken

COVENTRY HOUSE, CORRYMEELA

The Coventry House of Reconciliation at Corrymeela illustrates the initiatives carried out under the umbrella of the Community of the Cross of Nails in the late 1960s and 1970s. The Corrymeela Community at Ballycastle, Northern Ireland, was founded by the Revd Ray Davey as a Christian group to heal political and religious divisions in the province. In 1965 Corrymeela established itself at a holiday centre, which was then adapted and expanded. It became a Cross of Nails Centre in September 1971.

The opening of Coventry House in May 1976 was performed by Provost Bill Williams who, along with Canon Horace Dammers, provided much of the inspiration behind the initiative. The new building consisted of 30 bedrooms with a large gathering room at its centre. At the ceremony Ray Davey said:

> In an age when there is so much self-interest and cynicism . . . it is proper that we should pause and reflect on this magnanimity that a community in the heart of industrial England with so many problems and demands on their own doorstep, should think of us . . . Let all benefactors all over the world know how we feel about their great generosity. It is and will be a marvellous inspiration to us in such times as these, and an assurance that we are not alone.

Over the following 30 years Coventry House was home to permanent staff as well as over 300 one-year volunteers from many different countries, cultures and ages, who were able to learn to live together and support the ministry of the Corrymeela Community in reconciling the divided peoples of Northern Ireland.

But time and the ravages of the coast of County Antrim took their toll, and it was decided to build a new Coventry House. The £1.4 million energy-efficient residential block is again home to international long- and short-term volunteers, and begins to accomplish the Community's wish to 'create safe spaces where people of diverse backgrounds can come and meet each other, where there is an atmosphere of trust and acceptance, and where differences can be acknowledged, explored and accepted'. Irish President Mary McAleese opened it on 3 April 2009. The event was attended by many people associated with the Community, including, from Coventry, the Lord Mayor and Lady Mayoress, and John Stroyan, Bishop of Warwick.

Ted Hiscocks
Editorial Committee Member

hope that at least some of them, whether individuals or wealthy churches, might be sources of financial assistance, for there were many potential donors among them, both in America and in Germany. It remained a hope. Over the years the idea of such an 'order' has come to feel out of tune with the spirit of the age. Honoured people were grateful, and some remain among the Cathedral's closest friends, but 'the order' really remains as much of a fiction as the Common Discipline an aspiration.

Cardinal Josef Glemp, Primate of the Polish Church, on a goodwill visit to the Cathedral in February 1985. (left to right) Canon Peter Berry, the Primate, Canon Stephen Smalley.

With Canon Wright's return to Scotland in 1981 and the retirement soon after of the towering personality of Bill Williams, new times, more difficult times, dawned. The coffers were empty. A great deal of money had been spent – though not unwisely spent – at home and abroad. It was hard to find a new provost willing to take on this huge legacy. Vice-Provost Peter Berry valiantly kept all the flags flying, all the departments working, even the international outreach. It was possible because the spiritual dynamics that had driven the new Cathedral did not grind to a halt. After a long interregnum, Colin Semper came from being Head of Religious Broadcasting at the BBC to once again make the ship seaworthy. Remarkably laid back, he vowed to do the job in five years. Selling the grand Provost's House, living in a small flat on site, he balanced the books and before he left had amassed enough resources to appoint a new International Director. In 1986, with the Bishop's blessing, he offered me the job.

This was my dream job, built on a long international career. I already loved this cathedral. For the previous five years I had been head of the Division of International Affairs of the British Council of Churches, I had chaired Amnesty International UK, was a leading figure in the controversial Campaign for Nuclear Disarmament, a committed pacifist and even a Quaker. I was totally and very actively committed to the anti-apartheid struggle, expelled from South Africa as well as from the Soviet Union and other parts of the Communist bloc, yet – I hope justifiably – with a strong left-wing image and committed to dialogue with the Marxist world. Within three years the whole context would radically change. By 1989 both communism and apartheid were imploding. I would need to reinvent myself.

With me the Cathedral had taken a courageous gamble. Was my reputation a boon? Some thought so; many did not. Despite my achievements, my administrative abilities – I had warned in advance – were little short of abysmal. I would make up for that with my gifts of speaking and writing. With a loyal part-time secretary, almost no working budget and no guidance on how to proceed, I cheerfully went to work. I had not come to change things, but to build on them and at the same time to contribute my own insights, my own vision. My helpers and allies and caring critics were a small group of committed lay members of the cathedral community. It was listening to them and learning from them that made the work possible and rewarding. To name them all would be too much. However, not to name Allen and Mary Edwards would be impossible. The guiding spirits of the Chapel of Unity, they were my enablers and teachers of a living faith that embraces the world. They embodied love in action. Heather Wallace, who for a period freely gave all her time, was an inveterate helper and someone to stand up to me – as few did – without fear.

An unachieved aim which had also been Kenyon Wright's dream was to enable the whole cathedral community to own the international ministry of this unique cathedral. My gifts of communication did not suffice. Maybe the greater integration of the world beyond Britain into the regular liturgical life of the Cathedral might have helped. Perhaps that was simply expecting too much. Foreign visitors often had expectations of the world vision of this community that it could not match.

Colin Semper was succeeded as Provost by John Petty in 1988. He was a man of exceptional kindness, a totally dedicated parish priest. He loved the grand occasions – and there were many – but left the big vision to others. A team player, he led modestly from behind. Disciplined, with a military background, he served each aspect of

MURDER AT HUCHENFELD AND ITS AMAZING CONSEQUENCES

Of all the German centres of the Cathedral's Community of the Cross of Nails the story of Huchenfeld, a village just outside Pforzheim, is a remarkable example of murder most foul, turning to reconciliation most profound.

An East German Lutheran pastor with a brave record of resistance to many injustices retired to West Germany, to the village of Huchenfeld where his son lived. There he unearthed a story that the villagers did not want known. Soon after an air raid on Pforzheim, as devastating as Dresden's, a British reconnaissance Flying Fortress was hit by anti-aircraft fire. Its wing ablaze, the captain ordered his crew to bail out. His own parachute had jammed. He flew on, expecting to die but, surprisingly, the fire went out and he landed safely behind Allied lines.

The nine who bailed out came down near the village of Huchenfeld on the edge of Pforzheim. Two, some distance from the others, were taken prisoner in an orderly way. But anger at the devastating British bombing of Pforzheim was running high, and a local Nazi officer rounded up the remaining seven and locked them in the cellar of the village's town hall. The next morning he put pistols into the hands of young members of the Hitler Youth, probably 15 or 16 years old, and drove the airmen through a jeering crowd into the village churchyard. In the confusion, two managed to escape into the forest and were later lawfully taken prisoner. Five were murdered. Soon after the war the Nazi officer was tried by a British military court, sentenced to death and executed.

Some 40 years later Pastor Heinemann-Grüder, who had retired to the village and heard rumours of what had happened, was determined not to let things rest until there had been a public acknowledgement of this lynching and a memorial placed to the victims. He faced a great deal of hostility but he persevered. Knowing of Coventry's work for reconciliation with Germany, he invited me to the village to discuss all this with the mayor and others. The village council was not willing to erect a memorial. Those boys might still be around and they had never been held to account. Failing that, Heinemann-Grüder persuaded the church to act. A memorial plaque on the church wall would be solemnly unveiled, just feet from where the men were killed. This would follow a Eucharist in the church at which I was invited to preach.

Once this was agreed, the Mayor was shamed into officially associating the whole village with this act of penitence. The *Independent* and the *Mirror* co-operated in finding the widow of one of the murdered men. She was deeply moved and readily agreed to come to the ceremony. Other relatives were not found. The British Embassy sent a diplomat. The bodies of the murdered airmen had been buried by the British War Graves Commission not far away.

At the Eucharist one man who came to receive communion was crying bitterly. I quietly tried to comfort him. His were not the only tears that day. But through his tears he managed to say to me: 'I'm so ashamed, I was one of the boys who killed them.' He had come for forgiveness, almost 50 years later. After the service I shared this with Marjory Taylor, the widow of Flying Officer Harold Frost, who had come from England. Her immediate response was: 'Find him. I'd so much like to put my arms around him and forgive him.' We did not find him, nor did anyone know him. He had gone quickly, and evidently did not live locally.

All this was published in several British papers. On a sheep farm in North Wales, the aged surviving captain of the aircraft, Wing Cdr John Wynne, read the story. Until then he had never been told the fate of his crew. He was moved beyond measure, wrote to the Mayor, asking what he could do to express his gratitude to the village. A new kindergarten was being planned. He agreed to come to its opening and brought as his gift a Welsh rocking-horse. The children queued to ride it in a wonderful village festival. That led to the twinning of the villages of Huchenfeld and Llanbedr and to an annual exchange visit of school-children that continues to this day. In an RAF publication the two who had escaped now also read the story. They too have become friends of Huchenfeld and a part of this remarkable reconciliation story.

Without Kurt Jürgen Heinemann-Grüder and his stubborn insistence on penitence being seen to be done, there would be no story to tell. He died on 4 November 2010, aged 90.

Paul Oestreicher

the Cathedral's life but did not dictate what it should be. He totally supported a person as different as I was. That could never have been easy. Liberality characterized John Petty. He was proud of his cathedral for all people, of all convictions and all nations, and tried to greet them in their own tongue. Hi! – to the many Americans. I felt he was my emissary to the CCN USA. My priorities were European, more East than West, and then South African.

Much of the most creative work arose from needs of the moment. The Netherlands were torn by a debate over whether two very old men, Nazi war criminals, should stay in Breda prison until their death. The humanitarian case for their release after half a century of imprisonment was overwhelming. But in the light of public opinion, the government was reluctant to act. John Petty and I visited these old men.

Long ago they might have shown no mercy. There was all the more Christian reason to show it now to them. A plea from Coventry broke the log jam. They did not live much longer but died in their own homes. Such a mission was very close to John Petty's heart.

As apartheid was collapsing I was summoned to what might have been the most important mission of my ministry. A low-level war with much violence and many deaths had broken out in Natal between the African National Congress and the Inkatha Party of the Zulu Chief, Mangasuthu Buthelezi. Would he establish an independent Zulu state and preside over it? I knew him well as a devout Anglican from much earlier days when he came to London to find finance for a Zulu newspaper. He was my guest in the Southwark diocesan conference house of which I was chaplain. To those like Margaret Thatcher who thought of Mandela and the ANC as terrorists, Buthelezi was the acceptable face of black South Africa. He was, therefore, anything but my hero. Yet I liked him. He knew and respected me, though his shady advisors probably told him that I was not good news when I came as an emissary of the Bishop of Natal and of Archbishop Tutu to help persuade him to come in from the cold and join the first democratic government of South Africa. We prayed together. Many lives hung on his answer. Twice I was flown in his personal plane to his tribal seat of government in Ulundi. All this without a word of publicity anywhere. Of course, it took far more than one person from Coventry to change the course of history, but a trusting personal relationship wedded to what Coventry stood for in world opinion was one important factor in this reconciliation story. Buthelezi joined the new South Africa and the killing ended.

That did not conclude Coventry's commitment to the new South Africa. Over the last decade a whole series of Cross of Nails Centres has been established in various parts of the country. Archbishop Tutu, dancing down the

Archbishop Desmond Tutu addressed a full Cathedral at the start of Coventry Peace Week in 1989. © Tom McIlroy.

nave, paid a memorable visit to the Cathedral, as did the last apartheid-era President, F. W. de Klerk, reconciled with Nelson Mandela, his successor.

It was not long after my arrival in Coventry that a professor from the School of Peace Studies at Bradford University came to see me. The School had commissioned a sculpture to symbolize its work. It was simply called *Reconciliation*. The aged sculptor Josefina de Vasconcellos had expressed the hope that a replica might also be placed in the old Coventry Cathedral. Its message meant a lot to her. The professor brought a miniature version with him. But it would not be cheap. Perhaps we might find a sponsor. We did, in the person of Richard Branson, who was enthusiastic. But that was not all. I had begun to wonder why, when Germany had been so central to the Cathedral's life, Japan – though there had been one visit – hardly seemed to feature. Why not, we thought, offer another replica to the people of Hiroshima? Richard Branson readily took that on board, literally on board one of his own flights to Tokyo. The Lord Mayor of Coventry and the Provost, along with Richard Branson, presented the sculpture to the Mayor of Hiroshima. It has found its place at the entrance to the city's Peace Museum. This dual placement of the sculpture – at Coventry Cathedral and in Hiroshima – was, for the artist, by then well into her nineties, a dream fulfilled.

The story of the sculpture did not end there. Josefina wanted it placed where the Cold War had ended, where the Berlin Wall had been. The Cathedral acted on her wish and brought it to the Versöhnungskirche, the 'Church of Reconciliation', already a Cross of Nails Centre. A new, modest chapel, it straddles a site where the Wall had been and where the Communist authorities had dynamited the nineteenth-century church that had stood in no-man's land. Yet one more site for the sculpture was found: the grounds of Stormont, where erstwhile deadly enemies now rule Northern Ireland together. The Cathedral is in debt to the sculptor, who died aged 100 in 2005, and to Bradford's School of Peace Studies. One might well say the Cathedral has appropriated this work of art, so closely is it now associated with the Cathedral's mission. In miniature form, with the artist's blessing, it serves as an alternative symbol to the Cross of Nails, not burdened, when presented to Jews and Muslims and others too, with what are to them the negative connotations of a cross.

The journey to Hiroshima did not stand alone. It created a new sense of relationship with Japan and with the Japanese Embassy in London. In turn that led to friendship with a remarkable, reconciling woman, Keiko Holmes, who enabled former British prisoners of war to return to Japan to meet their former captors. They had often suffered grievously and yet found forgiveness a liberating experience. There are many contexts in which others were the reconcilers, and the Cathedral was privileged to be associated with them.

In a further way, during my years in Coventry, a work of art came to enhance the Cathedral's international significance and associated the Cathedral with Coventry's twin city of Volgograd, once Stalingrad, its battle the traumatic turning point of the Second World War. Dr Kurt Reuber was a German army surgeon during the long winter siege that virtually destroyed the city. The death toll was huge. At Christmas 1942, deep in a dug-out, Kurt Reuber, who was also a Lutheran pastor, invited some of the surviving soldiers to celebrate the birth of Jesus. To enliven that bitterly cold, bleak place, he drew a Russian mother and her child, a reflection of his love for the Russian people, so cruelly treated by his nation. This drawing came to be called the Stalingrad Madonna, surrounded by the words 'LICHT LEBEN LIEBE Weichnachten 1942' ('Life – Light – Love, Christmas 1942'). The surgeon, artist and pastor went into Soviet imprisonment together with the 9,000 German survivors of the siege. Like most of the others, he did not survive for long. Providentially, the Stalingrad Madonna did survive, flown out of the siege on the last plane to Germany.

The Stalingrad Madonna became a significant icon in post-war German church life and found its place in West Berlin's Cross of Nails Centre, the Kaiser Wilhelm Memorial Church, a ruin preserved as in Coventry, with a significant modern church beside it, which in effect became West Berlin's Cathedral. Kurt Soppa, the church's pastor, presented a replica of Kurt Reuber's Madonna to Coventry Cathedral at John Petty's installation. It forms the altar piece of the Cathedral's only new chapel, which was dedicated on the fiftieth anniversary of the Blitz by the Bishops of Coventry and Berlin and the Archbishop of Volgograd – Anglican, Lutheran and Russian Orthodox, truly international and ecumenical and a profound symbol of love in the midst of hatred. In what was Stalingrad's surviving Orthodox cathedral, now at the edge of Volgograd, there is, at the entrance to the iconostasis,* one of the very first Crosses of Nails, still the raw iron nails that lay in the ruins.

Akin perhaps to Stalingrad, which changed history, is Ground Zero in New York, where the World Trade Center stood. At its edge stands St Paul's Chapel, the Episcopal centre that provided the desperately needed pastoral care to innumerable people at the time – and still today. There, too, visitors can see Coventry's Cross of Nails, part of CCN USA, with its message of healing and peace.

After the Fall of the Wall in 1989, it was in Dresden's Deaconess Hospital that the Cross of Nails Centres in East and West gathered to formally launch CCN Germany to which, at the time of writing in 2010, some 60 centres are now affiliated. German church life is hard to imagine without this richly varied ecumenical network. And there are now its offshoots, made possible by the commitment of German Christians looking East, in Slovakia, Poland and Belarus.

This is not the place to tell the stories of the world's Cross of Nails Centres, be it in North America, Europe or South Africa. Nevertheless, they are part of Coventry's

THE REBUILDING OF THE FRAUENKIRCHE, DRESDEN

The bombing of Dresden by Anglo-American Allied forces on the night of 13 February 1945 was perhaps the most significant the Second World War air raid on a German city. After the war, the decision was taken to preserve the ruins of the main church – the Frauenkirche – as in Coventry, but in Dresden the ruins were left untouched as a war memorial; there was no attempt even to clear the piles of masonry.

Following the reunification of Germany in 1989, an initiative to rebuild the Frauenkirche gathered momentum, and in January 1993 reconstruction began. Much could be written about the 12-year rebuilding, and the international effort that raised the €180 million cost. In the UK the project led to the establishment of the Dresden Trust, whose initial aims were the promotion of religion and the rebuilding of the Frauenkirche as a memorial to all who died in aerial bombardments throughout the war. The Trust's first project was to make the cross that surmounts the bell-shaped dome capped by a cupola.

The rebuilt Frauenkirche, Dresden, has a cross of nails on the High Altar.

The cross, which is gilded and stands on an orb, was made by Alan Smith, of the London gold and silversmiths Grant MacDonald. For Alan this commission was particularly poignant as his father Frank had taken part in the bombing of Dresden in 1945. Once finished, the cross and the orb toured the country. It was exhibited in Coventry Cathedral from December 1998 to March 1999, and a service was held there in February 1999 with the German Ambassador, the Mayor of Dresden and two German bishops present. A reminder of that time is a model of the cross and orb in the Cathedral undercroft.

On 14 April 2005 the day came for the lifting of the cross and orb into position. John Coker recalls:

The Neumarkt Square in front of the church was packed, and we were welcomed enthusiastically by the local people, 'Thank you for coming' they said. A band played while we waited for the ceremony to begin. The Burgomaster introduced the Duke of Kent. He made a good speech in excellent German and referred to the 35,000 people who had been killed in the city 60 years before. At the end of the speech the crane driver started the lift, and we watched as the structure was raised into position. Precisely at the top there was applause; cheers rang out as did the cathedral bells. Then we went inside for a formal service.

Ted Hiscocks
Editorial Committee Member

story. One story stands almost alone, that of Dresden's Lutheran cathedral, the Frauenkirche, the 'Church of Our Lady'. A symbol of the destruction of Dresden, known once as the finest Baroque building north of the Alps, it remained a venerated ruin throughout the years of Communist rule. Many wanted to preserve the ruin as a holy site. Yet in 1992 the city appealed to the world to help rebuild it, in an extraordinary artistic and architectural undertaking. The British response came not only from Coventry but from people throughout the nation, from the Queen to the now very old widows of the airmen who had bombed it. The great golden Orb and Cross that tops it out, which was crafted by the son of an RAF bomber pilot, was the gift of the British nation, organized by the Dresden Trust of which the Bishop of Coventry was a trustee. A Cross of Nails now stands on the Frauenkirche's altar, the only thing that is not a replica of what was there before. This is a partnership that resonates deeply with the German people – and with many in Britain who grieved at Dresden's fate. Some in Germany wanted the Frauenkirche to remain a ruin as a witness to the suffering of war and a memorial to those peace and human rights groups to whom the ruin had become a place of pilgrimage during Communist times. Happily, with most Germans, they now celebrate the rebuilt church as a symbol of peace and reconciliation.

There is another German city of great historic beauty, even if less well known. Würzburg was also devastated by Allied bombs. It has chosen to be a Cross of Nails city, its cross taken each year in procession to a new location for that year, a parish, Catholic or Protestant, or some social institution. For one year it was Würzburg's prison. The Cross of Nails support group took its ministry into the prison. That work goes on. Significantly, all the Crosses of Nails for new centres around the world are now made in Würzburg's prison workshop.

It has never been easy to assess how much the work of the international ministry has meant at any given time to the cathedral community itself. In 1993 the Finance Committee decided that there was no longer enough money to employ an International Director. This committee made policy on all issues. The residentiary canons were not members of it, though they were generally present. I was told that I would need to find another job. I took a gamble and announced that I would raise the money for the work in Germany. With the help of the retired minister of a Cologne deanery, who had worked for many years in England, a German charity was set up to fund Coventry's international work. I chaired it and he, Martin Hueneke, administered it. All my instincts told me that this would not fall on deaf ears. Over a decade, the money needed was over-subscribed by a combination of gifts from church provinces and from individuals. This passed almost unnoticed in Coventry. When I retired at the end of 1997, enough money had accrued to advertise for a successor. It is not an exaggeration to say that German Christians rescued Coventry's international ministry into the next century.

One further debt is owed to the German churches. For some 15 years the Lutheran Church of Bavaria seconded a young pastor, man or woman, to work half-time as a member of the Cathedral's staff and half-time as an assistant chaplain at Coventry University. This gave them valuable ecumenical experience and certainly enriched the Cathedral's life. It was a practical implementation of the Meissen Accord, an agreement between the Church of England and the Protestant Church in Germany, for the first time making an exchange of ministries canonically possible. Of those who came from Bavaria, Oliver Schuegraf stayed much longer than the others and made an outstanding contribution to the Cathedral's life. So much did he become 'part of us' that he was able to become a Coventry ambassador to the CCN in North America, South Africa and Germany itself. Not satisfied with that, he wrote the Cathedral's story and reflected on it theologically. As already mentioned, this excellent German book is now on the market in an English translation. One fruit of all that is that Oliver is now the ecumenical officer at the national headquarters of the

German Lutheran Church. In him the Cathedral and the Church of England now has a wise, influential and knowledgeable friend.

On my retirement in 1997, great changes were afoot, greater than one might expect from any new director. Andrew White was a remarkably gifted charismatic Christian, conservative in his theology and in his politics, a highly successful parish priest from South London and an influential local Conservative councillor. He was already a significant international figure in Christian–Jewish relations. Before his ordination he had trained and worked as a technician in hospital operating theatres. With all that, he came with immense charm, powers of persuasion and was the youngest canon residentiary in England. Of partly Indian ancestry, he was also a multiple-sclerosis sufferer.

A larger-than-life figure, Andrew came with clear ideas of his vocation as a reconciler on a broad canvas. He would need far more money than the Cathedral could get its mind around and he had the charisma and faith to raise it. He recruited staff. At one point there were 12 people working with him. While remaining the focal point for the CCN around the world and delegating others to travel widely, he turned the ICR into a considerable powerhouse. Like other gifted people, he sat loose to worldly authority. His accountability was to God. He quickly acquired a high media profile and urged me to stay on and support his work. His sympathies were much wider than his own convictions might suggest. To a greater extent than before, he drew the Bishop of Coventry into his work, though not necessarily taking his advice. His embrace was as large as he was.

This new age for the ICR quickly came to be centred on the Middle East. The reconciliation of Jews, Muslims and Christians in Israel and Palestine was Andrew's 'God-given task'. The politicians in this long-running tragic conflict must learn – and he would seek to teach them – that they disregard religion and the religious leaders at their peril. Religion was both one cause of the conflict and one essential key to its resolution. He loved Jews and Muslims as much as he loved Christians, and not just Christians of his own kind. Essentially, he would have to win the trust both of the religious leaders (and not just the liberal ones) and of the politicians. Members of the Israeli cabinet knew they had a friend in him. So, before long, did Yasser Arafat. He did not simply operate with a Coventry label, but soon wore the mantle of the Archbishop of Canterbury's envoy. When Archbishop Carey retired, he chose to continue to have Andrew as his protégé. That patronage was important to both of them.

Encouraged by the Foreign Minister of Israel, Andrew White summoned some of the Middle East's most important religious leaders to confer with him. The outcome was the Alexandria Declaration of Religious Leaders in the Holy Land. Those who signed it committed themselves to the rejection of violence and bloodshed, to work together for a just peace and to reconciliation in Jerusalem and the Holy Land, to support a truce based on the Mitchell-Tenet Plans*, to call on both sides to desist from any kind of demonization of the other, and to bring up future generations in that spirit. This Declaration was unprecedented. The effect on history of this huge achievement, however, remains an open question.

Inevitably, international work at this level of intensity left the home base wondering. It had never been easy to make the people at the Sunday Eucharist feel that this was their show, the more so when the liturgy itself seldom related to it. The big man himself was seldom there. And another big change was in the offing. On John Petty's retirement, John Irvine, one of the creators of the Alpha Course*, arrived as Coventry's new Dean. His charismatic evangelical ethos was a break with Coventry's liberal tradition. The ICR and the CCN were clearly not his first priority. In what form would the international ministry now survive?

Bishop Bennetts was determined that it should, but that it needed to be more accountable and firmly anchored. He and the Dean appointed Canon Justin Welby as Co-Director alongside Canon White. The Bishop had two aims. One was to bring some stability and order to the development and running of the ICR, but as importantly to release Andrew to work in the Middle East while Justin focused on Africa. Justin Welby had none of his colleague's flamboyance. Prior to his ordination he had worked in the oil industry in many countries including Nigeria and therefore brought a new area of experience to the international team. In addition, he had many years experience of Africa, in a large number of countries. Andrew had vastly developed the work in Nigeria where reconciliation ministries were desperately needed. The Bishop himself became directly involved, through the existing diocesan partnership with Kaduna.

It was here that violence had led to more than 300 deaths, with Christians and Muslims in bitter contention. Might the religious leaders be able to stem the violence? Something like the Alexandria Declaration was needed and might just turn the tide. In 2002 the Kaduna Peace Declaration of Religious Leaders was signed and a standing working group was formed to oversee its implementation. Coventry's ICR undertook to continue supporting the process. The Declaration really did help to reduce the violence, even though the underlying problems were far from resolved. This was not merely a top-down initiative. Grassroots groups such as the Muslim–Christian Dialogue Forum were supported, to give peace a better chance. To all this was added some measure of practical humanitarian help. Justin took over the work in Africa, while Andrew focused on the Holy Land and increasingly Iraq. The two areas worked in very different ways. Justin was much more at grass roots, in the background seeking to facilitate more than to do. Much was achieved in this way with CCN centres in Burundi, and leading members of the rebel and government forces enabled to talk together and make progress towards peace. In the Niger Delta, considerable steps were made in enabling progress in Ogoniland, site of the execution of Ken Saro-Wiwa, one of Africa's great lost leaders. Muslim and Christian leaders were brought together in Kenya, pre-empting conflict on religious grounds, but all was behind the scenes. Andrew's genius was to capture the imagination of major figures, and lead bold and transforming events. Both kinds of involvement are needed.

This was a period of remarkable cathedral activism in the Middle East and in Nigeria. It was sustained by a large and expensive home base. The ICR was a hub of

President Olusegun Obasanjo of Nigeria receiving the Coventry Peace Prize (inset) in the Ruins on 14 November 2005.

dedicated people driven by the deep conviction that they were making a difference to the world. Sadly, the sums required could not be sustained in the absence of a charismatic and compelling figure such as Andrew White.

The upshot was a radical change of gear. At the end of 2004 the ICR budget ended with a note warning the Chapter that funds were running short. In 2005, to the dismay of those who knew and valued their work, most of the ICR/CCN staff were made redundant. Canon White had worked for seven years, Canon Welby for three. They had been at the heart of a programme of personal diplomacy, unparalleled in any cathedral anywhere. Sadly, it had to end. Justin Welby was now made Sub-Dean and Canon for Reconciliation Ministry and took a greater part in the Cathedral's administration, assisted by Martin Hayward. For some time Canon Stephen Davis led the work as Director of International Ministry, especially in the Niger Delta. Much healing of hurts at home, both practical and pastoral, had to happen, and took place even while some aspects of the work were continued, with the CCN in the Middle East, and with direct involvement in Nigeria, including in Plateau State, where a major area of conflict was at a turning point, in part owing to ICR's continued involvement.

Canon White, drawn as passionately as ever to his understanding of conflict resolution, now felt impelled to move his mission to Iraq, independent of English church structures. The Cathedral's international work as it had been was entering a new phase, more in line with its traditions. Time would be needed to rethink what should now be done and who should do it.

Since then, Andrew White's story is no longer part of the Cathedral's. It is an Iraqi story, which he has told and goes on telling to a large Christian public. As the 'Vicar of Baghdad' and under a mainly American umbrella – having from the outset believed in the rightness of the allied invasion – he is father to a large Christian community, hostage negotiator and above all a Christian who believes that peace and good government lie largely in the hands of religious leaders whom he believes he can influence. Totally unafraid, he is convinced that God has entrusted him with a unique mission. It is costly in more ways than one. God, he remains confident, will provide the means. Within the framework of his Foundation for Relief and Reconciliation in the Middle East, he pursues a charismatic vision which is rooted in the Coventry conviction that all, without exception, must be loved. Close to the people in power, heavily reliant on security, yet much loved by many, he goes on, undeterred and widely celebrated.

Was this remarkable Coventry story then over? Not really. This was only one brave charismatic interlude during which much, too much, had been ventured. Icarus* had flown too high, his wings had been singed. The bird of heaven had to come back to earth. Could the home base now do nothing much more than offer an annual peace prize to a deserving peacemaker and revive an annual peace lecture from a wise guru, eminently worthwhile things though these are? A long, long breath had now to be taken. A new vision takes time. Why should the Holy Spirit always be in a hurry?

As I look back and reflect, it is clear to me that Coventry's deserved reputation has been an inspiring story of healing historical wounds. That remains a pastoral and deeply Christian vocation. Much healing remains to be done, and not only in far-off places. It has not, however, been a prophetic ministry that speaks the truth to power – in love. Some have regretted that. The campaigners in the great causes of the last half-century have not found a ready ally in the Cathedral and its leaders. The brave band in the Lord Mayor's Peace Committee, led by Dr Madeleine Sharp, has generally, over many years, struggled alone, although the Chapel of Unity has given them a foothold outside the cathedral mainstream. Provost Williams set a pattern: his cathedral would not join anyone else's cause, would not expose itself to the hurly burly of conflict. It would determine its own peaceful flight path, part of no squadron. Causes were for others to pursue, demonstrations for others to march on. I respected that, even when part of me wished it were not so.

When, jointly with the University across the square, then still called the Polytechnic, the Cathedral hosted the Convention of END – the Campaign for European Nuclear Disarmament – in 1987, it did for a moment appear to put its neutrality on hold. Here was an assembly of critical intellectuals from across the European spectrum campaigning against the Cold War, against nuclear arms in East and West and for greater freedom in the Warsaw Pact states. A cathedral full of political slogans was an unexpected sight. The open and tolerant Provost Petty felt just a little out of his depth. For once peace also meant protest. MI5 must have had its ear to the ground, while the invited 'diplomats' from Eastern Europe suspected the whole thing was financed by the CIA. Prophets like the radical historian E. P. Thompson were not part of the normal cathedral scene.

Unique in a very different way was an initiative from within the heart of the cathedral community that gave the lie – and continues to do so – to the idea that the international ministry of the Cathedral was entirely run by paid specialists with hardly any grass-roots involvement. Jane and Martin Williams were, in the profoundest sense, children of this cathedral, deeply imbued with its spirit. When Romania threw off its dictatorship, Jane and Martin showed how much two people with imagination, limited resources and a lot of love could do to transform the lives of people. Their story is told in their own words on page 227. It is in fact much more than a postscript. Perhaps it is the story that matters most. It is about a very different kind of leadership. I am humbled that it began in my time and content that I did nothing to make it happen.

Jane Williams fills her water bottle at one end of the village trough while horses drink from the other end. In Dacia, Romania, this trough is the village's only water supply. See 'Coventry Cathedral in Romania', p. 227.

I have said that on the closing down of the ICR as it had been, a long breath would need to be taken. It was. Many in the CCN centres around the world began to wonder, was 'their' cathedral still there? Martin Hayward was doing what one person could do to keep contacts alive. It was clear that decision-making was not solely a matter for the cathedral leadership. Already in Colin Bennetts, the Bishop had become integral to the cathedral process and gave himself heart and soul to it, at real personal expense. A new bishop was awaited.

A new director with a new title was appointed, a Canon for Reconciliation with a brief that was both local and global, that would seek to make the Cross of Nails and all it stands for as much of a reality in Coventry, in the diocese and in England as abroad. The brief was to integrate the best of what had been with many things that had been missing. The task would be holistic in a way that it had not been. Flying on healing missions was not ruled out, but there was healing to be done on foot in the backstreets, as in the past. It would need to be a teaching ministry involving the whole cathedral community. And it would have to be humble enough to recognize that what could be done could only be done in co-operation with others, others in the diocese and in the city, in other churches, in Coventry's two universities, and challengingly today, in other religions. No more going it alone.

Was there someone to match that brief? Imaginatively and bravely the Bishop, together with the Dean, appointed David Porter whose credentials were remarkably fitting. A Christian political scientist from Northern Ireland, David Porter had been at the heart of one of the most challenging peace processes in modern times. What is more, he was neither ordained nor an Anglican, but a Baptist with Anabaptist* roots. Such a man as a leading canon in an Anglican cathedral breaks with every introspective tradition and is a reconciliation story in itself.

Every story of sin and redemption, of death and resurrection has a kairos* moment at its heart. For me it came in November 1990, 50 years to the day after the Blitz, after the fire in Coventry that lit a flame of love. It was a divine liturgy. Walking solemnly into the ruined Cathedral came Her Majesty Queen Elizabeth the Queen Mother, who had come with her husband King George VI half a century earlier to comfort a stricken city. Beside her walked Richard von Weizsäcker, President of the Federal Republic of Germany, respected far beyond Germany as perhaps no other German politician has been, a leading Christian lay man. Queen Mother and President walk through the Ruins to the altar and there, together, they pray the Litany of Reconciliation, both in German and in English. They turn, descend the steps and go through the screen of angels and saints into Basil Spence's tribute to a new future.

There is a great silence. Paul Leddington Wright, the Cathedral's Director of Music, goes to the piano. The Blitz 50 years ago is recalled. Hitler's bombers had code-named it 'Moonlight Sonata'. Ludwig van Beethoven's solemn melody fills a sacred space. Hundreds of wilted leaves descend on the people from on high, one leaf for every person killed in Coventry on that moonlit night. Drop, drop, slow tears.

The President's words are words of penitence, of the shame of his nation. But also words of gratitude and friendship, of reconciled history. He presents to the Queen Mother, to the British people, to this cathedral, a Bell of Peace, a gift from the German nation inscribed in English and in German. It has been rung ever since to preface the Cathedral's prayers for peace. Her Majesty the Queen Mother presents to the German President a Cross of Nails for the German nation to treasure. Even if not yet in every mind and heart, the war is over.

* Denotes an entry in the Glossary

Notes

1 W. E. Rose, *Sent from Coventry: A Mission of International Reconciliation*, Wolff, 1980.

2 Merrilyn Thomas, *Communing with the Enemy: Covert Operations, Christianity and Cold War Politics in Britain and the GDR*, Peter Lang, 2005.

7 A CHURCH AMONG CHURCHES

A Personal Reflection

COLIN BENNETTS

The Cathedral and the Bishop

I only ever crossed swords on one issue with John Petty. The then Provost and, later, Dean claimed to have the best job in the Church of England. I insisted that I did. That claim was not based on pride but on a sense of privilege, and that sense of privilege came in no small measure from the unique story that is Coventry Cathedral, a story that inspires the world and that continues to shape the diocese and its people. I was invited to be part of that story when I was installed on Palm Sunday 1998 as the eighth Bishop of Coventry. From the outset I was profoundly humbled by the quality of spiritual leadership offered by my predecessors and awed by the challenge of making the Coventry narrative relevant to the approaching new millennium.

The worshipping life of a bishop can, at times, feel quite nomadic. He belongs in all the parishes, but can only ever be present in one, and that usually for just a fleeting visit. It is in the parishes that much of his time is spent. This reality is quite at odds with the popular perception that the bishop is more often than not to be found in his cathedral. I have lost count of the times that members of parish churches have thanked me for coming, adding that they would come and see me one day soon in the Cathedral. On most Sundays, other than major festivals, the Cathedral is a delightfully bishop-free zone.

For all but four years of my ordained ministry I had been part of a local community, either in a parish, an Oxford college or a large cathedral. I now needed a spiritual base that would sustain me in a much more peripatetic ministry. During my ten years in Coventry the Cathedral provided that base at the early morning Communion service on Tuesdays or Thursdays. It offered a real sense of rootedness, a healthy antidote to what was otherwise a somewhat fragmented pattern of public praying.

Ordinations are regular diocesan events in the Cathedral's life. The three bishops taking part in 1994 are (left to right) Keith Arnold, Simon Barrington-Ward and Clive Handford. © Coventry Telegraph.

When I presided at the Easter Day Eucharist the week following my installation, the Provost greeted me with the words, 'Bishop Colin, welcome to *your* cathedral.' Such an unambiguous reception is, sadly, not as common as one might hope. From all that I hear on the grapevine, not every bishop is so fortunate in his relations with the cathedral Chapter. On countless subsequent occasions I was made to feel warmly welcome, not only by the clergy but equally by the stewards, vergers and musicians. This was certainly the case at high-profile public events, but no less so at those more intimate midweek services where I was receiving ministry rather than giving it. John Irvine, the current Dean, has continued to develop that sense of inclusivity and corporate ownership by welcoming not just the bishop, but all visitors from the diocese to '*your* cathedral'. The ancient Benedictine tradition of hospitality, the tradition which is the spiritual ancestor of the new Cathedral, is still very much alive and in evidence.

The Cathedral and diocese

So from my perspective it all felt rather cosy. But was I seeing the whole story? Throughout the Church of England, cathedrals are often seen by the parishes through less than rosy spectacles. They are regarded as privileged institutions, overstaffed, self-assured, impervious to change, and out of touch with ordinary parochial needs. It is assumed that cathedral congregations consist either of troublemakers who have fallen out with their local vicar or half-hearted Christians who want to avoid commitment and who sit quietly behind a pillar being entertained by beautiful music. Cathedrals don't generally contribute financially to the diocesan coffers, and the dean and at least two canons are independently funded by the Church Commissioners. Then there are issues of geography. Whatever the size of the diocese, there always seem to be complaints that the cathedral is too far away, or inaccessible because there is nowhere to park, or even that it is too dangerous to risk going there after dark. The most telling local version of this excuse is that the Coventry ring road, with its treacherous entry and exit points, keeps more people out of the city than the medieval walls ever did! Geographical remoteness, real or imagined, can all too easily lead to a sense of irrelevance if not alienation. And finally there is the old chestnut about the kind of worship found in cathedrals. A perennial problem at diocesan events is whether to stick to the traditional musical fare with semi-professional choir and formal liturgy, or to import a worship band and attempt a more informal style, knowing that any attempt at compromise will probably alienate the vast majority. The whole idea that the cathedral can in any real sense be the Mother Church of the diocese seems increasingly far-fetched and anachronistic. What may, perhaps, have been true for the Middle Ages is certainly not the case in the twenty-first century.

It is tempting to claim that Coventry Cathedral is far removed from this cynical stereotype, and, indeed, there is much that can be said in its defence. It is, for example, a fact that certain diocesan bishops have to pay thousands of pounds from their expense accounts to 'hire' their own cathedral for ordination services. By contrast, Coventry, a new cathedral with none of the medieval endowments of some of its sisters, has always been more than generous by absorbing those costs itself. The Cathedral's generosity towards the diocese can equally be seen in its willingness to respond to parish needs for Sunday preachers. It is rare to see a full complement of canons on a Sunday morning, and that is not because some are having a lie-in. This same generosity was evident a few years ago when the Dean became priest-in-charge of an inner-city parish until such time as a replacement was found. It turned out to be one of the cathedral lay staff who was ordained to that role. There is no doubt that the Cathedral Liaison Officers* (CLOs), set up by John Petty, did much to improve relations between the Cathedral and the parishes. Likewise the inclusion of a Reader representing the parishes of the diocese at the major Sunday Eucharist goes some way to bridging a gap that will probably always exist in some measure.

Modern worship in a modern building. Coventry Cathedral liturgy embraces the whole spectrum of worship. The statue on the left is by Elisabeth Frink.

CUTHBERT BARDSLEY, BISHOP OF COVENTRY 1956–76

The ashes of Cuthbert Bardsley (1907–91), along with those of Ellen his wife, have been interred below the high-altar cross, a few metres from the consecration stone which he 'signed' in 1962. This was a fitting tribute to a man whose ministry of precisely 20 years at Coventry had seen the laying of the foundation stone of the new building, its completion and consecration (a very rare, if not a unique, achievement); the appointment of Bill Williams (Provost), Joseph Poole, Stephen Verney, Simon Phipps and Edward Patey as the team to establish the new ministry; and the consecration of nine new churches and chapels across the Coventry Diocese. His impact on the wider Church over 40 years of ordained ministry was such that Donald Coggan (Archbishop of Canterbury 1974–80) was moved to write a biography.

The Rt Revd Cuthbert Bardsley, Bishop of Coventry, talking to pupils and the chairman of King's High School, Warwick, before the school's 90th anniversary service in 1969. © Coventry Telegraph.

It has been said that Cuthbert was born to be a bishop. He came from a cleri-cal family that had already produced three bishops. After parish ministry in London he became Provost of Southwark, and then, in 1947, Bishop of Croydon and bishop to the armed forces for eight years. As such, his impact was immense, perhaps best illustrated by a reunion service held for those whom he had con-firmed while Bishop of Croydon: no church was big enough to contain all those who wished to attend. The Davis Theatre was used for 4,300 people but that still left 1,000, and half of these were accommodated in Croydon parish church.

From addresses to large gatherings, to chance meetings with people in cri-sis, Cuthbert's earlier ministry was a suitable preparation for the challenges he faced later in Coventry, where the eyes of the Anglican Church and at times an even larger international audience would be upon him.

'We need a new vision, a new sense of vocation, a new belief in ourselves – above all, a new belief in Christ.' So said Cuthbert at his enthronement as the fifth Bishop of Coventry on 5 May 1956. Less than two months earlier he had been present for the laying of the foundation stone. Then on 25 May 1962 the new building was consecrated in the presence of HM the Queen, representatives of 57 nations, and a wide variety of church leaders. The great day was more than memorable theatre with Cuthbert in the lead role: he had prepared for it by enormous attention to detail, and by organizing networks of prayer across the diocese and beyond, to ensure that the Cathedral was 'filled with prayer, saturated with prayer'.

Ted Hiscocks
Editorial Committee Member

In matters liturgical, Coventry is anything but stuffy or elitist. Of course, the offices are conducted with a certain dignity but never with the nit-picking fussiness found in some places. In its relatively short history it has not adopted a fossilizing approach to worship but one of innovation. From its Consecration in 1962 onwards there has been no lack of experimentation in music: Benjamin Britten and Graham Kendrick have shared the same platform, albeit not at the same time. Rupert Jeff-coat, an outstanding composer of contemporary church music, wrote some of his most imaginative works for the cathedral choir. Paul Leddington Wright and the St Michael's Singers have made Coventry one of the most televised cathedrals in the land, and Kerry Beaumont continues to set an international standard for organ recitals. For some years a liturgical dance group adorned the regular worship. The annual Coventry Jazz Festival, which takes place in the Ruins, often spills over into the Sunday morning worship in the form of a Jazz Mass. The Cathedral also hosts

St Michael's Singers conducted by Paul Leddington Wright being filmed for one of their regular appearances on the BBC's Songs of Praise *in 2000.*

the International Church Music Festival every two years, drawing church musicians from all over the world. One of my frustrations in latter years was not being able to secure entry visas for some of the participants from African countries that the Home Office did not approve of. That sense of loss was shared by all who took part. Nor have the dramatic arts been absent. The Coventry cycle of Mystery Plays* is staged regularly in the Ruins, while younger members of the congregation have from time to time added their own brand of drama to the Sunday worship.

Coventry is probably unique among English cathedrals in its breadth of worship styles. These range from a said service of Holy Communion according to the Book of Common Prayer through to a semi-charismatic, informal Prayer and Praise service. In between are the main choral services of Sung Eucharist and Evensong. An encouraging trend in recent years has been the cross-over of congregational members, growing numbers attending both the choral and informal services. In a diocese that is varied but without ecclesiastical extremes it is good to see the Mother Church modelling similar variety. Are there many cathedrals where a conservative evangelical dean and a modern catholic precentor have worked so well together with such evident mutual love and respect?

A conventional view of the role of cathedrals is that they offer the bishop a base or springboard for mission in the wider diocese. Here, too, there can be no complaints.

Music often fills the Ruins. Visitors pause to listen to the jazz at a festival in support of Amnesty International held in 1991.

It has been my privilege to see the building full to capacity for a number of diocesan gatherings when it was not merely the size of the building that made it the most convenient place to meet; it was also the spiritual context that added a significant and challenging backdrop. The theme of death and resurrection is ever present, whether at an ordination service when parishes flock to support and pray for their new clergy, or when equally large numbers come for a confirmation service. Sometimes numbers can be a problem, even in such a large building. There came a point a few years ago when candidates at the Advent Confirmation had to be limited to 120 for fear of the occasion becoming too much like a production line. Such big events really helped underline the catholic nature of the Church, stretching the understanding of individuals beyond the merely local and parochial to the reality of the Body of Christ throughout space and time. Individuals from distant parishes or from smallish congregations immediately knew themselves to be part of something very much bigger. The Cathedral enabled them to overcome their sense of isolation and gave them a confidence in the wider purposes of God for them and his Church. The cathedral staff were always magnificent in their welcome to these events, not only on the night itself but also at the preparation and follow-up days when the bishops would meet with the candidates in *their own* cathedral.

One of the outstanding happenings of the last decade was the series of addresses on the Ten Commandments given by J. John, an international evangelist and honorary lay canon of Coventry. A sense of fun combined with serious teaching made these evenings hugely exciting, drawing people from parishes right across the diocese, packing their cathedral to overflowing. There is little doubt that under today's more stringent health and safety regulations many would have been turned away at the doors. There was a delightful absence of anything exclusive to one theological style or church tradition. The Cathedral proved an excellent venue for celebrating that great swathe of truth that we share in Christ rather than emphasizing sectarian differences. Much the same could be said for the teaching days linked with the 'Growing Healthy Churches' programme, which ran for five years in the parishes and came to a united focus in the Cathedral. Again and again the Cathedral proved to be the most natural environment for celebrating our oneness in Christ, part of God's people in this part of the West Midlands.

It is not always easy for bishops to exercise their teaching role when their public ministry is largely peripatetic. At the very end of my time in office, the Dean invited me to give a series of Bible readings at the Sunday evening Cathedral Praise service. It is for others to judge how effective they were, but I do have some regrets that I had not made better use of the Cathedral for similar occasions much earlier in my ministry.

The evangelist J. John filled the Cathedral on ten evenings during May to July 2000.

The Cathedral and conflict

Coventry is, perhaps, unusual in that its cathedral is in some senses 'owned' by those of other faith traditions and none, especially those who live in the city. The Ruins, for example, were a natural venue for a spontaneous interfaith prayer vigil on the night of the invasion of Iraq in 2003. The annual service of repentance and reconciliation held in recent years each August to commemorate the final ending of the Second World War brought together ambassadors and senior military men from Japan and Britain as well as 'ordinary' folk who still had memories and scars from that conflict. More recently, the Lord Mayor's Peace Committee has used the Chapel of Unity for a service commemorating the bombing of Hiroshima on 6 August. The juxtaposition of that event with the feast of the transfiguration never ceases to amaze and humble us all. The national significance of Coventry Cathedral was highlighted in March 2000 when the Queen, accompanied by Tony Blair, the then Prime Minister, along with leaders of the main opposition parties, unveiled the national memorial to those who died on the Home Front during that same war.

It is hard to speak of Coventry without at some stage also mentioning the Second World War, not surprising given its remarkable history. In the eyes of some, the Cathedral has been too obsessed with that war. This problem is compounded by the number of visitors, and in particular school groups, who want to see war relics. The old gas masks are sometimes more popular than the tapestry! Much of the older folk memory in the diocese concerns either the bombing of the Cathedral in November 1940, when people watched the flames from miles away, or the procession of the Cross of Nails around the diocese prior to the opening of the new Cathedral in 1962. This procession was designed as an act of consecration for the whole diocese prior to the dedication of the new building. Those heady days are brilliantly captured in Bishop Stephen Verney's book *Fire in Coventry,* republished in 2010. Many parishes bought into that symbol of forgiveness, reconciliation and peace, and they became members of the worldwide Community of the Cross of Nails. Others appear not to have been moved by this symbolic act and remained aloof. This later gave rise to the criticism from some that 'Coventry Cathedral has reconciled the world but divided the diocese'.

Ever since the war there has been a significant succession of Canons for International Ministry, each with their own unique experience, gifting and emphasis. The very first clergy appointment that I made in 1998 was that of Andrew White to be jointly funded by the Cathedral and diocese. Paul Oestreicher had exercised a remarkable ministry in South Africa, as well as in Germany and Eastern Europe, but times were changing; the anti-apartheid struggle and the Cold War were virtually over, and a new sense of direction for this ministry was needed. Very quickly Andrew's grasp of the interreligious conflicts in Israel/Palestine and in the Middle East, and his vision for reconciliation there, was endorsed by the Cathedral community.

In 1999 I was invited, along with Andrew, to lead a small delegation of bishops to Baghdad to report on the effects on ordinary people of the UN sanctions policy. This visit led to some remarkable two-way traffic between Coventry and Baghdad. For example, I shall never forget Paulos, the Chaldean* Archbishop of Mosul (Old Testament Nineveh) standing in the Ruins of the Cathedral and singing first in Aramaic and then in English, 'I have decided to follow Jesus . . . no turning back.' We then shared the Eucharist together and he gladly received the sacrament from me.

THE BENEDICTINE TRADITION AND THE COMMON DISCIPLINE

The first Coventry Cathedral, its ruins extensively excavated as part of Coventry's Phoenix Initiative millennium project, goes back to 1043 when it was founded as a Benedictine Abbey by Leofric, Earl of Mercia, and Godiva, his wife. The Benedictine order had its roots in the Rule of St Benedict, written in the early sixth century for the monks of Monte Cassino Abbey in what is now Italy.

The Benedictine Rule consists of 73 short chapters on how to lead a good Christian life and how to run a monastery. The Rule has had a profound influence on succeeding generations of Christians, initially across Europe but later much further afield. In 1964, Pope Paul VI named St Benedict as patron saint of Europe.

Mindful of these Benedictine origins, Provost Williams set out a Common Discipline for the staff of the Cathedral in 1967. Worship, study, prayer, recreation, food, drink, relationships, money and even sleep were all covered; and 'wives of members . . . invited to accept the spirit of the Discipline'! Other bodies, such as the cathedral congregation and Cross of Nails Centres, were urged to adapt it for their own use. At a personal level everyone was encouraged to have a 'consultant' to help them on their Christian journey.

Crosses of Nails were handed out almost as souvenirs after the war years, but under Provost Williams crosses were usually given to places where there was an active Christian reconciliation ministry, and a relationship with the Cathedral already established. Such relationships quite often relied on personal friendships. However, many Cross of Nails Centres took their linkages seriously, and so began the Community of the Cross of Nails (CCN) with Coventry acting as the 'Mother House'. Today sufficient centres thrive in Germany and the USA for there to be semi-autonomous regional groupings.

So what are the hallmarks of a CCN Centre? A ministry of reconciliation relevant to its own situation, perhaps involving practical projects; a common programme of work, prayer and study; and a common discipline for Christian living. One feature of this discipline which has been widely followed is the Foyer groups. These are random groupings of around eight members who for some six months commit to sharing a simple meal once a month, usually in one another's homes. Their purpose is to enable community members to get to know each other at a deeper level.

Ted Hiscocks
Editorial Committee Member

Canon Andrew White.

He seemed amused when I expressed surprise as well as delight at this since, technically, we were not in communion. He reminded me of the conditions under Saddam Hussein in Iraq and gently chastised me for allowing mental space for 'such trivial historic differences'. In 2008, Paulos was murdered by Muslim extremists for being a Christian, a fate that is increasingly common for that beleaguered minority in 'post-liberation' Iraq.

Later, Justin Welby and Stephen Davis, a lay canon of the Cathedral, found themselves involved in some of the bloody struggles in West Africa, setting up a significant interfaith dialogue and engaging in conflict resolution, often in highly dangerous places. A fuller account of this work will be found in Paul Oestreicher's chapter of this book.

The Diocese of Coventry, as distinct from the Cathedral, while basking in a certain amount of reflected glory, remains largely untouched by this work. In some extreme cases there is almost a sense of resentment that this ministry has such a high profile in the diocese. It is not always appreciated that the funding for the Cathedral's international ministry, including all the project work in Africa and the

Middle East, is raised entirely from external sources and does not cost the diocese a penny. The fact that much of this funding has, in the past, come from the Foreign and Commonwealth Office and other Whitehall departments indicates the value that the government places on this critical ministry. The diocese is only responsible for the cost of the canon's post itself. That misunderstanding has to be clarified almost every year when the diocesan budgets are being discussed.

Various attempts have been made to earth this international ministry in the everyday lives of parishes but the response has been at best patchy.

In January 2001 I signed a companioning agreement, along with Bishop Josiah from Kaduna and Archbishop Mar Severios Malki Murad of the Syriac Orthodox Church of Jerusalem, Jordan and the Holy Lands. This agreement committed our three dioceses to a partnership described in the following terms:

> As companions we wish to follow our Lord Jesus Christ in his Way. We understand our partnership to involve listening to each other, praying for each other, learning from each other, challenging each other. We hope to share in each other's spirituality, culture and life, and in the mission of God's Kingdom together.

A practical outcome of this was a two-way exchange of clergy, and later, in the case of Kaduna, some serious lay involvement in projects like well-digging and the equipping of a field clinic. The sad fact is that, although these links have to a certain extent worked well at the episcopal level, they have never really filtered through into the bloodstream of the diocese. One glorious exception to this is the profound commitment of Jim and Ann Saxton to the Diocese of Kaduna. This couple from Finham visit Nigeria regularly and at one time spent six months in Kaduna, Jim helping to set up IT systems and Ann teaching in the cathedral school. They also collected a significant number of theological books for the cathedral library and regularly arrange for Nigerian teachers to visit the UK. A few individual parishes continue to show great commitment, notably the Mid-Fosse group, led by John Burrell, which has raised money for the digging of wells in rural areas. The diocese has regularly allocated money to facilitate the links, but on the whole they are more theoretical than actual. Had there been more money and human resourcing it might have been different, but in reality the links have not yet matured into anything very substantial.

The Cathedral, as well as the diocese, has had to evaluate the ministry of the International Centre for Reconciliation, not least because most of the larger-than-life characters have now moved on to new ministries elsewhere. When strong personalities are present there is always a danger that long-term fruit may prove to be ephemeral. One positive result of this period of reflection has been a serious attempt on the part of the Cathedral to apply some of the lessons learned on the international scene to the more local needs of the City and Diocese of Coventry. In 2006, a small team led by Justin Welby, now Bishop of Durham, started working successfully with the West Midlands police to defuse community tensions within various immigrant groups in the city. This work is now being taken forward by David Porter, the current Director for Reconciliation Ministry. The same team that was working with the police also provided very effective mediation in one of the larger parishes of the diocese where a dangerous gulf had opened up between the vicar with his perceived inner circle and other parishioners. Short courses on the management and resolution of conflict are now offered to parishes in the diocese.

The Chapel of Unity

The heyday of structured ecumenism was probably the 1960s and 1970s. Those were the days when there was the serious expectation of organic union with other Christian denominations, not least between Anglicans and Methodists. The Anglican–Roman Catholic International Commission (ARCIC*) was soon to raise hopes that at least some of the ancient differences with Roman Catholics, often based on anachronistic misunderstandings, might be resolved. So it comes as no surprise that the Chapel of Unity formed part of the original concept for the new Cathedral. A well-founded biblical doctrine of the Church insisted that we should 'never do alone that which is best done together'. The visible unity of the Church was an essential prelude to the fulfilling of Jesus' prayer in John 17 'that the world might believe'. Disunity was seen as sinful and scandalous. The theory still holds true, of course, but theological fashions change and something of the original passion has been lost.

It might also be argued that something of the original vision for the Chapel of Unity was either lost or, perhaps, never fully understood. In the early days the Chapel had a full-time Free Church minister, Geoffrey Beck, who was, to all intents and purposes, a member of the cathedral staff. However, the fuller vision was not simply about various denominations coming together for worship; it also envisaged a social service centre, ministering to the community ecumenically. Such a centre was even part of the architectural competition but was abandoned on economic grounds. The ecumenical movement and its dream had always stood on twin pillars: faith and order, and life and work. The Chapel without the 'life and work' pillar left the vision unfulfilled. Something of the spirit of the original vision was maintained by the dogged commitment of various lay people, notably Dr Allen Edwards, whose prophetic witness to social justice, while not always sitting comfortably with the cathedral establishment, nevertheless symbolized the non-existent community service centre. Chris Burch, during his time as Precentor, also did much to model this essential fusion of faith and works through his chairing of the City Council's Anti-Poverty Forum, while at the same time offering practical support to those ministering in areas of severe social deprivation. The distinctions between cathedral, city and diocese can often be usefully blurred.

Christian people on the whole no longer attend ecumenical gatherings and much of the steam for organizational church unity has run out. To many, therefore, the very existence of the Chapel of Unity is at best anachronistic and at worst a nuisance. Technically not part of the Cathedral proper, the Chapel of Unity's independent constitution and at times its maverick actions are an irritant to the smooth running of the Cathedral. Many will recall the occasion when Vincent Nichols, then Roman Catholic Archbishop of Birmingham and now translated to Westminster, came to speak in the Chapel only to find that the large turnout meant the meeting had to overflow into the Cathedral proper. For much of the time, though, the Chapel is used by an ageing congregation of ecumenical enthusiasts, still amazingly faithful to the vision but rapidly dwindling in strength.

Some would argue that its very raison d'être was subverted from the beginning because Bill Williams invited Christians of every denomination to receive communion at the cathedral altar, contrary to the practice of the Church of England at the time. However, others would applaud that gesture, seeing it as prophetic and certainly in advance of its time. That spirit of Godly anarchy appeals to those whose patience with the hierarchy has run out and who long to break free from the constraints of institutions which seem to be more beholden to law than to grace. A good current example of this would be the movement in Germany known as 'Wir sind Kirche' ('We are Church'), where the rules forbidding intercommunion between Catholics and Lutherans are deliberately flouted in the belief that only a grass-roots rebellion is likely to liberate Jesus' disciples from anachronistic disciplines. Such actions bring into focus the ongoing question as to whether the shared Eucharist is the ultimate goal of unity or whether the bread and wine are meant to be food for the journey.

But the Chapel of Unity is still there, in the Cathedral but not of it. There can be no doubt that a radical reappraisal is needed if the Chapel is to find a new purpose for the future. But the urgent need for Christians to be one has not gone away. Could the Chapel of Unity perhaps have something to say to the current dilemmas facing the Church of England and the wider Anglican Communion? Ecumenism is, of course, not simply a matter for separated denominations. The C of E itself has for centuries held together Christian disciples who have differing understandings of what it means to follow Jesus. Church history shows that breaking away from the mainstream is rarely the long-term solution to internal disputes. The unity of a diocese under the leadership of the bishop is a principle that was severely shaken for some by the ordination of women to the priesthood. It will be shaken even more vigorously by the consecration of women bishops.[1] For many, the acceptance of openly gay or lesbian clergy is a step too far, a watershed that demands separation. Yet this too is an issue that will not go away.

It is, of course, stating the obvious to say that most of these current divisions are not primarily about gender issues but are caused by confusion over the issue of authority, and specially the authority of the Bible. Hermeneutics* is the technical term for the disciplines which shape how we, in twenty-first century, are to read texts that in some cases go back 3,000 years. It was in the course of one of the private consultations with Anglican Primates that I hosted with the Cathedral that the idea of an international project on hermeneutics was born. This has now evolved into a very successful study course, 'The Bible in the Life of the Church', which David Moxon pioneered. David is the Archbishop of New Zealand, and it was in the Chapel of Unity that we celebrated the Eucharist that was the culmination of our time together. It seems fitting that Justin Welby, then Dean of Liverpool, and I, in so-called retirement, were asked by the Archbishop of Canterbury to continue something of this work. We are two of six Pastoral Visitors to the Anglican Communion who visit various provinces at the invitation of the local primate. We are called to function as conciliators and advisers in situations of particular tension across the Communion. Central to this work is the attempt to keep dialogue going between various factions with a view to maintaining the highest degree of communion possible in situations of disagreement or tension. To date, this work has taken Visitors to the United States, Canada and various African provinces. In many respects it is a direct fruit of the long-established ministry of Coventry Cathedral and very much in keeping with the original spirit of the Chapel of Unity.

How is it possible to preserve the unity of the Spirit in the bond of peace when so many issues are surfacing that point to fragmentation rather than healing? Could the Chapel of Unity contribute to this process by being a place to hear once again St Paul's plea to 'let the same mind be in us which was also in Christ Jesus' (Philippians 5.5)? This 'mind' is not necessarily about agreement in all things; rather, it is a call to humility and servanthood after the pattern of Jesus who emptied himself and became obedient to death on the cross. It enables Jesus' disciples to do what St Paul urges elsewhere, to 'prefer one another in love' (Romans 12.10). This is what is to inform our relationships within Christ's family. The need is not so much for a fresh vision as for one that is refreshed by the Spirit, one that will capture the hearts of the younger generation and restore something of its original purpose to this rather odd adjunct to the Cathedral.

It may be said the one small step towards internal unity was taken in 2003 when the diocesan and cathedral administrations started to share the same office space on Hill Top. Traditionally quite separate, there was the hope that this move would

Youell House (named for Cathedral benefactor Alf Youell – inset) was built over the remains of the chapter house of the Benedictine Abbey – Coventry's first cathedral – as part of the City's Millennium Project known as the Phoenix Initiative, and it houses Cathedral and Diocesan offices.

not only lead to a more streamlined and cost-effective operation but that it would also incarnate a very important theological principle. Interestingly, other dioceses have now begun to take up this idea. While recognizing the need for clearly defined boundaries in such an operation, I am firmly of the opinion that there is yet much more to be done in the sharing of resources and expertise that will meet the criterion of 'never doing alone that which is best done together'.

A significant birthday

The need for regular self-examination is obvious both for individual ministries and for corporate institutions. A birthday is no bad time to do this. In his sermon at the twenty-fifth anniversary celebrations of the Cathedral in 1987 the then Archbishop of York, John Habgood, preached on Isaiah 40.31 – 'Those who wait for the Lord shall renew their strength, they shall mount up with wings like eagles, they shall run and not be weary, they shall walk and not faint.' He suggested that the time had come for Coventry to 'learn how to walk'. There seems to be something in the DNA of Coventry Cathedral that enables it to fly high with people and projects that are exciting, spectacular and often groundbreaking. The Cathedral has always had a prophetic role in relation to the diocese, the nation and, indeed, the world. This prophetic edge must never be lost. But these excursions into the stratosphere always need to be balanced by times of sober assessment and evaluation. We do well to remember that whether we are walking, running or flying, the secret of fruitful discipleship, of effective Kingdom-building, is 'waiting on the Lord who renews our strength'.

Self-examination is not much use unless it leads to improvement and change. That is a task for the current generation to work on, not those of us who have had their time and moved on. But on behalf of past generations let me assure the cathedral community that we do not forget you, and long to see a renewed flourishing under God of this very special place with its very special people.

Thanks be to God!

* Denotes an entry in the Glossary

Note

1 The Cathedral's support for the ordained ministry of women found symbolic expression internationally when the first Anglican woman diocesan bishop worldwide, Penny Jamieson from Dunedin in New Zealand, and the first woman Lutheran bishop worldwide, Maria Jepsen from Hamburg in Germany, were present at the ordination of 35 women as priests in the Cathedral on Saturday 23 April 1994.

8 ONE MAN'S LIFE IN THE CATHEDRAL

The View from the Pew 1962–2012

'ADAM'

'The Cathedral is appealing for help with all the visitors who've turned up. Why don't you volunteer?'

It was 26 May 1962 – the day after the Consecration.

The speaker looked across the room at Adam who sat at the family table slowly eating a piece of cake. Adam's mother was reading aloud from that day's Coventry Evening Telegraph, *hoping to catch the interest of her teenage son.*

Adam mulled it over. In recent years a visit to the ruined shell of the old Cathedral had been a highlight when showing family visitors around Coventry city centre. During those visits Adam had witnessed the gradual birth of the new Cathedral building as its bright orange sandstone walls rose slowly alongside the old.

Mum's words struck a chord. A Junior Member of Warwick Road Congregational Church, Adam had only ever been inside an Anglican church as a tourist. But if help was needed, why not give it a try – even if it meant working for a denomination different from his own. After all, the visitors were coming to Coventry, his city, and no true Coventrian would want the visitors to leave with a bad impression.

Adam had watched the Consecration Service on television. The news programmes had shown a helicopter placing the flèche* on the roof. He had read beforehand about the controversies over the tapestry and the modern architecture of the new building. Yes, if he volunteered he could see what all the fuss is about as well as do his city a good turn.

Adam walked to the Cathedral. He pushed his way through bustling crowds of eager tourists who jammed the Cathedral Bookshop. Within minutes Judith Barnes, the manageress, placed him behind a shop counter selling cathedral guide books and souvenirs.

Adam did not know then that this was a decision that would change his life. A decision that would lead to a deepening of his personal faith and to life experiences in Coventry and around the world of which he would never have dreamed.

Adam joined the community of Coventry Cathedral.

Coventry Cathedral community in 1962

The Consecration of Coventry Cathedral on 25 May 1962 was preceded by massive publicity. The old Cathedral Church of St Michael, Coventry, had been the first (and, in the event, the only) cathedral to be destroyed by bombing during the Second World War. News of the November 1940 Blitz on Coventry resounded around the world in its day, so it was not surprising that the dedication of the new Cathedral received similar national and international news treatment. After all, Coventry Cathedral was the first twentieth-century English cathedral to be designed by a single architect, and then to be built and consecrated in his lifetime.

Early in May the BBC showed the film *Act of Faith*, telling the Cathedral's historic story. The Consecration Service itself was broadcast live on BBC television and was reported by news organizations internationally. Interest in the new Cathedral and anticipation of its impact were so great that the BBC installed by way of gift a permanent nave floodlighting capacity for future broadcasts – a lighting system that is still in use 50 years later.

The publicity was bound to attract visitors – but nobody anticipated the size of the response. From the day of the Consecration there were queues of curious visitors anxious to glimpse the interior of the building. The visitors were so keen that many were prepared to wait an hour or longer to enter. Visitor numbers were so great that at first they walked in a circle around the nave between services in a huge crocodile, four abreast, at the rate of 2,000 an hour. The side chapels were roped off to ease the flow. In 1962 it was estimated that 3 million visitors passed through the Cathedral in the first 12 months. The aisle carpets that initially protected the black Kerrymount marble in the floor wore out under this pressure and were discarded after six weeks' use.

By each afternoon during the summer months the queue of visitors ran from the Cathedral entrance up the length of St Michael's Avenue, around Holy Trinity Church and doubled back on itself. One of the duties of the vergers was to create a gap in the visitor queue at the top of St Michael's Avenue some 45 minutes before a service so that the visitors knew which of them would gain access to the building to

For ten years after the Consecration tourists filled the Cathedral Porch and often queued for two hours or more at the height of summer along St Michael's Avenue before they entered the building. © Richard Sadler FRPS.

The St Michael's needleworkers (formed originally by Judith Poole in the 1960s) maintain the robes and the kneelers as well as creating original items for use in the Cathedral.

look round as tourists before the visitor doors closed and the service doors opened to the congregation.

As 1962 ended, Provost Williams looked back with some amazement at a level of interest that no one had foreseen:

> The Bookshop has provided material to satisfy the vast demand of visitors for material. So guileless were we in preparing the stock for the Bookshops that, thinking we were very adventurous, we prepared a stock in May which we thought would last for two months. The public appetite consumed it in less than a week![1]

Coping with thousands of visitors required great efforts by a large cathedral community that was not only committed to that task but also prepared to do something about it.

Cathedral guides

An army of cathedral guides interpreted the building for the visitors as part of a guides' organization that was military in its precision. Training had begun in January 1962 with a series of lectures on the building, covering the works of art, its history and meaning. Lectures covered tactics for dealing with visitors. Potential helpers were told that guides and stewards should never tell tourist visitors that the Cathedral was 'Closed for a service' – the Cathedral was always 'Open for a service, and if you wish to look round you may do so afterwards'.

It had been anticipated quite early in 1962 that guided tours would be impossible, so a rota was devised that covered ten hours a day and identified twelve guiding stations around the nave. Whenever a new rota appeared, guides rushed to book their favourite guiding station for the duty period that they could give.

Visitors came to Coventry Cathedral for many different reasons. Some were interested in the modern architecture, or in wartime history, or the message of reconciliation, or liturgy – or just to see what the fuss was about. But no matter what the reason for their visit, their presence presented an opportunity for mission and outreach. The guides recognized the importance of their interpretative work in a ministry using the building as a teaching aid of the Christian faith.

> A cathedral has many duties to perform, with a primary obligation to the diocese of which it is the Mother Church, and the city and community within which it is situated.
>
> But this summer has made it abundantly clear that there is also a ministry to the visitors, which is a major responsibility.

Everything must be done not only to welcome them, but to interpret as clearly as possible, the Cathedral's particular witness to the basic truths of the Christian Gospel.[2]

Chain of Prayer

During the summer months of the tourist season the nave hummed with the noise of shuffling feet, the buzz of conversation, the cries of children and, sometimes competing with that volume, the sound of cathedral guides interpreting the building to the moving line of visitors. While all that activity carried on, at the centre of the nave there was always at least one person kneeling in prayer; someone in the middle of all this excitement meditating and oblivious to the surrounding activity.

The Coventry Cathedral Chain of Prayer was started by Canon Stephen Verney, the Diocesan Missioner. In February 1962 he wrote to every incumbent in the diocese asking them to approach their congregations to recruit people willing to spend just half an hour each month in prayer in their new cathedral. Over 300 volunteers came forward from all corners of Warwickshire – they travelled from Wootton Wawen and Stratford, Nuneaton and Rugby, every point of the compass – in a Chain of Prayer that was co-ordinated by Leslie Bartlett.

Their aim was to offer to God continuous prayer throughout the day – prayers of thanksgiving, prayer for the needs of the world, prayers for each other. The kneeling figures in the Cathedral nave were a reminder to visitors that the building is a house of prayer and not an art museum. The sight of someone praying in the nave was itself a witness that helped and encouraged others to pick up a cathedral prayer leaflet and kneel before God. The Chain of Prayer also united the family of the diocese in a continuing act of prayer for one another.

Strangely, those who prayed in the centre of the nave experienced a greater sense of privacy there than in the Chapel of Christ in Gethsemane, the Cathedral chapel originally designed for private prayer. The conversations of the visitors were more distant and less intrusive.

Cathedral stewards

Many of the visitors who shuffled round the Cathedral as tourists joined the congregation at services and often filled the building to capacity. Throughout 1962 there was standing room only at Saturday Evensongs at 5 pm, a situation that continued through the 1960s. All seats were taken and people stood in the aisles to hear the cathedral choir – up to 2,000 people in what today would be viewed as a health and safety nightmare.

These massive congregations called into action from the cathedral community another army of volunteers – the cathedral stewards. This group of local volunteers, drawn largely from the cathedral congregation, was formed in 1958 to assist the events that were then being held in the Cathedral Ruins. In the new Cathedral building, 20 cathedral stewards were needed for each special service. Stewards were needed to help with seating, with the offertory and they were also trained to deal with evacuation emergencies. At each service the stewards were supported by the attendance of at least one of the five cathedral churchwardens. In the early years the churchwarden on duty was often John Collier, the Provost's Warden, whose eagle eyes could allegedly spot trouble at a hundred yards.

In the months immediately following the Consecration, special services were held for every kind of group, and the stewards' duties were very heavy. There were services for children in schools throughout Coventry, for church schools, for Sunday schools, for Commonwealth young people, local government representatives, Mothers Union, rural deaneries, Christian Endeavour, the medical profession, the armed forces, pensioners, Young Wives, social services, Rotary International, architects and so on.

Joseph Poole, the Cathedral's Precentor, created masterpieces of liturgy to suit each group. On 8 June 1962 worship was offered at the 'Service of the Arts' by Edric Connor in song, with Betty Lawrence at the piano and Curly Clayton on guitar, by the cathedral choir, by the Orchestra da Camera and by students of the Royal Ballet School directed by Dame Ninette de Valois. This was a celebration of the arts of poetry, drama and music, attended by senior school pupils from across the city – a fine example of Joseph Poole's mastery of liturgy.

Some days there were special services in the morning, the afternoon and the evening. There were so many special services in the months following the Consecration that by August 1962 there was a visible fog in the air of the nave caused by a build-up of the smoke from the large sanctuary candles. For several months the six candles mounted on their Hans Coper candlesticks either side of the altar had burned almost continuously.

The foggy atmosphere exposed a minor design defect of the building. The original design relied on a flow of air into the nave from the doors of the great west screen, but that flow alone proved to be insufficient. A year later ventilation fans were installed in the nave roof and in the undercroft, and the problem has never returned.

Practical duties

Behind the scenes and away from the very public duties of the guides and stewards, members of the cathedral community tackled many practical jobs around the building and its offices. Coping with the sheer numbers of visitors created a whole range of different tasks, and the congregation responded willingly to this challenge. In his summary of the summer's activities, tribute was paid by Canon Patey:

> This hectic Cathedral Summer has brought into being an operation of voluntary service of the highest possible order. Men and women and young people have given themselves with sacrificial generosity as stewards, ushers, odd-job men, secretaries, removers, guides, booksellers, caterers and much else. A gigantic undertaking has been initiated, on the strength of voluntary work of rare calibre and devotion.[3]

Paul Skelton, a cathedral volunteer, uses his carpentry skills to repair Cathedral furniture. This practical help was in the tradition of volunteers going back before the Consecration.

THE FRIENDS OF COVENTRY CATHEDRAL

In 1918, St Michael's parish church became the 'new' Coventry Cathedral. Sixteen years later, in 1934, Coventry joined a popular new movement among cathedrals to set up its own 'Friends of . . .' association, an independent charity with subscribing members who elect a governing council. They receive a newsletter and can join in a programme of events. All funds raised are used to support projects at the Cathedral.

The first gift to the Cathedral, of £80, was made in 1935 for two chorister scholarships. Over the years varied gifts have been made, including major items such as the open-air stage in the Ruins, the Lady Chapel screen, commissioning of a 'tolling bell' in the tower, and many smaller items from crockery, shrubs for the gardens, to batteries for the PA system!

John Viner, Secretary of the Friends of Coventry Cathedral, presenting new surplices to the cathedral choir for its tour of the USA in 1984. This is one of many gifts by the Friends since the organization was founded in 1934. © Edward Ockenden.

In 1934, the Friends of Coventry Cathedral was rooted in parishes across the new diocese, encouraging individuals to make an enduring link with their Mother Church, but within six years, the Friends had lost their cherished cathedral in one devastating night of bombing. The enforced adoption of a radical new building and ministry outlook must have taken a bit of befriending for some members, but under the media spotlight, membership grew to 1,500 as the new Cathedral was consecrated in 1962.

Dynamic ministers organized activities for people to join directly. As such, the role of the Friends as an independent support club gradually declined. While many cathedrals developed their Friends at the core of fundraising efforts, Coventry set up a Development Trust for this purpose in 1991. This further diminished the distinctive value and role of the association, and the fortunes of the Friends have fluctuated with the vision and energy of a willing core of organizing volunteers. The year 2008 marked a low point when folding the association was seriously contemplated. However, this moment of crisis prompted a positive revival in fortunes. The seventy-fifth anniversary in 2009 was a true occasion for celebration. The Friends is currently enjoying a positive growth in membership, activities and income. Giving to the Cathedral is at an all-time high.

Against a backdrop of growing financial challenge, the Cathedral needs all the supporting friends it can find, and the true value of nurturing long-term relationships through a vibrant Friends of Coventry Cathedral is again being recognized.

Peter Woodward, Chairman of the Friends of Coventry Cathedral (2008–)
Friends of Coventry Cathedral: www.friendsofcoventrycathedral.org.uk

An educated laity

In 1962 the guides and the stewards were the obvious and visible signs of cathedral community activity on the nave floor. Hidden from sight elsewhere in the building and beyond in the city, the Cathedral's ministry of engagement with the world was carried forward by the cathedral community in many differing ways. Some examples:

- Each month some 200 people attended the Congregation Meeting in the lecture hall. They heard talks on topical issues and caught up with news of the latest initiatives taken by staff members. In the early years of the Cathedral's life the staff team was learning with the congregation about the role of a cathedral in the twentieth century. The staff took the opportunity of the monthly meeting to explain their excitement. The meetings allowed Provost Williams to share his inspiring international vision with the community as he developed the Cathedral's unique ministry of reconciliation.

- Between those monthly meetings and in addition to many special services there were lectures and talks to attend. In 1962 topics included 'Fundamentals of the Christian Faith' (a series anticipating the Alpha courses) and 'Men, Women and God', ten talks examining personal relationships at all ages, family life and marriage.

- Each week five or six hundred people attended Saturday evening organ recitals by internationally known organists who came from the Vatican, from Notre Dame, Paris, and from all over the world.

- The Cathedral's Drama Director, Martyn Colborn, arranged a programme of plays, workshops and poetry readings.

- Each month the Missionary Committee organized a different display by an established charity on the west screen noticeboards with a collection taken in support.

- The Cathedral's Film Society showed the occasional feature film, and George Clark, Works Superintendent, trained volunteer projectionists in the mysteries of the lecture hall's 16mm projector eventually housed in a great wooden 'tardis'. On Saturday afternoons, visitors could freely attend one of two showings of the John Laing Film Unit documentary on the construction of the new Cathedral, built by that firm.

- There were cathedral home groups throughout the city – Bible study groups, a healing ministry group, a science and religion group, a group at Stephen Verney's house for university students home on vacation, a Friday night youth group led by Nigel White. The Junior Church teachers met to plan their Sunday school programme, and the choirboys' parents gathered to plan their fundraising strategy for future choir trips abroad. The cathedral bread-makers (founded by Joseph Poole and Mary Edwards) met to support new members who were struggling with the recipe for loaves to use at the Communion on Sunday.

- A hospitality roll from among the cathedral community (later co-ordinated for some years by Gwladys Tonge) provided accommodation that the staff could offer to visitors from distant churches with which the Cathedral was forming links. Girls from the National Cathedral School in Washington and young people from the diocese of Alabama visited regularly through the 1960s. The visitors not only helped the Cathedral to manage its visitors, but they also helped their hosts to think internationally.

Provost Williams spoke regularly at the monthly meetings. His appreciation of the breadth of all this activity made each listener feel part of an all-encompassing vision of the way Christianity can work in the world. The cathedral community was living and working in the city and far beyond just as its predecessor community of Benedictine monks had been concerned for the whole of life in the eleventh century.

Adam joined the army of cathedral guides with enthusiasm. His name was put forward by Ken Fell (a pre-war cathedral chorister) and he was vetted by John Gallois, chief guide. It was tactfully suggested that he should remove his Christian CND badge while on duty to avoid unnecessary confrontations, and he was handed the guides' lecture notes to study before taking up his duties.

Adam's favourite guiding positions were behind the Bishop's throne or in the Lady Chapel. During school terms he could manage guiding one evening a week after school until the Cathedral closed at 7 pm. Then he would help the duty verger to secure the building for the night.

One afternoon in term-time Adam came to the Cathedral with his group of Bablake School sixth-formers to attend the Service of the Arts. He started to attend the 10.30 Communion, and Bob Turner, another volunteer, helped him to unravel some of the mysteries of Anglican liturgy with which he was unfamiliar. What on earth was a 'ninefold Kyrie'*?

Adam joined the stewards. It was hard work but it also enabled him to attend concerts by the Berlin Philharmonic, the Vienna Boys Choir, Yehudi Menuhin and other leading musicians. He met a variety of people whose offerings contributed to the Cathedral's life, such as Dame Flora Robson (actress), Harold Ratcliffe (master mason), Robert Harris (actor), Patrick Reyntiens (glass artist), Dorothy Tutin (actress), Anton Dolin (ballet choreographer) and 1960s pop stars Adam Faith, Cilla Black and Cliff Richard, among others.

Adam changed. His eyes were opened and he realized that his faith had applications in every aspect of his life. Being a Christian was not just a question of Bible study and attendance at church. His faith had real-time applications at home, at school, at work and across national boundaries.

For Adam, Christianity suddenly made sense.

The origins of the Cathedral community

Today the Cathedral has a roll set up in accordance with the Cathedrals Measure 1999 to include members of the congregation, all volunteers and staff. The total congregation membership is 310.

In 1962 the equivalent electoral roll listed almost 1,000 members. In addition to the members of the electoral roll there were several hundred additional volunteers and active supporters of the ministry. These were people who did voluntary work in some capacity at the Cathedral but who worshipped in their own church, possibly of a different denomination. Active supporters of the ministry in 1962 numbered almost 1,500.

Such a difference in numbers between then and now merits examination.

In the 1960s the Coventry Cathedral electoral roll was not simply a formal legal requirement of ecclesiastical law. In the Cathedral it was used proactively as a membership register for active members of the cathedral community. Membership was a sign of personal commitment to the ministry. It was not exclusive and Anglican members could at the same time retain their membership of the equivalent electoral roll of their own parish church. The Cathedral had inherited an electoral roll from its origins as the former parish church of St Michael, Coventry, which had been its status until the founding of the Coventry Diocese in 1918.

The diocesan boundaries are largely the same as the boundaries of the traditional county of Warwickshire, going from Atherstone in the north to Long Compton and Shotteswell on the Oxfordshire border in the south. Members of the modern community roll are drawn largely from within the city of Coventry and its immediate vicinity. It was quite different in 1962 when the Cathedral drew large numbers of regular supporters from much farther afield in the diocese, from Nuneaton (10 miles), Stratford-upon-Avon (20 miles) and so on.

What was the reason for this widespread support across the diocese? The building of the new Cathedral received a great deal of publicity in the build-up to the Consecration, and this publicity inevitably sparked off curiosity in some people sufficient for them to visit. But by itself that does not explain why large numbers of people came to Coventry from outside the city and committed themselves to the ministry of Coventry Cathedral.

The answer lies partly in what happened in the wider diocese before the Consecration. Bishop Cuthbert Bardsley took up his appointment as Bishop of Coventry in 1956. He was a man on a lifetime mission. He saw his role as Bishop 'to relate the mind of God to the needs of a very needy world, and to proclaim God's message in terms that will be understandable to people who are bewildered by the world as they find it'. He came to Coventry just as building work started on the walls of the new Cathedral. One of his important early tasks was to appoint a staff team of clergy for the new building.

In 1958 announcements were made of the appointments: Bill Williams (Provost), Joseph Poole (Precentor), Simon Phipps (Industrial Chaplain), Edward Patey (Canon Residentiary) and Stephen Verney (Diocesan Missioner). This was the core team that worked together to forge the future pattern of the ministry of reconciliation at Coventry Cathedral.

Bishop Bardsley invited Provost Williams as team leader 'to do one of the most worthwhile pieces of work in the Church of England'. Provost Williams was a surprising choice. He was far from being an establishment figure, and in many ways was quite the opposite. He came to Coventry from St Mary's Church, Southampton. He had been brought up in South Africa and on his arrival in England had found an established church that he felt behaved more like a gentlemen's club than a tool of God's mission. This view had a profound impact upon the formative years of the new team ministry.

Provost Williams and the new Coventry team spelled out the limitations of our unchanging, traditional parish system in a society that has been changing constantly since the industrial revolution of the eighteenth and nineteenth centuries. Provost Williams spoke of the ways in which people had abandoned the geographical 'community' as traditionally defined, and had adopted new models of community – at work, in leisure pursuits, in shared-interest groups, in common employment needs, in common loyalties of different kinds and so on. While these changes had taken place all around it, the Church of England had remained untouched by them and had failed to adapt.

> The Church has a vast and increasing need to understand these other communities, so as to understand more clearly the pressures under which individual people have to live. There is clearly a pressing need for the Church to have areas of ministry specially focused upon these special sources of pressure.
>
> The parish is not the only unit for the Church's ministry. It is and always will be an essential complement to the whole range of the Church's concern for people, but in the modern age it represents only a limited penetration into the life of twentieth century man.[4]

These thoughts were shared by the cathedral team as they sought to make their cathedral 'an instrument of strategic coherent thinking and activity'.[5]

Stephen Verney was a team member as well as Vicar of Leamington Hastings and Diocesan Missioner, becoming a canon residentiary in 1964. After his appointment as Diocesan Missioner in 1958 he met regularly with groups of fellow clergy in the diocese. Three years before the dedication of the new building, Canon Verney found groups of clergy in the diocese who wanted to know how to prepare themselves and their parishioners for the Consecration. In his own words, 'a consecrated Cathedral demands a consecrated people'.

The clergy met together regularly to ask what they should do. Before long they were finding God together and a course of action emerged. They grew in friendship between themselves and invited groups of laity to join them in prayer, study and fellowship. In the year before the Consecration this movement was joined by whole parishes across the diocese, encouraged by Bishop Bardsley and the cathedral staff team.

The movement of the Holy Spirit through the diocese reached a climax on the eve of the Consecration. For 40 days and nights, the Cathedral Cross of Nails had made a 100-mile pilgrimage by foot from parish to parish across the diocese. On the eve of the Consecration it was carried from St John's Church, Fleet Street, Coventry, to the entrance of the Cathedral Ruins. Hundreds of people gathered to see Bishop Bardsley hand over the Cross to Provost Williams who carried it into the new building and placed it in the high-altar cross, where it remains today. 'It seemed to bring with it into the Cathedral the prayers of the whole diocese. The Cross of Nails was the cross triumphant. Christ reigned from the tree.'[6]

The question being asked of the many pilgrims across the diocese was, 'What is the Spirit saying to the Churches?' The answer for many of them was to act immediately to support the ministry of the Cathedral as it reached out towards the new communities of our society that lay beyond their local parish boundaries.

The cathedral team of clergy made the building a place of Christian experiment, guided by the Holy Spirit and involving lay people in all aspects of its ministry. This exciting approach attracted support in great numbers from lay people from other denominations as well as from across the diocese. It was those people who swelled the numbers of the cathedral community in 1962 and made the building such a powerhouse.

The clergy encouraged daily worship. The Cathedral's early morning Communion services followed by breakfast were not timed for clergy comfort, but were held at 7 am, 7.30 am and (on Tuesdays) at 6.30 am – arranged in this way to facilitate worship before the start of the working day. The Bishop often attended on Mondays.

Canon Verney tells the story of the 'consecrated people' in his book *Fire in Coventry*. It is a book that tells of the work of the Holy Spirit in Coventry Diocese in a way so inspiring that the book was reprinted and redistributed throughout the diocese by the current Bishop of Coventry after his installation in 2009. It is the story of the Holy Spirit at work in the modern age.

In the 1960s, even if you were not an active supporter of the Cathedral's ministry, you would have been aware of the Cathedral's activities through the local media outlets. In Coventry, the local papers regularly reported not only the Cathedral's activities but also gave publicity to what was said from the pulpit. Here there were Christians who did not cut themselves off from the world in inward-looking religious piety but people who spoke out on matters of concern that were relevant to the person in the street.

The *Coventry Evening Telegraph* regularly reported sermons that tackled contemporary issues. Visiting preachers knew that their message might be reported and they chose their subjects accordingly. Press reports of this sort continued for the next ten years, petering off slowly towards the end of that time. A side effect of this reporting was the encouragement of local interest and support for the Cathedral. It helped to maintain community numbers. The changes since that time in the attitudes of our society towards the Church are brought home by the contrast between today's lack of interest in religion and a selection of 1960s' headlines from the *Coventry Evening Telegraph*:

'SCROOGE RIGHT ABOUT XMAS SAYS CANON' – Canon William Purcell, BBC Midlands Director of Religious Broadcasting, speaking about seasonal 'humbug'

'WARWICK RD. MINISTER ON "SIX" FAILURE' – Revd David Dale, Minister of Warwick Road Congregational Church, on Christian attitudes towards the breakdown of Common Market discussions

'CATHEDRAL SERMON ON THALIDOMIDE AGONY' – Canon Edward Patey

'REV SIMON PHIPPS ON VALUE OF CRISIS' – Revd Simon Phipps, Bishop's Industrial Chaplain, on the crises of conflict in the UK arising from its mixed economy

'WORLD LIVES IN CONSTANT FEAR – BISHOP BLOOM' – Bishop Anthony Bloom, head of the Russian Orthodox Church in England, on international tension

'PROVOST ON PROBLEM OF "KEY CHILDREN"' – Provost Williams on working parents

'CATHEDRAL SERMON ON BEHAVIOUR OF YOUNG PEOPLE' – Revd J. O. C. Alleyne, Chaplain of Clare College, Cambridge

'COVENTRY MINISTER ON NEEDS OF HUNGRY' – Revd R. J. Hamper, Minister of Queen's Road Baptist Church

'"STUDY POLITICAL MANIFESTOES" – CHRISTIANS URGED' – Revd R. J. M. Collins, Minister of Wyken Congregational Church

Adam, the first student verger in 1963.

Adam spent much of his spare time helping the cathedral vergers. John Wickens, Provost's Verger, taught him the intricacies of maniples* and dalmatics*, the colours of the church seasons and showed him how to lay out vestments. He held the camera bag while Richard Sadler photographed the building for new cathedral guide books.

There was fun too on social outings for the vergers and their helpers. On a visit to see Becket at the Gaumont Cinema, Birmingham, the scene when the four knights hammered at the door of Canterbury Cathedral was greeted with suppressed laughter at the comment, 'They wouldn't have got in if John Collier was on the door!'

In 1963 Adam was summoned to meet Provost Williams who invited him to become the Cathedral's first Student Verger. He took up this post at the same time as the appointment of John Cook, the replacement for Rex Jarvis, second verger. Adam always wore his Coventry cassock with pride.

Why a cathedral congregation?

At the time of Coventry's Consecration it was not automatically the case that cathedrals would have a permanent congregation where lay people had a say in their running. Some ancient cathedrals were administered by a chapter of clergy who led worship each day, morning and night, whether or not there was a lay congregation present. Unlike more recent foundations, those cathedrals had no geographical parish from which to draw a congregation. So if a cathedral tried to recruit a congregation it risked the accusation of poaching from the adjoining parishes. It was a commonly held view in the wider Church that cathedrals existed as venues for big diocesan occasions, and apart from that they were there to add to the rivers of prayer that had flowed upwards from them for centuries past.

This was not the case in Coventry. Provost Williams and the Coventry team thought differently. They wanted to achieve effective outgoing work, and that requires a formal and committed congregation to succeed.

The congregation through the years

In the early 1960s, members of the congregation involved themselves in all aspects of the Cathedral's ministry. There was an annual parish meeting, but the administration was generally handled through the monthly congregational meetings and occasional full-day conferences. Many of the Cathedral's office staff (numbering 82 at its peak) were fully integrated into congregation activities. This helped communication both ways, and enabled enthusiasms to be shared. At the end of 1964 the congregation members took stock of their structure and purpose in a series of meetings in which they sought ways to create a deeper unity as well as more active service. A group structure emerged from these meetings with some groups studying, some researching, others doing ecumenical work or international work or social work and so on.

> Such a group structure is beautifully flexible. Like the cells of a body, each group can be a different shape and adapted to a different task. They can meet often, or less often, as they wish, but each becomes a centre of Christian life . . . this is the original structure of the Christian Church which we are re-discovering. It is the structure for unity and service which Jesus Himself adopted, when He called twelve 'that they might be with Him, and that He might send them forth'.[7]

The excitement of the Cathedral's experiments in ministry and the publicity that they received continued to attract new members to the Cathedral throughout the 1960s. Peter Spink was appointed Chaplain to the cathedral community in 1968. To strengthen bonds between members he initiated 'houseparties' at home and overseas so that for a period of two or three days members could meet together without the pressures of daily involvement and learn together. In the year after his appointment his reflections on his time in Coventry acknowledged the importance of reaching out to life beyond the church walls:

> Those who worship in a cathedral normally elect to do so for particular reasons. In the case of our own Cathedral, my first eight months here have taught me that a very powerful motivating factor is a desire to be effective witnesses in contemporary society: this in a situation where there is opportunity through a team ministry to bring witness to bear at all levels of society.[8]

Not everyone in the cathedral congregation felt comfortable at first with Canon Spink's 'houseparties'. These were gatherings that went beyond the cell groups of earlier years, and broke down individual personal barriers that had been easier to

A REVOLUTIONARY CONSTITUTION

If the modern architectural lines of Coventry Cathedral were revolutionary then so was its constitution. In the post-war period there was no standard constitution for cathedrals in the UK, and the team led by Provost Williams created something appropriate to the twentieth century.

They believed that the most effective way for a cathedral to work is to maximize the use of the different skills of both clergy and laity. The strengths of the clergy lie in their skills of ministry; lay people who work in industry and commerce bring to the table financial acumen and practical administrative experience to benefit the Church. The Cathedrals Measure 1963 gave scope for change, and the new Coventry Cathedral Scheme received the royal assent by Order in Council on 20 December 1967. What was revolutionary was the separation of powers between clergy and laity, and the level of involvement of laity in the governance of the Cathedral – a level significantly greater than in all other cathedrals.

The 1967 constitution gave to the clergy (through the office of the Provost) full control of worship and day-to-day administration. The administrative and executive body of the Cathedral was its Council, which operated through the Finance Committee. The clergy met weekly to plan the ministry, and the Finance Committee met monthly to work out how to finance it! The Finance Committee was chaired by the Provost, and other members were the Bursar, five churchwardens, a chapter representative, a bishop's nominee and someone elected at the annual parish meeting. This was a predominantly lay body dealing with practical financial matters. The Coventry system worked extremely well, as long as the chairman was able to distinguish between matters clerical and matters administrative. The five churchwardens were fully involved in the Cathedral's finances, which enabled them to take immediate action whenever necessary to rally support from the congregation.

In the last decade of the twentieth century the public outcry at Hereford Cathedral Chapter's decision to sell the Mappa Mundi, and the internal disputes in Lincoln Cathedral gave rise to a commission and eventually to the Cathedrals Measure 1999. This required each cathedral to set up a Transitional Council whose sole job was to draft a new constitution based on a set model. At Coventry the new Constitution and Statutes came into effect on 24 September 2000. The most public aspect of the change was the replacement of the title 'Provost' with 'Dean'. The Chapter became the main administrative body, but there the balance of control at Coventry tipped towards the clergy, whereas in many older cathedrals lay people were taking a part in governing for the first time. Meanwhile, the Council was recast as primarily a monitoring body, and a College of Canons was introduced. These three form the Corporation of Coventry Cathedral.

Martin Williams, Ted Hiscocks
Editorial Committee Members

The Abbot of San Miniato, Florence (a Cross of Nails Centre), with a Cathedral houseparty led by Canon Peter Spink in 1975. © Ted Hiscocks.

maintain in smaller, shorter meetings. David Shaw from the congregation recognized the difficulties facing people like himself when confronted with a houseparty:

Some of us came to these with misgivings. Almost all of us left with a conviction of their value. For here, there were certain marked advantages. The numbers were rather larger than the regular groups tended to attract. People were mixed up in new ways and new relationships were forged and, perhaps most important of all, they were together under one roof for much longer than they had ever been before. Once more, we were getting to know and trust one another and we were discovering truth together . . . Many would say that they have come away from these houseparties with fresh understanding and renewed purpose.[9]

In September 1970 the Bishop spoke to the whole cathedral community when it gathered for a residential weekend at Keele University. Attended by some 300 residential members, as well as by day visitors, it was the houseparty to beat all houseparties! The Friends of the Cathedral were invited, and one of their number who travelled from Cumberland summed it up:

It was no quiet weekend of retreat. It was a battle conference . . . I was filled with a compelling sense of purpose such as I have never known before, although the 'pull' of the Cathedral has been increasingly in my life as time and opportunity to visit Coventry have come my way.[10]

That anonymous Friend particularly enjoyed the Saturday evening entertainment at Keele, which introduced Mick (Jim Gillespie) and Nick (Norman Williams) who, in the roles of Epstein's St Michael and the Devil, came down from the cathedral wall with an irreverent commentary on cathedral life that 'made one laugh until one ached'.

The tenth anniversary of the Consecration was celebrated in style. The Gala Night on 25 May 1972 started with an unusual Eucharist celebrated around a central altar. For the first time, worship was enhanced by liturgical dance performed by members of the congregation directed by Margaret Stevens of Reigate. That dance led to the formation of the St Michael's Dancers, as noted in Chapter 3.

The Bishop led the community in an act of rededication, after which the congregation were handed balloons as they followed a Highland piper from the nave and through the streets to the birthday party. It was a time for looking back over the first ten years of the Cathedral's life and at the ministry that had maintained its momentum and the size of its support. Edward Patey (by then the Dean of Liverpool) returned to preach at the tenth anniversary service:

A few swallows do not make a summer, so it would be premature to talk confidently about a religious revival. But there are enough signs on the horizon to kindle hope, and it has been the particular privilege of Coventry Cathedral in the first ten years of its life to reflect, within one place and through one ministry, many of those tokens of the renewal of the church which are beginning to give encouragement to Christian men and women the world over.

It is not for Coventry to make any unique or special claim in this matter. I doubt whether anything has been discovered here, these last ten years, which has not been discovered elsewhere.

But one thing is certain. The pattern of renewal has been focused in this place with a clarity and an intensity which has given Coventry in its first ten years of history a place of unique influence among the English Cathedrals of our time.[11]

That year appreciation of the impact of the Cathedral's ministry through its first years was voiced again by Lord Rootes, linking the strength of both the ministry and the architecture when he spoke at a ten-year reunion of the 1962 Festival Committee:

> I believe that the names of Spence, Laing, Sutherland, Piper and Hutton, if not others, will be remembered 500 years from now, not in footnotes in dusty, seldom-read tomes on 20th century ecclesiastical architecture, but as men of vision and genius who together created a living work of art which will have endured because they and the Cathedral's ministry met the present by looking far into the future, without ever losing sight of religion's first and last end.[12]

These were tributes to a ministry that had only achieved what it did with the commitment and support of large numbers.

Pastoral work

By the tenth anniversary, congregation numbers had started to decline, and the decline continued over the following years. In 1980 there were 230 households on the electoral roll, of which 40 were outside the city boundaries. With fewer numbers it was more difficult to maintain the same levels of activity, and more difficult for members of the more scattered congregation to meet other than at cathedral functions. This made it harder for clergy to keep track of their individual needs. Pastoral work became far more difficult with such a widespread congregation.

In the Cathedral's early years, before and after the Consecration, each member of the clergy team took responsibility for the pastoral care of those people within the areas in which he worked. The weekly staff meeting each Monday included worship, Bible study and the opportunity to report particular needs of members of the congregation, among other things. Initially there was also a chaplain in post with special responsibility for the congregation: John Alleyne at the time of the Consecration was followed by Roy Boole.

Stephen Macdonald was the next chaplain, and to enable widespread consultation about congregation matters and easier dissemination of congregation news he instituted the St Michael's Committee – a body selected, not elected, from among the different interest groups within the community. This body met monthly and continued under the name Community Advisory Team (known as CAT) until the new cathedral constitution of 2000 established the modern St Michael's Committee, whose members are now elected in rotation at the Annual Meeting.

By the mid-1970s the Cathedral's funds could no longer maintain the staffing levels of the past. By that time there was no chaplain for the congregation and responsibility fell to Canon Stuart King appointed as Canon Pastor in 1977. To help with pastoral care he instituted a system of Area Wardens in each area of the city, and each warden maintained contact with around 15 congregation members in his or her locality. The wardens' role survives today in the Link Neighbours. A publication called *Compass* became a useful guide for newcomers to the spread of community activities.

In pastoral work, as in all other areas of ministry, each clergy member brought his own talents to bear on the work. Stuart King was a skilled musician. At cathedral parties he had people competing to 'name the tune' of hymns that he managed to disguise in a range of musical styles. His piano and organ duets with Paul Leddington Wright brought another dimension to many services.

Social activities

Drama and music have always played a large part in the life of the cathedral community, as noted in Chapter 3. In the 1960s and 1970s many plays were performed under the direction of the Cathedral's drama directors. In the 1960s, for several years, Professor Van Kussrow brought drama students from Valparaiso University, USA, to study religious drama for a year of their course based at the Cathedral in conjunction with Lanchester College, later to be Coventry University. The students directed productions involving the congregation as part of their course.

Particular musical highlights by the community and for the community over the years were the pantomime *Dick Whittington* and the play *Cabaret*, both performed in the lecture hall. *Fiddler on the Roof* was a community musical performed in the nave. 'Mick and Nick', mentioned above, were also revived from time to time on party occasions, and had no difficulty finding subjects for further irreverence.

In the early years, the highlight of the Cathedral's social life was the annual cathedral ball. The monthly congregation meetings were themselves partly social occasions and partly business. As years went by and with changing fashions the ball

Coventry Cathedral football team was formed in 1999 by Neil McGowan and Chris Shilton and continues to field a team in local leagues.

was replaced by an annual fiesta on the birthday of the Consecration, and later by smaller party gatherings.

Adam immersed himself fully in cathedral life. As well as a verger, he was a representative for young people on the first St Michael's Committee. As the years went by he became a member of the Cathedral Council and later an elected churchwarden, a post he held for some 20 years.

Adam married on 14 November 1970 – a date also with significance in the life of the Cathedral as it was the thirtieth anniversary of the Coventry Blitz. He met his wife at the Cathedral, where she had been a member of the congregation since her childhood.

In his work at the Cathedral, Adam undertook many different tasks apart from the duties of the offices he held. Some of those tasks involved speaking about the ministry at Deanery Synods and at other distant church gatherings; he compèred congregational social events and reviews; he met the Queen Mother; he directed Brigitte Bardot to her seat at the funeral of Jill Phipps (killed protesting against animal cruelty); he presented a Coventry Cross of Nails to the church in Modra, Slovakia; and at the service to commemorate the dedication of the Home Front memorial he

*was privileged to lead the Queen and her consort down the aisle. A miscellaneous
selection of Adam's highlights!*

*Adam's sons joined the cathedral choir. As choristers they toured at home and
abroad taking the good reputation of Coventry cathedral choir with them. Adam
helped the choir by acting as tour manager across the USA, in South Africa and in
Italy, where they sang at an audience with the Pope.*

Financial decline

By the time of the retirement of Provost Williams in November 1981 the financial
position at the Cathedral was so weak that it only permitted community activities
that were self-funding. The community was shrinking and ageing, and as a result
appeals to it for financial help could no longer be relied upon to produce such large
support as in the past.

Peter Berry took charge of the Cathedral temporarily for a year and organized
it on this basis before the appointment of Colin Semper in 1982. Provost Semper
launched the Silver Jubilee Trust in 1983 in a quest for outside funding, and that
initiative was continued by his successor, Provost John Petty, with the appointment
of David Burbidge to head what was renamed the Development Trust. In 1918, Coventry Diocese had been established with an endowment of £10,000. The Cathedral
Trust was tasked with the creation of an endowment fund of several million pounds
– a fund sufficient to guarantee the building and its ministry for all time. The Trust
made substantial progress along this route until the Chapter found itself unable to
maintain balanced budgets, and diverted Trust energies into raising funds to cover
current expenditure. The results of the 2012 Golden Jubilee Appeal are awaited with
hopeful anticipation.

Pastoral work continues

Stuart King was appointed Canon Pastor under the leadership of Provost Williams,
when the financial decline was starting to bite. When Stuart King left, the Cathedral's
funds were insufficient for immediate staff replacement. Fortunately, two ordained
members of the cathedral community who were already giving their time voluntarily
took up the reins in the following years and attended to the pastoral needs of the
congregation – Jim Tysoe and Norman Williams. The secondment of the Revd Dr
Paula Whitmore by the USA Disciples of Christ, California, was a further help. She
initiated a group from the congregation to study *Faith in the City*, the Archbishop

of Canterbury's report that resounded through the Church of England and led to the establishment of the Church Urban Fund. To gain experience and insight into the problems of the inner city, members of the congregation took on voluntary tasks with organizations working there – housing organizations, youth clubs, day-care centres. This was the start of the ongoing link with Norton House, Hillfields, in the provision of meals for homeless people. When she left after three years in Coventry, Paula commented that 'the Cathedral congregation is its most abused and underused resource'.

As the Silver Jubilee Appeal progressed, the financial strains eased, though they have never disappeared altogether. The cathedral Chapter recognized the need to strengthen and support the congregation with a full-time appointment. David Carrette was recruited to the staff as Canon Pastor in 1988. He inspired a monthly cathedral magazine, *The Pilgrim*, edited by Mary Viner. To bind the community together it offered a forum for writing of a more serious nature than the weekly service sheets allowed, and to bind Cathedral and diocese it included news contributed by parishes near and far. The following January, David's sudden death from a heart attack shocked everyone.

His successor as Canon Pastor was Gerald Hughes. He was an experienced parish priest from Coventry Diocese who was already well aware of the Cathedral's needs. Gerald Hughes worked hard with the cathedral volunteers and with all ages in the congregation. One of the services that he encouraged was the 'Journey to Bethlehem', a Christmas service for children held on the afternoon of Christmas Eve.

'Journey to Bethlehem' had been started by Sheila Leddington Wright and Jane Williams as an interactive service for the children of the Cathedral's junior church/youth group. The children were encouraged to come along and to bring their friends to re-enact the Christmas story. During the service and with many children dressed in costume they walked to the inn (at the Chapel of Unity steps), then to the fields (around the high altar) and finally to the stable (at the font). At the stable, Gerald Hughes used his talents as a member of the Magic Circle to bring the Christmas story to life, adding his own magic to the magic of the story.

This Christmas Eve event continues to this day and has grown in popularity each year. Children arrive in costume an hour before the service, asking to be Mary or Joseph. Jesus is always a newborn baby. At the early services Nigel and Tina Guthrie put together a small music group to play. That musical offering has grown over time into today's 60–70-member ad hoc orchestra directed by Paul Leddington Wright, as well as incorporating a choir drawn from across the cathedral community. Congregation numbers have grown from the 30 or so who watched Gerald Hughes' magic tricks for it to become the best-attended service of the Christmas season. For many musical students returning to their Coventry hometown from university to play or sing on Christmas Eve, it is the event that signals the start of their Christmas.

Declining cathedral finances meant that the staff numbers continued to reduce – yet the same amount of day-to-day work was still required to keep the Cathedral going. When Vivienne Faull was appointed as Canon Pastor in 1994, she had also to take on the responsibility of deputizing for the Provost. There could no longer be someone with care of the cathedral community as a sole responsibility. The day-to-day administration of the Cathedral and the need to fulfil its diocesan commitments meant that Canon Faull had only a day and a half each week to devote to congregational matters, as she readily acknowledged. The same work pattern continued in 2000 with the appointment of Stuart Beake, who, as Acting Dean, took charge of the Cathedral during a 12-month interregnum. By this time the long-time lack of support showed in strains across the community, and his skills and experience in practical reconciliation were called upon to good effect.

With the support of CAT (Community Advisory Team) the life of the community was maintained, with a programme of worship, education and social events. The CAT monthly meeting was an opportunity to share the needs and aspirations of the congregation and to plan and organize the events that kept the community together.

The appointment of Dean John Irvine in March 2001 heralded an adjustment in the focus of congregational life. Dean Irvine was one of the team that had devised and developed the Christian teaching courses that led to the worldwide Alpha* movement. His emphasis on the need for a personal commitment to faith, and his addition of evangelical worship services to the pattern of cathedral life appeals today to new members for reasons quite different from those of the past. In Canon Tim Pullen the Cathedral also has a Canon Pastor with sole responsibility for the community. Both he and Dean John Irvine reach out through Alpha courses*, through their teaching and through modern evangelical worship to help new Christians to find their Saviour and to strengthen the personal faith of those who are already on that road. Building up the Church is a long-term strategy, but there are already signs of growth as more newcomers are welcomed into the cathedral community.

What has happened in 50 years?

In the last 50 years the cathedral community has moved from large numbers of people taking part in hectically busy experiments in Christian mission during the 1960s to a less busy rhythm of life with fewer activities as numbers diminished and as the 'baby boomers' grew in age. This pattern of change is not simply the result of the gradually fading publicity that followed the Consecration. In the last 50 years there have been huge changes in British society, in the role of the Church at large and in the way in which Christianity is perceived.

As far as the Church in general is concerned, Provost Williams' views on the inadequacy of the parish system are now widely accepted among those responsible for the mission of the Church. The Church can no longer simply stand there and expect people to come along to their local parish church to hear the Gospel, which is what happened in the past. The declining numbers testify to this. Today Christians must take the message of Christ out of their churches into the workplace, to the leisure activity, to the meeting place, wherever people gather – because they cannot expect non-believers to come to them. If they do not do this, then there is little hope for the future of the Church.

Under the 2000 Cathedral Constitution lay people play a significant part in the Cathedral Chapter. From left to right: Canon Stuart Beake, Ted Hiscocks, Tom Walls and Margaret Sedgwick in discussion at a Chapter Away Day in 2002.

There are signs of growth in movements like Alpha* which have particular appeal to people with a knowledge of Christianity deep within them that can be re-awakened. But we must not deceive ourselves. There is now a generation growing up without any knowledge of or belief in Christianity, and its ignorance, coupled with the increasing materialism of our society, creates a barren desert for the growth of any faith. The Church in general is deemed irrelevant by the population at large. In Coventry, the Cathedral rarely makes the news other than in discussions about tourism or possibly when it launches another appeal for more funds. The same is true for churches of all denominations. It is difficult to find any news story today that includes Christian comment on a current topic such as happened in the 1960s with the Cathedral, as mentioned earlier. That is hardly surprising, however, because with a concentration on teaching the Bible it is unusual today for the cathedral pulpit to be used for cutting-edge thinking on topical subjects.

In the lifetime of the Cathedral the Church of England has lost its place at the heart of the establishment and in the hearts of English people. It has become embroiled in arguments about the role of women and about sexuality. It demonstrated a closeness to Mammon when it lost millions on the stockmarket, and, as if to make the point more strongly, it then looked to its shrinking congregations to make up its losses.

Our country has become more secular. In the 1990s our politicians had to decide if the country was still Christian enough to keep Sunday special. Now, each Sunday, many more people pay homage at the supermarket than worship in church. Today we are part of a multicultural society. When Prince Charles becomes king the coronation oath is more likely to declare him 'Defender of Faith' than 'Defender of the Faith'. All these changes have reduced the role and the importance of the Church in our society, and they impact upon Coventry Cathedral today.

The City of Coventry itself has changed during this period. In the 1962 'motor city' there were nine car production lines working round the clock and helping to create a city of almost full employment, with wages well above the national average. Today there is no car manufacturing in the city, and unemployment in the West Midlands is greater than the national average. Richard Farnell has written on these issues in Chapter 5.

What hope is there for the cathedral community in the future? People have always joined cathedral congregations for different reasons. For some people a cathedral takes its identity from its glorious music in the cathedral tradition, about which you can read elsewhere in this book. In Coventry the music tradition has been maintained, and its music of the highest quality continues to attract support. But this is at great financial cost. The support of Coventry's music and worship takes almost one-quarter of its income. Without serious growth of income, can this be sustained?

Another segment of any cathedral congregation is made up of 'refugees' from local parishes. They are Christians who cannot cope with the changes introduced in their parish church; perhaps they disagree with changing churchmanship; or maybe they object to the intrusiveness of some stewardship campaigns. Some have felt

COVENTRY CATHEDRAL IN ROMANIA

Jane Williams is a child of Coventry Cathedral. As a member of the cathedral Sunday school that met in the undercroft before the Consecration she recalls being carried by Provost Bill Williams at the end of the service as he encouraged the children after their classes. It was the international vision of Bill Williams that inspired Jane to take direct action in the years that followed.

After the Romanian Revolution of Christmas 1989, horrific conditions were revealed when the borders opened. In 1994 Jane and Martin Williams travelled the 1,500 miles from Coventry to Sibiu, Transylvania, to see what help they themselves could offer. That was the start of a long-term commitment by members of the cathedral community.

At first, the need for direct practical aid was paramount. Ordinary Romanians were starved of food and lacked what we would consider daily necessities. Jane and Martin launched appeals for clothing, medical supplies, food and building materials. Volunteers from the congregation helped to sort out the vast amount of aid that arrived. After two years, an education aid project began with the aim of improving living conditions for ordinary Romanians, so that children would no longer be abandoned to the so-called 'orphanages'. Jane Williams developed training courses for nurses and devised the first course of antenatal classes to be held in Romania – classes that were later adopted for use by the Association of Romanian Midwives.

Jane took with her to Romania a professor from Newman College, Birmingham, to start links between his university college and the University of Sibiu. The first Romanian Early Years programme has now started. Senior staff of the hospital acknowledge that these health education programmes of the last ten years for staff, mothers and mothers-to-be have played a major part in updating hospital practices and patient attitudes, with the effect of reducing abandonment.

The Coventry Cross of Nails was presented to the project in 1996. Ten members from the cathedral congregation travelled to Romania to help complete the building where the Cross of Nails was kept. The dedication ceremony was attended by Orthodox priests and Nonconformist ministers – fellow Christians who had never before met in the same room, let alone prayed together. It was a special occasion – real reconciliation in action.

Recently members of the cathedral congregation sponsored local third-year university students to spend their summer working at a Health Centre in Sibiu where deprived children with complex health and behavioural problems live.

> The students reported life-changing experiences. The Centre Director appreci-
> ated not only the benefits to the children, but also the sharing of skills with her
> untrained staff.
> The work continues.
> There is further information from www.sharecharity.org.uk.
>
> *Martin Williams*
> *Editorial Committee Member*

overworked in their previous church; some are searchers who want to be anonymous for the time being. A cathedral offers you the opportunity to maintain your
faith while hiding behind a pillar and nursing your spiritual bruises. Those people
will still join the cathedral community, but in numbers far smaller than in the past
as the secularization of the country continues.

Many people were attracted to Coventry Cathedral in the 1960s by its outreach
ministry and by its application of Christian theology to the problems of the day.
Provost Williams wrote about cybernetics. Ted Heath addressed the congregation
on his vision of Europe – even before he took the country into the Common Market.
Simon Phipps worked for six months in a Coventry car factory, an experience that
enabled him to talk about industrial relations in language understood by all sides.
These are but a few examples.

Forward thinking of this sort often leads to controversy, and controversy is something with which many Christians do not want to become involved. Where is the
Christian viewpoint on recent legislation governing same-sex relationships, the role
of greed and capitalism in the international credit crisis, the Afghanistan war? How
should other faiths be viewed? These are some of the topics on which ordinary
Christians seek help, but about which the Church does not speak out. Sermons
confined to biblical teaching will not attract these people.

The international work of the Cathedral is a ministry peculiar to Coventry because
of its history, and that work will continue to gain supporters for the Cathedral as
long as it is maintained. The Community of the Cross of Nails unites many thousands of people across Europe, the USA and the rest of the world – people who share
together the aspiration and spirit of reconciliation. Each Friday at noon they say in
their own language the words of the Litany of Reconciliation that lies at the heart of
the Cathedral's ministry.

Finally, signs of growth in Coventry are to be found in new members who join after
discovering Christ through the teachings of the Cathedral Praise – non-traditional,
evangelical worship held in the setting of the Cathedral. Coventry Cathedral's com-

munity has changed substantially over the last 50 years, just as the world has changed around it. Now it is adapting to its new secular environment. Who knows what the next 50 years will bring?

Adam continued his regular support of cathedral worship and community activities, and at the same time his involvement in the ministry took new turns.

In 1984 he was invited by Colin Semper to revive Network *magazine, to be a readable, annual report on events in the Cathedral's ministry, with attractive illustrations that would appeal to a wide readership. He soon discovered that no one kept a suitable photo record of the cathedral ministry, so he then started to create one himself – a task that he continues.*

Adam put his professional legal training to use as a member of the Transitional Council that was appointed under the Cathedrals Measure to devise the new cathedral constitution. To ensure the success of St Michael's Committee, the new body created by this new constitution and representing congregation, staff and volunteers, he led it for its first two sessions.

Lay history in the making. This was the first meeting of St Michael's Committee after its creation by the new Cathedral Constitution in 2000. The Committee provides the cathedral congregation, volunteers and staff with a voice on the Cathedral Chapter.

On 14 July 2001 his installation in the Cathedral as an honorary lay canon was an unexpected honour. As someone who had spoken out for proper recognition of the role of laity in the church, he was 'hoist with his own petard', in the words of Bishop Colin Bennetts.

Today on the fiftieth anniversary of the Consecration Adam looks back with tremendous gratitude. That first day spent in the Cathedral Bookshop in 1962 led to life-changing faith experiences that still resonate within him.

In 1981 Provost Williams retired with an air of reluctance. Adam knew that Coventry Cathedral's ministry was the flower that Provost Williams had nurtured and tended – something that was so precious to him that he could hardly bear to leave it to others.

Before his final service Adam spoke to him quietly at the back of the church:

Coventry Cathedral has lit a burning candle within me and within many thousands of others whose lives have been touched by its ministry. No one can ever tell the full extent of its impact. Like the ripples from a stone thrown into a pond, you never know where the ripples end. But the candles carry on burning, and the ripples are still travelling on.

* Denotes an entry in the Glossary

Notes

1 Provost Williams, in *Coventry Cathedral Review*, December 1962.
2 Canon Edward Patey, in *Coventry Cathedral Review*, September 1962.
3 Canon Edward Patey, in *Coventry Cathedral Review*, September 1962.
4 H. C. N. Williams, *Coventry Cathedral in Action*, Religious Education Press, 1968.
5 Williams, *Coventry Cathedral in Action*.
6 Donald Coggan, *Bishop Bardsley: Bishop, Evangelist, Pastor*, Collins, 1989.
7 Canon Stephen Verney, in *Coventry Cathedral Review*, February 1965.
8 Canon Peter Spink, in *Network*, April 1969.
9 David Shaw, in *Network*, April 1970.
10 Anonymous Friend, *Network*, January 1971.
11 Dean Edward Patey, cathedral sermon, May 1972.
12 Lord Rootes, reported in *Network*, July 1972.

CONCLUSION: A SERIOUS HOUSE

Celebrating and Learning from 50 Years

CHRISTOPHER LAMB

In the early 1990s I went to one of the Sikh temples in Coventry to ask them if they would be prepared to support and give money for work among the homeless in the city. This was work associated with the name of Dr Amal Dharri, an Asian Christian doctor who had been murdered in 1981 in a random racial attack. They listened to this story with great interest, and gave generously to the work. But it was not I, the Christian minister, who quoted the Bible, it was one of the Sikh speakers. He told his fellow-Sikhs that Jesus Christ had said 'Father, forgive them, for they know not what they do.' He was sure that the murdered Dr Dharri, who was a Christian, would have said the same. I am not sure if I, as a visitor in the gurdwara, would have felt free enough to say something like that, because it might have sounded too much like proselytizing. But anyway I didn't need to, because the witness to Jesus Christ was being made by the Sikh. How did he know about it? He knew because he had been in the Ruins of the old Cathedral and seen the words FATHER FORGIVE carved behind the old altar, and he knew the story of the cross made of nails. The building had made its own witness to the theme of reconciliation, and there was nothing more I needed to say.

My work then was in reconciling majority and minority communities in the City and the diocese, based on the Cathedral and continuing the pioneer work of Canon Peter Berry. But everyone associated with the Cathedral in the last 50 years has in one way or another been engaged in the same task of reconciliation. Is it possible to gauge how successful it has been? Has reconciliation been a slogan rather than a genuinely motivating principle? John Petty reported that at a deans' meeting a colleague from another cathedral said to him: 'We are all searching for our particular mission. You in Coventry have had yours given to you.' Have we been a Reconciling People?

Much of the work of a cathedral will not in fact vary very greatly from one diocese to another. There will be the daily services to hold, the special ones to prepare for, the visitors to greet and talk to, the building itself to maintain and secure, exhibitions and special events to plan, and staff and the regular congregation to care for, and to help to grow in faith. As in any other situation it is easy for these tasks to become routine, and for the building to lose its special character through familiarity. But in words already quoted from Philip Larkin, who was baptized in the old Cathedral in 1922, this is 'a serious house, on serious earth'. Coventry has the huge gift of the physical demonstration of a house of God ruined and rebuilt, itself a symbol of hope in the living Lord. For over 50 years the ruined and rebuilt house has been used to focus attention on the ruinous conflicts that have destroyed human lives and on the possibility of bringing forgiveness, peace and reconciliation in the name of the Prince of Peace. 'Blessed are the peacemakers, for they shall be called the children of God' (Matthew 5.9).

Reconciliation at the heart

From Provost Howard's adoption of 'Father Forgive' as the 'logo' for the cathedral Ruins to the work of Andrew White in the Middle East and Justin Welby in Nigeria, Coventry Cathedral has been continually engaged, often in startling and creative ways, in the work of bringing peace to the nations. Paul Oestreicher's account of the story in this book can only be a partial record of what has been attempted and achieved. 'Adam' has given us a sense, in his chapter, of the essential support to this work provided by the congregation. He has shown too how ordinary cathedral worshippers have also been international pioneers in their own way, even if, as Bishop Bennetts notes, this has not been something which has entered the 'bloodstream of the Diocese'. At home in Coventry itself, outreach in industrial mission, interfaith relations and many other areas has been chronicled by Margaret Sedgwick – all work which attempted to cross domestic frontiers and create bridges of understanding. Richard Farnell has noted how this waxed and waned according to available finance, and how the Cathedral came at times to be seen by the City as a convenient 'public utility' rather than a symbol and icon of hope and new life. But other factors have been at work here, not least the institutional decline of the Church as a whole, and recent overt hostility to the Christian faith by a variety of public figures.

Apart from all this high-profile and sometimes frenetic activity, what is at the heart of the Cathedral's ministry? What is a cathedral for? It has always been acknowledged in Coventry Cathedral that the possibility of peace between human beings is the result of a prior peace with God. But whether in the daily routine of worship and simply keeping the Cathedral going, or in the complex and tortuous work of negotiations to bring together mutually antagonized communities, whether in Coventry or Nigeria, it is easy for the vertical dimension of our own reconciliation to be, if not forgotten, then over-shadowed. 'God has reconciled us to himself through Christ, and has given us the ministry of reconciliation; that is, in Christ, God was reconciling the world to himself . . . So we are ambassadors for Christ' (2 Corinthians 5.18–20). It is only because we are reconciled as it were vertically with God that we can be of any use in the horizontal reconciliation of our fellow human beings. In fact, without that Godward dimension and consciousness, then we are no more than a rather amateur outfit attempting complex tasks of conflict resolution, with the distinct possibility of leaving matters worse than we found them.

Here is the rationale behind the change in the character of the cathedral ministry that came with the appointment of John Irvine as Dean. Here is a man who is unafraid of labelling himself an evangelical, a conservative and a charismatic. Clergy often shy away from the labels that are used to describe the differing emphases and convictions in the Church. They may claim to be impatient with (or even superior to) the arguments that have divided Christians. Others don't want to be pigeon-holed, and their opinions second-guessed and maybe dismissed in advance of them being heard. They don't want to be put in a box, whatever it is marked. John Irvine belongs rather to those who stand for a definite tradition within Anglicanism, and are not afraid to say so. The result of his coming to the Cathedral has been an emphasis on inviting people to consider Jesus Christ as their personal saviour in traditional evangelical language, presented in the form of the Alpha course* and experiments in more informal worship. This has been new to Coventry Cathedral's understated style of personal devotion, and the response from some long-standing members of the congregation was initially negative. They complained of a reiteration of basic beliefs and the absence of a wider vision. It was good to see new people coming into worship, but they missed the liberal openness to social and political issues of previous years. There was a fear that new appointments to the clergy staff might be conservative evangelical clones, in spite of the early appointment of a precentor from the Catholic tradition.

Evangelicalism and religion in the UK

This may say more about the ghetto-ized subcultures within the Church of England than about the real issues at stake. Some analyses of the religious culture of England in the twenty-first century suggest that the old 'catholic', 'liberal' and 'evangelical' labels of intra-Christian discourse are all equally irrelevant to the prevailing secular mood. Callum Brown, in his doom-laden *Death of Christian Britain*, proclaims:

> The evangelical narrative has decayed . . . The search for personal faith is now in 'the New Age' of minor cults, personal development and consumer choice. The universal world-view of both Christianity and identity which prevailed until the 1950s seems impossible to recreate in any form.

And again:

> For the generations growing up since the 1960s, new ethical concerns have emerged to dominate their moral culture – environmentalism, gender and racial equality, nuclear weapons and power, vegetarianism, the well-being of body and mind – issues with which Christianity and the Bible in particular are perceived as being wholly unconcerned and unconnected. At the same time, the social implications of conventional religious culture – respectability, sobriety, observance of social convention, observance of the Sabbath – have been rejected *en bloc*.[1]

Others would dismiss this analysis as way off course, and evidently unaware of the vitality shown in Christian organizations like Greenbelt and publications like *Third Way*, which combine orthodox Christian conviction with all the concerns expressed daily in the media, together with a keen appreciation of the arts. Callum Brown, perhaps more familiar with his native Scotland than England, may have been misled by the noisy secularism of popular culture. However, the media is an immensely powerful player in moulding public attitudes and there is a current fashion of rejecting religion as at best irrelevant and at worst inimical to the public good. This tendency has been vastly strengthened by Islamic radicalism despite the (largely unreported) condemnation by Muslims of the terrorist crimes committed in their name. Untold damage has been done by the widespread reports of child abuse by some Roman Catholic priests, and that church's former attempts to preserve its reputation by concealing the facts. Since Callum Brown wrote in 2001, Richard Dawkins has published *The God Delusion* (2006), and Christopher Hitchens *God Is Not Great: How Religion Poisons Everything* (2007), both best-selling books rubbishing the idea of God altogether. Richard Farnell notes in his chapter how 'the 1970s and 1980s saw a growing acceptance of the notion that faith is a private matter and that religion has no place in the public square of politics and policy making'. It has taken a Muslim author, Dr Ataullah Siddiqui, to document the reluctance of senior civil servants to accept religious bodies as a significant force in public life.[2] It is at least arguable that it is the insistence of British Muslims on their religious rather than their ethnic identity that has begun to change the attitudes of British governments towards faith, and that secured, for example, the inclusion of a question about faith for the first time in the 2001 census.

Hostility or indifference?

So is the anti-religious fashion simply blind to the real significance of Christian faith in twenty-first-century Britain? Believers of course would say 'Yes', but the socio-logical situation is complex. Though there are claims that the institutional decline of the churches has bottomed out, and that church attendance in London is actually on the increase, there seem to be currents flowing in different directions. A recent survey of Generation Y, 300 young people involved in church youth and community projects, has concluded that:

> for the majority, religion and spirituality was irrelevant for day-to-day living; our young people were not looking for answers to ultimate questions and showed little sign of 'pick and mix' spirituality . . . On the rare occasions when a religious per-spective was required (for example, coping with family illnesses or bereavements) they often 'made do' with a very faded, inherited cultural memory of Christianity in the absence of anything else . . . In this respect they would sometimes pray in their bedrooms. What is salutary for the Church is that generally young people seemed quite content with this situation, happy to get by with what little they knew about the Christian faith.[3]

Is indifference to faith better than hostility, or simply the mark of a generation that has not yet woken up to any of the serious questions in life? In the survey the young people were asked to say which statement about God best represented their own views, and 43 per cent ticked the box that said 'I don't know what to think'. If this is an accurate picture of young people with some church affiliation, however slender, what of those entirely unchurched?

It may be that the truly committed religious believers are, and always have been, a small minority and that the mass of people simply follow the trends laid down for them by the dominant voices in their society. Even in America, with its much higher church attendance and its overtly believing political leaders, the actual degree of reli-gious knowledge is reckoned to be surprisingly limited. According to recent research by the Pew Forum on Religion and Public Life, those best informed on religion in the USA were atheists and agnostics, Jews and Mormons.[4] Most Christians were indifferent to their lack of knowledge and 'coasted' through the drama of religion as though it were cultural wallpaper.

If this is widely the case then perhaps it does make sense for the Cathedral and other Christian churches to focus on the fundamentals of the faith for the few who will take them seriously, and become the 'movers and shakers' of society. Evangelism should be the first priority. In different language ('evangelization' rather than 'evangelism'), this also seems to be the view of Pope Benedict XVI, who has been reported as in favour of a smaller, slimmer and far better informed and committed Catholic Church in Europe, a church that will bring about real changes in society, rather than a large but flabby church that may claim a Catholic identity but is highly selective about what it chooses to believe and practise from the Catholic tradition.

Questions for the future

Yet I am not sure we can leave it there. It is vital to nurture the roots of faith, and to bring new people within the sound of the gospel. As already noted, a Christian call for reconciliation among peoples can only be driven by a prior reconciliation with God. But the Jesus of the Gospels, the key to that reconciliation, is a figure of huge and startling sympathies, and of the most generous and far-reaching vision imaginable. Can the Cathedral afford to be locked into evangelicalism? The evangelical movement in the Church of England is currently dominant and still growing, despite its unjust association in the popular mind with American-style fundamentalism, creationism and homophobia. It is also subject to its own internal tensions over the role of women as priests and bishops, and the question of homosexuality. All religious traditions in the twenty-first century, whether Jewish, Christian, Muslim or Hindu, are experiencing a revival of traditional orthodoxies and a rejection of more open, liberal attitudes in favour of what is perceived as a more authentic, less compromised religious stance. In the Christian churches, 'back to the Bible' movements attract the idealism of young people, and their taste for being engaged in something clearly counter-cultural. There are always those who like to swim against the tide. Despite the evidence about 'Generation Y' above, we may presume that British youngsters are no exception. An uncompromising message will draw a number of them.

But a cathedral must offer more than a faith they may well outgrow. Does not a theologically diverse staff team provide the breadth of spiritual nurture a cathedral congregation has a right to expect? In the words of 'Adam' (Martin Williams) in this book:

It is difficult to find any news story today that reveals Christian comment on a current topic such as happened in the 1960s with the Cathedral as mentioned earlier. That is hardly surprising, however, because with a concentration on teaching the

Bible it is unusual today for the cathedral pulpit to be used for cutting-edge thinking on topical subjects.

If we lose the wider perspective we shall also lose the inquiring minds. Richard Farnell refers to the 'twin Christian vocations of citizenship and discipleship'. Canon Kenyon Wright, reflecting on his own experience of the Cathedral in the 1970s, writes:

> If I were asked to sum up succinctly the purpose of the Coventry 'experiment', I would say it was to provide a space for the whole of our society (as well as internationally) in which the crucial issues of the time could be honestly faced; the wounds of the past healed in reconciliation; the values of the gospel and the 'Kingdom of God' applied to all areas of life; and the future shaped together.[5]

What have we learnt from 50 years? Is a verdict possible?

It is tempting but perilous to sit in judgement on one's forebears. We did not inherit their situation or their assumptions; we have not sat where they sat; we did not face the problems and opportunities they faced; and our knowledge of the outcome of their decisions is a privilege they did not have when they made them, and is in any case partial. Nevertheless, it is wise to try to learn from their apparent mistakes, and to celebrate and hopefully to build on their achievements.

In the light of the recurrent financial crises of Coventry Cathedral since 1980 it is reasonable to ask: why was no money saved in the early years so that work begun then in such hope could be sustained? Knowing that Coventry Cathedral did not have the endowments of the older foundations, why was nothing put aside? Although there were numerous appeals for funds it was not until 1983 that a serious attempt to provide endowment for the future was made in the Silver Jubilee Trust, relaunched in 1991 as the Coventry Cathedral Development Trust. You would have thought that Joseph's interpretation of the Pharaoh's dream – seven fat cattle meaning seven fat years, seven lean cattle meaning seven lean years – was sufficiently familiar to the clergy of the 1960s. Instead, money was spent as it came in, and when it no longer came in such quantity the Cathedral's finances were allowed to wane in tandem with those of the City.

Bill Williams would no doubt robustly defend his policy of expanding the ministry and therefore the expenditure of the Cathedral in response to what he saw as unique and unrepeatable opportunities. Certainly the worldwide reputation of Coventry Cathedral and its message of reconciliation is his legacy under God. He and his team put Coventry Cathedral on the map in a way that fully matched the drama of its destruction and rebuilding. It is this that has in the long run enabled the more recent international work of Paul Oestreicher, Andrew White and Justin Welby. But we have also seen how work on that scale could not be sustained.

At the time of writing, our government is busy looking for ways to cut public expenditure, and churches are no strangers to the exigencies of financial constraints. These compel new thinking on priorities, in itself no bad thing. The Cathedral has been through the same process several times, which at least has ensured that no dimension of ministry has been allowed to continue unexamined. But there have been inevitable losses.

Ministries now missing

Margaret Sedgwick in this volume has noted the way in which successive provosts/deans have determined the shape and direction of the Cathedral's ministry. This is no doubt inevitable and proper, what we expect from gifted leadership. The downside is that changing priorities means that some work is abandoned altogether. This is what happened to the healing ministry begun by John Petty, which included the remodelling of 7 Priory Row to provide a suite of rooms for counselling and prayer. These are now used as meeting rooms for church committees, though it must be added that prayer and the laying on of hands for healing is offered, as in many churches, in the regular services. A Drama Department and liturgical dance were also features of the Cathedral's ministry at one time – dance until 2007, as John Brassington recalls in Chapter 3.

Some work pioneered by the Cathedral was in the course of time taken over by other bodies. This was true of the industrial mission work begun by Simon Phipps, which changed its name successively to Ministry in the World of Work, and then **WORK**CARE. For many years it has been an ecumenical body, which sadly often means that its impact in Anglican circles is less than it might be. It has been argued by Trevor Cooper, a former senior industrial missioner, that despite the prophetic vision of Bill Williams,

the priority placed on personal piety and spirituality still seems to take precedence over the need to understand the influence of secular institutions, with their political and economic priorities, and the effect on the attitudes and behaviour of individuals . . . The churches appear to be more concerned with preservation of religious practices and the behaviour of individuals, than with the ethics of society at large.[6]

Would that be so if industrial mission was still part of the Cathedral's ministry?

Another area of work which was once part of the Cathedral's ministry was community relations, the offering of Christian engagement and insight in the taxing arenas of racial justice and interfaith relations. While the latter in particular is recognized as relevant to Canon David Porter's current responsibilities as Director for Reconciliation Ministry, earlier work in this area was led full-time by Peter Berry and Christopher Lamb, in a diocesan–cathedral partnership. In those years the Cathedral became, for those of other faiths, the guarantor of a positive and sympathetic attitude from the Christian churches towards other religious traditions. This was maintained in the spirit of the good neighbour without any compromise of fundamental Christian conviction. Now that Islam and other faiths continue to present such a series of basic questions to Christian faith, would it not be good for the Cathedral still to have such experience at hand? In a sense it is still physically at hand in the Coventry Multi-Faith Centre, built by the City Council in the new development over the ruins of the original Benedictine abbey, but the Centre lacks any staff who can make it effective.

Kennedy House is another case of a ministry now missing, its story told in Margaret Sedgwick's chapter. Perhaps it should not be mourned, as a venture of its time and that time passed, though lack of adequate management seems to have been a besetting problem. It is difficult to imagine young people from across the world being drawn to Coventry today in the way that they were in the 1960s. Keith Parr is now doing remarkable work with teenagers of a very different sort. Nevertheless, an ageing congregation needs the vitality of Christian young people, who themselves need a place of their own where they can find their own way forward in the faith. Perhaps the new St Michael's House, located in the former Deanery, will prove to be a new form of the original vision. David Porter outlines plans for it in the following piece.

Bishop Colin Bennetts has noted that a radical reappraisal is needed if the Chapel of Unity is to find a new purpose for the future. The idea behind it seemed bold and imaginative in the 1940s, but despite the support of other churches at the time, it proved perhaps to be a case of Anglican 'you-come-in-ism', rather than genuine ecumenism. The real problem may have been the absence of the planned Christian Service Centre, never built for lack of money, though it was part of the detailed requirements for the new Cathedral given to the architects competing in 1951. Provost Howard records in detail how Bishop Neville Gorton received considerable Free Church support for his 1944 plans for a rebuilt cathedral which would include 'as an essential part of the Cathedral Scheme a Christian centre of service to the community', in which the Free Churches would be full partners, and 'a special Chapel of Unity attached to the fabric of the Cathedral itself with the Christian Centre'.[7] Wide enthusiasm was not, however, matched by equivalent giving to the appeal, and when Sir Giles Gilbert Scott's design for the Cathedral was rejected, and he resigned, the appeal had to be abandoned. Consequently the Chapel of Unity seemed to represent a Christian people who were ready to unite for worship but not to serve the wider community. It is significant that the encouragement of evangelism would have been part of the remit of the Christian Service Centre. Today the Chapel of Unity Commission declares it is actively working to promote it as a place for prayer and meditation as well as highlighting the work for social justice and care of the earth.

In the context of inter-church relationships we should also note that the Council of Covenanting City Centre Churches of Coventry, known as 'C6', ran successfully for some 15 years from its inauguration in January 1988, bringing together Anglican, Methodist, Roman Catholic, Baptist and URC churches.

The Centre of Studies was another venture that was perhaps in retrospect too ambitious, and like the Christian Service Centre defeated by the lack of finance. Despite initial success and acclamation in the mid-1970s it was a casualty of the recession of the early 1980s and has never been revived. Closer relations with Coventry University have only partially made up for this. Again, St Michael's House may continue the original vision in another form.

An age of austerity may bring us to see these ministries now missing as currently unaffordable luxuries, when the primary task is to re-establish in the harsher conditions of the twenty-first century the basic beliefs of the faith once delivered to the saints.

A time to celebrate

Nevertheless, we can justly celebrate all the ventures listed above as evidence of an imaginative, wide-ranging and deeply impressive spirit of inquiry and service marked by confidence in the God of the Christian Scriptures. Here is a faith not just in humanity and its capacity to rise above tragedy and disaster, the phoenix* from the ashes of the City of Coventry's self-image, but a faith in the incarnate Lord who gave himself up to death for truth, justice and redemption, and rose again to be with his people for ever. If, as some say, Coventry Cathedral hung on to the memory of the Second World War too long, or is better appreciated in the USA and Germany than in its own diocese; if it has sometimes been led astray by its own image, these are all the age-long weaknesses of an institution which like others is all too human.

More significantly, here is a cathedral that grabbed the attention of the nation and the world – and still does – and took a God-given moment to bring a Christian understanding of peace and reconciliation to many parts of a fearful world. The roads into Coventry proclaim that this is 'Coventry, city of peace and reconciliation'. It is a message that still needs to be heard. Here is a cathedral that – like others – has made itself a home for the arts and welcomed every attempt to create something beautiful for God. Perhaps most important for the future, here is a cathedral that has welcomed literally hundreds of thousands of schoolchildren over half a century, and given them an unparalleled glimpse of the realities of war, conflict, peace, reconciliation and a faith centred on Jesus of Nazareth, crucified and risen. Such sustained and imaginative witness in so many fields has had incalculable effect on numberless lives.

And of course the work goes on. The last words in this volume should be given to Canon David Porter, Baptist lay man from Northern Ireland and Director for the Cathedral's Reconciliation Ministry, as he describes the vision for Coventry Cathedral's future.

* Denotes an entry in the Glossary

Notes

1 Callum Brown, *The Death of Christian Britain: Understanding Secularisation 1800–2000*, Routledge, 2001, pp. 190, 196.

2 Ataullah Siddiqui, 'Inter-Faith Relations in Britain Since 1970: An Assessment', *Exchange* 39 (2010), Brill, Netherlands.

3 Sylvia Collins-Mayo, Bob Mayo, Sally Nash and Christopher Cocksworth (eds), *The Faith of Generation Y*, Church House Publishing, 2010.

4 'Religious Illiteracy – New and Not So New', www.ekklesia.co.uk, daily bulletin (accessed 5 October 2010).

5 Kenyon Wright, 'Cathedral of Peace', unpublished paper, July 2010.

6 Trevor Cooper, *Who Goes There? A Challenge to Humanity*, AuthorHouse, 2009, p. 20.

7 R. T. Howard, 'The Latter Glory: The House of Coventry Cathedral 1939–1958', unpublished, pp. 49, 50.

A NEVER-ENDING STORY

Every story should have an ending. But the Coventry Cathedral story of rec-onciliation is as open-ended as ever in a world still stalked by fear, hostility and conflict between its peoples and nations. The experience of the Cathedral's Chapter and people over the last 50 years shows that there is much that can be done by ordinary people doing extraordinary things to heal the wounds of the past and bring a greater awareness of what it means to live at peace with all people.

Their story is best honoured when, sharing a vision for a better, more Christ-like world, we commit ourselves to working out what that means for us in our time and place. Coventry Cathedral is a remarkable place and a powerful space in which to meet with God and be provoked about our part in the ongoing story of the Church's ministry of reconciliation. The events of its destruction and rebuilding inspire each new generation to give meaning and significance to Jesus' message of love for the enemy and forgiveness for those who do us harm.

Over the next ten years we will be developing the cathedral Ruins as an inter-national memorial to civilians killed, injured and traumatized by violent con-flict. In doing so we want to commemorate the unseen victims and engage in a challenging conversation with a world where civilian populations are deliber-ately targeted and terrorized as a weapon of war, and represent over 90 per cent of its casualties.

To start this process and mark the fiftieth anniversary, the gift of a statue from the Frauenkirche in Dresden is to be dedicated to the civilians killed in the Allied bombings of Germany. The capacity to acknowledge and embrace the suffering of our enemy is, more than any other act or gesture, a true sign that reconciliation has taken place and enemies have indeed become friends.

A second anniversary initiative is the setting up of St Michael's House as a learning community to equip a new generation for reconciliation ministry. Its focus will be on spiritual formation alongside intellectual development, skills-based learning enriched by theological reflection. Whether hosting honest con-versations, promoting debate or providing training courses its aim is to develop leaders with a better understanding of the challenges of reconciliation in today's world.

The Community of the Cross of Nails remains central to who we are, pro-viding a network of relationships across the world. At its heart is the need to heal the wounds of history, which not only result from conflict between cultures, peoples and nations, but also from long-standing alienation within and between

our task
is great,
but God
is greater

David Porter.

communities. The CCN's global partners meet to share their experience of learning to live with difference and diversity and affirm a practical commitment to building a culture of peace, praying for each other and providing support when necessary to churches in conflict or post-conflict situations.

As part of this network, International Cross of Nails Schools (ICONS) is a new initiative with the purpose of enabling young people to play their part as global citizens, confident in their own identity and able to celebrate diversity. It supports schools in helping them to explore what it means to be a person of faith and develop the skills to be part of a cohesive, equal and interdependent society.

Our vision to be a world centre for reconciliation must also inform our vocation as a reconciled and reconciling people in the community of which we are a part. The Cathedral serves the Diocese of Coventry and the City and communities of Coventry and Warwickshire. Dealing with difference within the Church, contributing to better social and community cohesion in local communities and living faithful responses to global poverty and environmental change, are all part of our witness. In the increasing diversity of our local contexts this requires a mature intercultural and interfaith engagement with all for whom this part of God's earth is home and with whom we share space.

The absence of reconciliation in our world demonstrates a profound lack of spiritual vision, political imagination and moral resource to find an alternative way to live with our differences and resolve our disputes without demonizing or even killing each other. Inspired by the story of Coventry Cathedral and a God who in Christ reconciles all things, can we imagine a better world where our enemies today become our friends tomorrow? Indeed are we ready to take the story one step further towards its end in the purposes of God for humanity and all creation?

David Porter
Canon Director for Reconciliation Ministry

APPENDICES

GLOSSARY

The architectural definitions are as used in Pevsner's *The Buildings of England*.
 * When used in the text these words are marked with an asterix.

Alpha Course	an evangelistic programme bringing enquirers together over a meal to learn about and discuss issues in the Christian faith
Anabaptist	literally 're-baptiser'. A radical Christian movement from the sixteenth century. Mennonites are the best-known example
anamnesis	literally 'memorial', especially the remembering of Christ's death and resurrection
Apocalypse	the revealing of hidden things; the Greek title for the book of Revelation
apse	semi-circular end of a chancel or chapel
ARCIC	Anglican–Roman Catholic International Commission, a group appointed by the two churches, which has met since 1970 to identify common beliefs
aumbry	recess to hold the consecrated elements or sacred vessels
Cathedral Liaison Officer	a parish representative appointed to keep in contact with the Cathedral
Chaldean	the Eastern Syriac Church in full communion with the Church of Rome
dalmatic	a vestment worn by a deacon at the Eucharist
flèche	literally an 'arrow', a slender spire
groin	sharp edge at the meeting of two cells of a cross-vault
hermeneutics	the art of interpretation and elucidating meaning
hieratic	(from Greek for 'priest') in a traditional religious form
Icarus	in Greek mythology the boy whose father made him wings from feathers and wax. He flew too close to the sun, the wax melted and he drowned

	in the sea
iconostasis	literally 'icon-stand', screen covered with icons in an Orthodox church
kairos	time or moment of opportunity, as contrasted with measured time
koinonia	literally 'fellowship'
Kristallnacht	the 'night of broken glass', a concerted Nazi attack on Jewish premises in Germany on 9/10 November 1938
mandorla	Italian for 'almond', so an almond shape created by the overlap of two circles
maniple	a silk strip formerly worn by ministers at the Eucharist on the left arm – now very rarely
maquette	a scale model, especially of a sculpture
Mitchell-Tenet Plans	plans proposed in 2001–2 to resolve the Israel/Palestine conflict
Mystery Plays	medieval enactments of Bible stories, recorded in Coventry from 1392
narthex	enclosed vestibule or covered porch at the entrance of a church
ninefold Kyrie	the Greek phrases 'Kyrie eleison, Christe eleison, Kyrie eleison' or 'Lord have mercy, Christ have mercy, Lord have mercy', each repeated three times
numinous	the experience of holiness, awe and fascination
phoenix	a mythical bird or fire spirit that lives for 500 or 1,000 years, then burns to ashes, from which a new identical bird is born
predella	step or platform on which an altar stands
reredos	painted or sculptured screen above and behind an altar
Stasi	Ministerium für Staatssicherheit (Ministry for State Security), the Secret Police of East Germany 1950–90
tetramorph	literally 'four figures', referring to the four figures of Revelation 4
tympanum	literally a 'drum', the surface between a lintel and the arch above it
via dolorosa	'the sorrowful way' – the route taken by Jesus carrying his cross through Jerusalem on his way to crucifixion

TIME CHART

History of Coventry Cathedral in perspective with events in the wider world

Coventry Cathedral	Coventry	Britain and the Wider World
1940 Air raid destroys Cathedral. King visits following day	1940 Air raid destroys city centre.	1940 First German air raids on London. Battle of Britain
1941 Appointment of Rebuilding Commission	1941 Donald Gibson first plans for rebuilding Coventry	1941 Japanese bomb Pearl Harbor. USA enters war
		1942/3 Siege of Stalingrad
	1944 Coventry twinned with Stalingrad	
	1945 'The Future of Coventry' exhibition and booklet show plans for reconstruction	1945 Bombing of Dresden. Germany (May) and Japan surrender (August)
	1946 Harry Ferguson opens world's largest tractor plant in Coventry	
1947 Harlech Committee appointed	1947 Twinning with Lidice and Kiel	
	1948 New Broadgate opened by Princess Elizabeth	1948 Gandhi assassinated. Jews proclaim State of Israel
		1950 Start of Korean War
1951 Basil Spence wins competition to design new Cathedral		1951 Festival of Britain
		1952 Death of King George VI
		1953 Coronation of Queen Elizabeth II. Armistice ends Korean War
1954 Licence to build new Cathedral		

Coventry Cathedral		Coventry		Britain and the Wider World	
1955	John Laing awarded contract to build new Cathedral	1955	Opening of Upper Precinct traffic-free shopping centre		
1956	Queen lays foundation stone			1956	Suez crisis
		1957	Coventry twinned with Belgrade	1957	Treaty of Rome creates EEC. USSR launch Sputnik
		1958	Opening of Belgrade Theatre	1958	Race riots in Notting Hill Gate
		1959	Coventry twinned with Dresden	1959	BMC Mini car. Opening of M1
		1960	Founding of Lanchester College of Technology. Herbert Museum and Art Gallery opened		
		1961	Jimmy Hill manager of Coventry City Football Club	1961	Building of Berlin Wall
1962	Consecration of new Cathedral			1962	Cuba missile crisis
				1963	Martin Luther King 'I have a dream' speech. President Kennedy shot in Dallas
1965	Willy Brandt opens Kennedy House	1965	Founding of University of Warwick		
		1967	Coventry City FC promoted to First Division. Chrysler takes control of Rootes	1967	Israeli/Arab Six Days' War
1968	*People and Cities* conference			1968	Enoch Powell 'Rivers of Blood' speech. Martin Luther King assassinated
				1969	Neil Armstrong and Buzz Aldrin set foot on the Moon
1970	Opening of Bardsley House	1970	Queen opens Walsgrave Hospital		
				1972	Bloody Sunday in Ulster. US troops withdraw from Vietnam

Coventry Cathedral	Coventry	Britain and the Wider World
		1973 Miners' strike. Three-day week
1974 Opening of Centre of Studies		
1976 Opening of Coventry House of Reconciliation at Corrymeela		
1978 Coventry Mystery Plays reborn	1978 Chrysler sells European operations to Peugeot	
		1979 Margaret Thatcher Prime Minister. Islamic Republic in Iran
1981 Provost Williams retires	1981 *Ghost Town* by Coventry band 'The Specials'	1981 Brixton and Toxteth race riots. First PCs marketed by IBM
1982 Colin Semper installed as Provost	1982 Coventry Festival of Peace. Pope John Paul II visits Coventry	1982 Falklands War
		1985 Live Aid concerts
1987 Silver Jubilee of Consecration. Provost Semper leaves Coventry	1987 Coventry City beats Tottenham Hotspur 3–2 in FA Cup Final	1987 'Black Monday' stock-market crash
1988 John Petty installed as Provost		1988 Lockerbie air disaster
		1989 Fall of Berlin Wall
1990 Queen Mother and German President at Blitz Remembrance Service	1990 Programme of events to mark 50th anniversary of Blitz on Coventry	1990 Nelson Mandela freed from prison
1991 Development Trust established		1991 Fall of Soviet Union
	1992 Coventry University founded	
1994 Ordination of women priests. Vivienne Faull Canon of Coventry Cathedral		1994 Opening of Channel Tunnel

Coventry Cathedral	Coventry	Britain and the Wider World
1995 *Reconciliation* sculpture installed in Coventry and Hiroshima. Queen distributes Maundy money at Coventry Cathedral		
		1997 Princess Diana dies in car crash
1999 Closure of Kennedy House	1999 Phoenix Initiative	
2000 Dedication of Millennium Chapel. Home Front Service. Dean Petty retires		
2001 Fire in undercroft. John Irvine installed as Dean		2001 9/11 – suicide planes crash into Twin Towers in New York
2002 Canon Andrew White helps enable Alexandria Declaration		2002 US-led invasion of Afghanistan sweeps Taliban from power
2003 Opening of Youell House		2003 Invasion of Iraq
	2005 Massey Ferguson and Jaguar close their Coventry factories	2005 London suicide bombings
2006 Financial crises. Redefinition of International Mission	2006 Peugeot closes Ryton car factory	
2012 Fiftieth anniversary of consecration		2012 London hosts Olympic Games

BISHOPS, PROVOSTS/DEANS AND OTHER STAFF OF COVENTRY CATHEDRAL

Bishops of Coventry

Mervyn George Haigh: born 1887, Bishop 1931–42, died 1962
Neville Vincent Gorton: born 1888, Bishop 1943–55, died (in office) 1955
Cuthbert Killick Norman Bardsley: born 1907, Bishop 1956–76, died 1991
John Gibbs: born 1917, Bishop 1976–85, died 2007
Simon Barrington-Ward: born 1930, Bishop 1985–98
Colin James Bennetts: born 1940, Bishop 1998–2008
Christopher John Cocksworth: born 1959, Bishop 2008 to present

Provosts/Deans of the Cathedral

Richard Thomas Howard: born 1884, Provost 1933–58, died 1981
Harold Claude Noel (Bill) Williams: born 1914, Provost 1958–81, died 1990
Colin Douglas Semper: born 1938, Provost 1982–87
John Fitzmaurice Petty: born 1935, Provost and Dean 1988–2000
John Dudley Irvine: born 1949, Dean 2001 to present

Other Staff

Precentors

Joseph Poole	1958–77
Stephen Smalley	1977–86
John Blackman	1987 (acting)
Michael Sadgrove	1987–95
Christopher Burch	1995–2002
David Robinson	2002–03 (acting)
Adrian Daffern	2003–10
David Stone	2010 to present

Organists/Directors of Music

David Lepine	1961–72	
Robert Weddle	1972–77	
Ian Little	1977–84	
Paul Leddington Wright	1984–95	Consultant 1995 to present
David Poulter	1995–97	
Rupert Jeffcoat	1997–2005	
Alistair Reid (acting)	2005–06	
Kerry Beaumont	2006 to present	

Head Vergers

John Wickens	1962–69
John Cook	1969–76
David Dorey	1976–82
Paul Timms	1982–92
John Hoseine	1992–94
Gary Schofield	1994–97
Martyn Dack	1997–2001
Duncan Withers	2001–03
Janice Clarke	2003–11

Residentiary Canons

Edward Patey	1958–64
Joseph Poole	1963–77
Stephen Verney	1964–70
Horace Dammers	1965–73
Peter Spink	1970–77
Peter Berry	1973–86
Kenyon Wright	1974–81
Stephen Smalley	1977–86
Stuart King	1977–84
Paul Oestreicher	1986–97
Michael Sadgrove	1987–95
David Carrette	1988–89
Gerald Hughes	1989–94
Vivienne Faull	1994–2000
Christopher Burch	1995–2002
Andrew White	1998–2005
Stuart Beake	2000–05
Justin Welby	2002–07
Adrian Daffern	2003–10
Yvonne Richmond	2006–09
Timothy Pullen	2008 to present
David Stone	2010 to present

BIBLIOGRAPHY

An annotated selection of books about Coventry Cathedral

Campbell, Louise, *Coventry Cathedral: Art and Architecture in Post-War Britain*, Oxford: Oxford University Press, 1996.
[Clarendon History of Art Series. Study of the creative process in the context of the wider debate on architecture and reconstruction in the mid-twentieth century.]

Campbell, Louise (ed.), *To Build a Cathedral, 1945–1962*, Coventry: A. H. Jolly, 1987.
[Catalogue of exhibition held at the Mead Gallery, University of Warwick: original works relating to the design and furnishings of the new Coventry Cathedral.]

Howard, R. T., *Ruined and Rebuilt: The Story of Coventry Cathedral 1939–1962*, Coventry: Council of Coventry Cathedral, 1962.
[Provost Howard's own personal account from the start of the Second World War to the Consecration in 1962.]

Revai, Andrew, *Sutherland: Christ in Glory in the Tetramorph: The Genesis of the Great Tapestry in Coventry Cathedral*, London: Pallas Gallery, 1964.
[The story of the tapestry based on conversations with the artist.]

Spence, Basil, *Phoenix at Coventry: The Building of a Cathedral*, London: Geoffrey Bles, 1962.
[The architect's own personal account from conception to the start of construction.]

Thomas, John, *Coventry Cathedral*, London: HarperCollins, 1987.
[New Bell's Cathedral Guides. The most substantial and comprehensive of a number of guide books (190 pages). Includes the history of Christianity on the site from the seventh century through to the construction of the new Cathedral and a walk-around tour of the ruins and new building.]

Verney, Stephen, *Fire in Coventry*, London: Hodder & Stoughton, 1964; revised Atlanta GA: Austin Publishing, 1996, republished with new introduction, Coventry: Diocese of Coventry, 2010.
[Interpretation of the significance of the new Coventry Cathedral to the people of the diocese and to the story of the contemporary Church.]

Readers may also like to know of

Banham, R., 'Coventry Cathedral – Strictly "Trad, Dad"', *New Statesman*, May 1962, pp. 768–9.

Beeson, Trevor, 'The Very Reverend H. N. C. "Bill" Williams' – Obituary, *Daily Telegraph*, 11 April 1990.

Brookes, A. J., *St. Michael's Church Past and Present with Brief History of Coventry*, Coventry, undated, *c.* 1910.

Campbell, L., Glendinning, M. and Thomas, J., *Basil Spence: Buildings and Projects*, London: RIBA Enterprises, forthcoming 2011.

Coventry Cathedral: Report of Lord Harlech's Commission, Oxford: Oxford University Press, 1947.

Daffern, Adrian, 'The Legacy of Canon Joseph Poole', *Friends of Coventry Cathedral Newsletter,* September 2009.

Demidowicz, George (ed.), *Coventry's First Cathedral: The Cathedral and Priory of St Mary. Papers from the 1993 Symposium*, Stamford: Paul Watkins, 1994.

Donat, J., 'Sir Basil Spence OM, on his work', *Listener,* 18 February 1965, pp. 253–5.

Gloag, J., *Sacred Edifice*, London: Cassell, 1954; originally published 1937.

Hammond, Peter, *Liturgy and Architecture*, London: Williams Clowes & Son Ltd, 1960.

Hitchcock, H. R., 'English Architecture in the Early 1960s', *Zodiac* 12, 1964, pp. 19–47.

Lambourne, N., *War Damage in Western Europe*, Edinburgh: Edinburgh University Press, 2001.

Lepine, David, *An Excellent Good Song: An Account of the Music, Choir and Organs of Coventry Cathedral*, Coventry: The Cathedral, 1968. [Pamphlet, 36 pages.]

Long, P. and Thomas, J. (eds), *Basil Spence Architect*, Edinburgh: National Gallery of Scotland, 2007.

Sadgrove, Michael, *A Picture of Faith: A Meditation on the Imagery of Christ in Glory*, Bury St Edmunds: Kevin Mayhew, 1995.

Spalding, F., 'John Piper and Coventry, in War and Peace', *Burlington Magazine,* vol. CXLV, July 2003, pp. 488–500.

Spence, Basil, 'The Cathedral Church of St Michael, Coventry', *RIBA Journal*, February 1955, pp. 145–51.

Spence, Basil and Snoek, Henk, *Out of the Ashes; A Progress through Coventry Cathedral*, London: Geoffrey Bles, 1963.

van Eck, C., *Classical Rhetoric and the Visual Arts in Early Modern Europe*, Cambridge: Cambridge University Press, 2007.

The West Window at Coventry Cathedral, Leamington Spa: English Counties Periodicals, 1962.

Williams, H. C. N., *20th Century Cathedral*, London: Hodder & Stoughton, 1964.

Williams, H. C. N., *A Vision of Duty: Sermons Preached in Coventry Cathedral*, London: Hodder & Stoughton, 1963.

Williams, H. C. N., *Coventry Cathedral in Action*, 36pp, Oxford: Religious Education Press, 1968.

Williams, H. C. N., 'Coventry Cathedral Policy and Organisations', *Coventry Cathedral Review*, January 1965, vol. 5, no. 2.

Williams, H. C. N., *The Latter Glory: The Story of Coventry Cathedral*, Manchester: The Whitehorn Press, reprinted 1985.

Church history

Beeson, Trevor, *The Deans*, London: SCM Press, 2004.

St Benedict's Rule, A New Translation for Today, York: Ampleforth Abbey Press, 1997.

Brown, Callum G., *The Death of Christian Britain. Understanding secularisation 1800–2000*, London: Routledge, 2001.

Casiday, A. and Norris, F. W. (eds), *The Cambridge History of Christianity: Volume 2 Constantine to c. 600*, Cambridge: Cambridge University Press, 2007.

Coggan, Donald, *Cuthbert Bardsley. Bishop, Evangelist, Pastor*, London: Collins, 1989.

Dunn, J. D. G., *Beginning from Jerusalem*, Grand Rapids MI: Eerdmans, 2009.

Gill, D. W. J. and Gempf, C. (eds), *The Book of Acts in its Graeco-Roman Setting*, Grand Rapids MI: Eerdmans, 1994.

Hastings, Adrian, *A History of English Christianity 1920–2000*, London: SCM Press, 2001.

Church and City

City of Coventry, *Coventry into the 21st Century: The Unitary Development Plan 1988–2001*, 1993.

Cooper, Trevor, *Who Goes There? A Challenge to Humanity*, Milton Keynes: AuthorHouse, 2009.

Cox, Harvey, *The Secular City*, Harmondsworth: Penguin, 1968.

Cray, Graham, *Disciples and Citizens: A Vision for Distinctive Living*, Nottingham: Inter-Varsity Press, 2007.

Davie, Grace, *The Sociology of Religion*, London: Sage, 2007.

Dinham, A., Furbey, R. and Lowndes, V. (eds), *Faith in the Public Realm*, Bristol: Policy Press, 2009.

Graham, Elaine and Lowe, Stephen, *What Makes a Good City? Public Theology and the Urban Church*, London: Darton, Longman & Todd, 2009.

Hodgkinson, George, *Sent to Coventry*, London: Robert Maxwell & Co., 1970.

Kendall, Catherine, *Living with Poverty: Coventry in the 1930's and 1990's*, Coventry: Steering Group to mark the visit to Coventry of Church Action on Poverty's Pilgrimage against Poverty, 5 October 1999.

Lancaster, Bill and Mason, Tony (eds), *Life and Labour in a Twentieth Century City: The Experience of Coventry*, Coventry: Cryfield Press, 1987.

Micklethwait, John and Wooldridge, Adrian, *God is Back*, London: Allen Lane, 2009.

Richardson, Kenneth and Harris, Elizabeth, *Twentieth-Century Coventry*, Coventry: City of Coventry, 1972.

Sandel, Michael J., *Justice, What's the Right thing to do?*, London: Allen Lane, 2009.

Spencer, Nick, *'Doing God': A Future for Faith in the Public Square*, London: Theos, 2006.

Spencer, Nick and Chaplin, Jonathan (eds), *God and Government*, London: SPCK, 2009.

Thoms, David and Donnelly, Tom, *The Coventry Motor Industry: Birth to Renaissance*, Aldershot: Ashgate, 2000.

Tiratsoo, N., *Reconstruction, Affluence and Labour Politics: Coventry 1945–1960*, London: Routledge, 1990.

Verney, Stephen, *People and Cities*, London: Fontana, 1969.

International issues

Rose, W. E., *Sent from Coventry: A Mission of International Reconciliation*, London: Wolff, 1980.

Thomas, Merrilyn, *Communing with the Enemy. Covert Operations, Christianity and Cold War Politics in Britain and the GDR*, Bern, Switzerland: Peter Lang, 2005.

INDEX